60
MINUTE
TAX
PLANNER

TITLES ALSO IN THIS SERIES

60 MINUTE TAX PLANNER

EDWARD A. LYON, TAX ATTORNEY

PRENTICE HALL PRESS

Library of Congress Cataloging-in-Publication Data

Lyon, Edward A.
    60 minute tax planner / Edward A. Lyon.
        p.   cm.
    Includes index.
    ISBN 0-7352-0106-4 (paper)
    1. Tax planning—United States—Popular works. 2. Income tax—Law
and legislation—United States—Popular works. I. Title.
    KF6297.Z9L96 1998
    343.7304—cd21   98-30377
                                                           CIP

Printed in the United States of America

This publication is designed to provide accurate and authoritative information in regard to the subject matter covered. It is sold with the understanding that the publisher is not engaged in rendering legal, accounting, or other professional service. If legal advice or other expert assistance is required, the services of a competent professional should be sought.

. . . From the Declaration of Principles jointly adopted by a
Committee of the American Bar Association and a
Committee of Publishers and Associations.

10 9 8 7 6 5 4 3 2 1

ISBN 0-7352-0106-4 (p)

ATTENTION: CORPORATIONS AND SCHOOLS
Prentice Hall books are available at quantity discounts with bulk purchase for educational, business, or sales promotion use. For information, please write to: Prentice Hall Special Sales, 240 Frisch Court, Paramus, New Jersey 07652. Please supply: title of book, ISBN, quantity, how the book will be used, date needed.

PRENTICE HALL PRESS
Paramus, NJ 07652

On the World Wide Web at http://www.phdirect.com

This book is dedicated to Mary, Molly, and Mary Claire,
my three priceless deductions.

ACKNOWLEDGMENTS

I'd like to thank the following people for their support and encouragement: Paul Caron, John W. Dean, Louis A. Epstein, Karl H. Kreunen, and Alex Mills. I'd also like to thank Ellen Schneid Coleman, Sharon L. Gonzalez, and Audrey Kopciak at Prentice Hall. Finally, I'd like to thank my agent, Rhonda Winchell, without whose support this book would not have been possible.

INTRODUCTION

In the time it takes you to read this sentence, Uncle Sam will collect a million bucks. On Wall Street, they call it a stone, and that's what it feels like when it's your turn to pay. In the hour it takes for this book to start cutting your taxes, the IRS will collect over $170 million. If you're a typical American, in the hour it takes for the book to start cutting your taxes, the IRS will collect nearly 50 cents just from *you*.

Taxes act as "resistance" on your finances. A sailboat gliding through the water fights friction from the water against the hull. A car speeding down the highway fights resistance from the wind. The faster the boat and the car go, the more that resistance grows. It works the same with taxes and money. Families working to raise their kids fight the resistance of taxes on their budget. Investors working to grow their assets fight the resistance of taxes on their growth. The more they make, the more they grow, the more their taxes climb.

HOW THE SIXTY-MINUTE TAX PLANNER WORKS

◆ ◆ ◆

The *Sixty-Minute Tax Planner* will help you cut the friction you face from taxes. You'll learn how to integrate taxes into your own financial plan. Pay the least amount of tax on your income. Take advantage of tax credits and other special breaks. And choose investments that boost your wealth without boosting the taxes you pay.

But saving taxes shouldn't be your first financial goal. What! A tax book telling you not to save taxes? Your goal should be to make and keep as much as you can *after* taxes. Sometimes taxes are just the price of success. Don't buy tax-free bonds just for tax-free interest, if you could make more after taxes from other investments. Don't stuff funds in an IRA if the tax you'll pay down the road is less somewhere else. And don't take out an enormous mortgage just for the tax break, if you can pay less after taxes with some other loan.

Saving on taxes is easy to do, no matter how rich you are. Just look at billionaire entrepreneur and political gadfly Ross Perot. When Perot ran for President, he filed income and wealth disclosures with the Federal Election Commission. His filing shows that he used tax-free bonds and tax-sheltered real estate to cut his taxes. His municipal-bond holdings alone included issues from 45 out of 50 states and income between $18 and $87 million. (Candidates report income and holdings in broad ranges.) Citizens for Tax Justice, a Washington tax-reform group, estimates that in 1995, Perot earned $230 million, and paid just $19.5 million, or 8.5% of his income, in tax. Perot could have earned far, far more, even after taxes, from any number of investments. Perhaps he just doesn't want to take risks with his money, but how much in lost opportunity could he be costing himself?

The *Sixty-Minute Tax Planner* is a guide to tax *planning,* not tax *preparation.* That's a crucial difference. Tax *planning* is making financial choices with an eye toward eventual tax consequences. It's taking steps today to cut your tax bill tomorrow. It means not diving in before you look for rocks in the water. Tax *preparation* is simply recording history and hoping for the best. As hockey great Wayne Gretzky says, "Most people skate to where the puck is. I skate to where it's going to be." This book will teach you to skate where the puck is going to be.

Finally, the *Sixty-Minute Tax Planner* helps you make tax choices for the real world. There are any number of computer programs that claim to tell you, down to the last dollar, whether to invest in an ordinary IRA or a Roth IRA. Similar programs tell you whether to buy a taxable mutual fund or a variable annuity. You can crunch the numbers until you are blue in the face. But these programs all depend on certain underlying assumptions—and in the real world, these assumptions don't always hold true. For example, if you're choosing between an ordinary IRA and a Roth IRA, you'll have to enter what your tax rates are—now, and during a retirement that may be 30 years away. You don't know what your tax rate will be 30 years from now! And tax choices aren't just dollars-and-cents choices. Tax choices are behavior choices. Let's say you're choosing between a mutual fund and a variable annuity. The calculator will probably assume you buy the mutual fund and hold it, through thick and thin. If you get nervous and dump your fund, all that careful planning goes out the window. The *Sixty-Minute Tax Planner* teaches you how these assumptions affect your decisions—and what will happen when those assumptions change.

We pay taxes all our lives. We pay tax on our earnings, our investments, and when we die, we pay tax on whatever's left. We pay income tax, payroll tax, property tax, sales tax, estate tax, gift tax, inheritance tax, booze and cigarette tax, tire tax, airplane tax, hotel tax, rental car tax . . . The list goes on and on. The average American family pays almost 35% of its income in taxes. The average American worker spends 2 hours and 47 minutes out of an eight-hour shift just to pay taxes.

The good news is, there's a lot you can do to control the biggest tax of all: the federal income tax. The *Sixty-Minute Tax Planner* gives you a Tax Tune-up Quick Check to help you save thousands in taxes and, yes, even put cash in your next paycheck. You'll accomplish your financial goals faster and more securely. Employing just one of the many successful strategies can pay for this book hundreds or even thousands of times over.

What could you do with thousands in tax savings? Take a vacation? Save more for retirement? Put your children or grandchildren through college? Do you think you can spend it better than the government?

The *Tax Planner* doesn't teach you how to file your return. It doesn't take you step by step through the Tax Code or Form 1040. If that's what you want, there are plenty of 600-page references on the subject. They're good books, full of solid information. They'll tell you everything you ever wanted to know about railroad retirement benefits, farm income, and gain on involuntary conversion of residential property. But in their attempts to be all things to all taxpayers, they can be dense, intimidating, and difficult to use.

The *Tax Planner* gives you what you *really* want: *strategies* to *cut* your tax bill and rescue your money from faceless IRS bureaucrats. You don't need to be a CPA, or even *have* a CPA, to take advantage of these strategies. You just need to know where your opportunities lie. Do you own your own home? Do you have an IRA? Do you invest in stocks, bonds, or mutual funds? The *Tax Planner* helps you make the most of these opportunities. Are you saving to finance your kids' education? Are you helping support your parents? Are you worried about long-term health-care costs? The *Tax Planner* helps you through these challenges with some relief from the IRS. The Dictionary of Tax Deductions in the back of the book can save you hundreds, if not thousands, just by reporting deductions you can already take.

While you're at it, learn a bit about why the tax system is the way it is and how you can use this knowledge to save yourself some cash. This might not make your tax bill easier to swallow. But if you understand how Congress uses the tax code to manipulate the economy, you'll have a head-start understanding on how to cruise through the economy with as little IRS drag as possible.

WHO SHOULD READ THIS BOOK?

❖ ❖ ❖

Anyone who pays taxes can profit from this book.

If you struggle each year to file your own 1040, you'll learn smart moves you can make now that will pay off for years to come. You probably already know how to fill out the forms. But forms alone are no road map to tax savings. First, the forms are designed to calculate your tax, not cut it. Second, the forms record history, not shape it. If you want to cut your taxes, you'll need to plan your future moves to leave as little for the IRS as you can.

This book shows you where to focus your efforts for maximum results. You learn how to prove your deductions. Finally, if matters get complicated enough, you learn how to hire a tax preparer to fit your needs and your budget.

You can use these same strategies to save thousands with your regular tax preparer. Professional tax preparers are experts at taking the information you provide and assembling an accurate return. But they don't get paid according to how much you save, and few are truly proactive advocates for their clients. Your tax preparer can help you tailor the recommendations in this book to your own unique situation. Still, cutting your taxes is like any other effort in life. The more you put in, the more you'll take out.

None of these recommendations will land you in jail. They're all IRS-tested and court-approved. Your tax preparer can be as conservative or aggressive as you prefer: He or she should be familiar and comfortable with each and every one of these strategies. (If not, find someone who is.)

If you manage your own investments through your retirement plan, mutual funds, or a discount broker, you learn just how much control you have over your taxes. You probably already know that municipal bonds pay tax-free income, that capital gains are more valuable than interest and dividends, and that tax-deferred compounding can multiply your returns. But did you know that every time you sell an investment, you trigger a "taxable event"? Trust me, this is one event that you don't want to be invited to. This book shows you how to invest with the least drag from taxes possible. You also learn which tax-deferred investments are appropriate for you and how to make the most of those that are.

If you use a stockbroker, financial planner, or investment manager to help manage your investments, you learn smart strategies to take to them. This *Tax Planner* can complement their knowledge and give you great ideas for them to put to work. You find straight answers to hard questions, without technical jargon, sales pressure, or high hourly fees. And the same rule applies to financial advisers as tax preparers: The more solid information you can give them, the more value you get from them.

You'll be able to judge their advice with more confidence. If your adviser suggests a variable annuity, you'll know how to compare that choice with mutual funds and variable life insurance. If he or she recommends switching from one fund into another, you'll be able to factor the burden of taxes involved.

This part of the book teaches you just enough about the tax system to understand the strategies to follow. You learn some of the definitions used throughout the book. Terms such as "adjusted gross income" might intimidate you at first. But words, not numbers, are the key to beating the system.

Start Cutting Your Taxes

◆ ◆ ◆

The *Sixty-Minute Tax Planner* isn't organized like most tax books according to tax forms. Instead, it's organized to fit your life, your choices, and your goals. The Tax Tune-up Quick Check is the heart of the book. This chart will tell you which specific strategies can help you save thousands in tax. Just turn to the appropriate pages to find your best strategies for cutting your taxes. If you own your home, for example, turn to Chapter 3 to learn how you can use a home equity loan to convert nondeductible personal interest into deductible home-equity interest. If you buy mutual funds, turn to Chapter 8 to learn the most tax-efficient ways to take advantage of these popular investments. Finally, review the Dictionary of Tax Deductions to learn how to write off dozens of everyday expenses.

Specific strategies may involve additional terms and definitions; if so, you find them with the appropriate strategy. If you get stuck, turn to the Dictionary of Tax Deductions. You'll find capsule refreshers of all of these definitions.

Not every chapter applies to every reader, so there's no need to review the entire book. It should take less than 60 minutes to start cutting your taxes.

Good luck!

CONTENTS

LIST OF TABLES AND WORKSHEETS

60 MINUTE TAX TUNE-UP QUICK CHECK

Family and Home		See Chapter
Are you getting married?	♦ Consider the "marriage penalty" ♦ File a new W-4 as early as possible the year you marry	2
Do you have children?	♦ File a new Form W-4 as early as possible the year a child is born ♦ Claim appropriate tax credits	2
Do you help support your parents?	♦ Claim parents as dependents ♦ Rent your parents a home ♦ File a Multiple Support Declaration	2
Are you getting divorced?	♦ Structure your divorce for tax savings	2
Has your spouse died?	♦ Figure new basis for joint property ♦ Claim "qualifying widower" status for the next two years, if eligible	2
Do you rent your home?	♦ Buy a home for tax savings and more	3
Do you own your home?	♦ Cut taxes with home-equity debt ♦ Minimize tax on second homes	3
Are you planning to sell your home?	♦ Avoid tax on the sale	3

Your Investments		See Chapter
Do you own taxable investments?	♦ Consider tax-advantaged alternatives — U.S. savings bonds — U.S. treasuries — municipal bonds — stocks — annuities — life insurance — real estate ♦ Write off investment expenses	6 14
Do you buy stocks?	♦ Decide which to hold in taxable accounts ♦ Minimize turnover ♦ Convert dividends to capital gains	7

Your Investments		See Chapter
Do you buy mutual funds?	◆ Cut tax on dividends and sales — keep appropriate records — avoid "buying the dividend" — convert dividends into capital gains — deduct sales "loads" — consult Morningstar Mutual Funds tax-analysis ratings — buy index funds and tax-managed funds	8
Do you own appreciated assets such as stocks or real estate?	◆ Avoid tax on capital gains	6

College Funding		See Chapter
Are you saving for college?	◆ Consider tax-advantaged savings — college IRAs — prepaid tuition plans — life insurance — shift income to children	11
Are you paying college tuition?	◆ Hope Scholarship tax credits ◆ Lifetime Learning tax credits ◆ Buy off-campus housing	11
Have you just graduated from school?	◆ Deduct student loan interest	11

Retirement		See Chapter
Does your employer offer a plan?	◆ Contribute to the plan	12
Do you need to save more?	◆ Make the most of IRAs ◆ Designate beneficiaries to make the most of tax deferral ◆ Choose which investments to hold in tax-deferred accounts	12
Do you plan to move when you retire?	◆ Buy your retirement home now	3
Are you retired?	◆ Manage your nest egg right ◆ Start collecting Social Security ◆ Protect your Social Security benefits	12

Your Job, Your Business, and Your Community		**See Chapter**
Does your employer offer these breaks?	◆ Flexible Spending Accounts ◆ Medical Savings Accounts ◆ Dependent Care Accounts ◆ Tuition-assistance plans	**4**
Are you self-employed?	◆ Write off business expenses ◆ Cut taxes with retirement plans	**4**
Do you have a hobby or valuable skill?	◆ Consider starting a hobby business	**4**
Do you volunteer or make charitable gifts?	◆ Write off volunteer expenses ◆ Make the most of charitable gifts ◆ Consider charitable trusts	**5**

When You File Your Return		**See Chapter**
Year-end tax planning	◆ Shift income to cut tax ◆ "Bunch" deductions ◆ Deduct expenses before you pay ◆ Avoid the AMT ◆ Avoid audit	**14**
Have you discovered deductions you overlooked in previous years?	◆ File an amended return to claim over-looked savings from previous years	**13**
Put cash in your next paycheck!	◆ File a new Form W-4 to put cash in your next paycheck	**13**

ONE

WHAT YOU NEED TO KNOW ABOUT THE TAX SYSTEM

THE TAX SYSTEM has a logic behind it, believe it or not. Most taxpayers see it as a numbers game, with visions of green eyeshades and long columns of intimidating figures. But any competent sixth grader can do the math. The tax system is really more about words than numbers. Should 401(k) contributions count as income? Should home-office expenses qualify for a deduction? For this taxpayer? For that one?

Tax pros don't spend their days hunched over adding machines. They help their clients plan their investments, spend their money, and live the good life with as little resistance from IRS friction as possible. They spend most of the year working with business clients, then scramble from February 1 to April 15, "the season," to churn out dozens or even hundreds of individual returns.

Here in a nutshell is the essence of the federal income tax: These definitions appear throughout the book, so pay close attention to the next few pages.

SIX STEPS TO FIGURING YOUR TAX

Add up your income from all sources to calculate "total income."

Subtract "adjustments to income" to calculate "adjusted gross income."

Subtract deductions and personal exemptions to calculate "taxable income."

Consult the table of "tax brackets" to figure your actual tax.

Add in any extra taxes such as self-employment or alternative minimum tax (AMT).

Finally, subtract any available "tax credits" and send a check to the IRS.

That's really most of what you need to know. The real issue isn't the arithmetic. It's what you include in income, what you deduct from your income, and where you invest to avoid reporting income at all.

Given how the system works, then, there are four main ways to control your taxes:

1. Buy Tax-Advantaged Investments That Don't Increase Your Income

You have more control over your investments than any other aspect of your return. You can buy investments that pay tax-free income and investments that pay tax-deferred income that you don't report until you cash out your gains. You can also buy investments that reward you with lower-taxed capital gains.

2. Make the Most of Adjustments to Income and Itemized Deductions

Adjustments to income and itemized deduction cut your tax bill by cutting your taxable income. You may be amazed to discover how much you can already deduct. The Dictionary of Tax Deductions at the back of this book can be an eye-opening gold mine.

3. Use Tax Credits to Lower Your Final Bill

Tax credits are even more valuable than adjustments to income and tax deductions because they cut your tax bill dollar for dollar. There are several valuable tax breaks for families with children and senior citizens. There are also investments that reward you with tax credits in addition to growth and income.

4. Shift Income to Other Taxpayers or Other Tax Years

If you can shift income from this year's return to someone else or a later year, you'll cut this year's tax bill. It's valuable just to squeeze another year's use out of your tax dollar. You've probably heard that "justice delayed is justice denied." In case of taxes, taxation delayed equals a tax cut. And if you can shift income to a lower-bracket taxpayer or lower-bracket year, you'll do even better.

Most of the strategies you find in the *Tax Planner* fall into one of these broad categories. You learn how to invest like the pros and avoid the IRS as a silent partner. You learn about deductions you never suspected. You learn how to save thousands over time. And, if you don't want to wait 'til next April 15th to reward yourself, you learn how to file a new Form W-4 with your employer (or adjust your quarterly estimates) to start capturing your savings in your next paycheck. You even learn how to file an amended return to save taxes from previous years.

WHAT IS INCOME?
❖ ❖ ❖

This might seem like an obvious question, but it's not. Thousands of taxpayers wind up audited for failing to report all their income, and thousands more waste millions in taxes on income that's not taxable to begin with. You need to know what sorts of income you actually have to report and what you can leave off your return. You also need to understand the difference between ordinary income and capital gains.

Ordinary Income

Ordinary income includes most of what we take for granted as taxable income.

- Wages, salaries, and tips
- Commissions
- Self-employment income
- Interest and dividends
- Pension and annuity proceeds
- Rents and royalties
- Alimony received
- Gambling winnings, lotteries, and game shows
- Barter
- Certain employee benefits (including the value of group life coverage exceeding $50,000)

Capital Gains

Capital gains are income from the sale or exchange of property: your house, your investments, even your business. Capital gains are taxed at lower rates than ordinary income, leaving more after tax for you.

Capital gains enjoy three significant advantages over ordinary income.

- Long-term capital gains are taxed at lower rates than ordinary income—no more than 20%, even for taxpayers in the top tax brackets.
- You don't pay tax until you "realize" your gain (actually sell your property), so you can choose when to pay the tax.
- If you hold on to your gains until you die, you avoid income tax entirely. Your heirs inherit the property with a "basis" equal to its value on your date of death. This "stepped-up basis" is an important tax- and estate-planning tool.

The Congressional Joint Committee on Taxation reports that capital-gains breaks in effect in 1996 were worth $31.6 billion. The committee further reports that breaks for home sales were worth an extra $20.1 billion. Changes made by the Taxpayer Relief Act of 1997, including even lower rates and a more generous exclusion for primary homes, should make capital gains more valuable still.

The starting point for determining capital gain is your "basis." Basis generally equals the cost of the property (including any commissions or other expense of acquiring property), adjusted for improvements or depreciation. Your basis in your house is the purchase price plus any improvements. Your basis in stock is the purchase price plus commission. Your gain in the property is the difference between your basis and your net proceeds from the sale of the property. Capital gains are divided into two categories: short-term (from property held for up to one year) and long-term (from property held for more than 12 months). Beginning in 2001, there will be a third class of capital gains for property acquired after December 31, 2000, and held for more than five years.

Short-term gain is taxed at ordinary rates. Long-term gain is taxed at 10% for taxpayers in the 15% tax bracket and capped at 20% for taxpayers in higher brackets. Property bought after December 31, 2000, and held for more than five years will be taxed at 8% for taxpayers in the 15% bracket and capped at 18% for taxpayers in higher brackets. (The 8% rate kicks in for post-2000 gain on assets held for five years regardless of when you bought the property; the 18% rate doesn't kick in until property is sold after 2006.) For more information, see Chapter 6, Tax-Advantaged Investments to Meet Your Needs.

In the 1970s and '80s, ordinary tax rates ranged as high as 90%, and capital gains were capped at roughly half of those rates. Tax pros spent countless hours working to structure investments to reward investors with capital gains, and converting ordinary income into capital gains became the tax-planning equivalent of spinning lead into gold. An entire tax-shelter industry sprang up to feed investors' appetites for tax savings, including the ill-fated limited partnerships of the 1980s. Unfortunately for buyers, these partnerships were sold on tax laws, not investment fundamentals, and most of the industry dried up with the 1986 tax reform.

There are two main reasons for taxing capital gains at a lower rate and tolerating the inevitable scheming to classify income as capital gains. The first is to encourage long-term investment. If you start a business and wind up hiring a dozen people, the nation's economy benefits more than if you simply put the cash in the bank. The second is to avoid taxing gains from inflation. If you buy a stock for $100,000, and the value just keeps pace with inflation, you're really no better off after 20 years than you were when you bought the stock. The value of your shares stays the same, in relative dollars. But if you sell the stock for $200,000, you'll owe real tax on $100,000 of gain. That's a nasty penalty for just holding on. Taxing capital gains at a lower rate reduces, but doesn't entirely eliminate, this penalty.

Each new Congress brings with it efforts to "index" capital gains to inflation. If you buy a stock for $100,000 and hold on until it reaches $200,000, but the value of your original $100,000 inflates to $150,000, then you'd pay tax on the $50,000 real gain and not the $50,000 inflationary gain. In theory, it's a great idea. Why pay tax on illusory, inflationary gains? In real life, though, indexing would make the tax system even more complicated. The recent debate over changing the Consumer Price Index shows that "inflation" isn't easy to define. Who's to say what inflation really costs? Should houses be indexed to a house index, and stocks indexed to a stock index? The new "five-year" capital-gains rate is a simplified effort to cut tax on inflationary gains. This wrinkle hints at the complications indexing would bring. The expanded $250,000 exclusion for gains on the sale of a primary home is another effort to cut tax on inflationary gains.

Capital gains are still an important planning tool, even with lower spreads. (In fact, the Taxpayer Relief Act of 1997 actually increased the spread and restored the benefit of lower rates to taxpayers in the 15% and 28% tax brackets.) The chapters on investing all reveal how to take advantage of lower capital-gains rates.

Passive Income

Tax-shelter promoters saved investors billions in taxes by structuring investments to throw off enormous "paper" losses—losses that don't actually cost investors cash—that the investors could write off against their other income. A partnership might raise $2 million from investors. The partnership would then borrow $20 million to buy real estate, or oil and gas, or cattle, or equipment to lease to business. The limited partners weren't personally responsible for repaying the loan. But they got to write off the interest the partnership paid. In some cases, they could write off more than their entire investment— each year! Eventually, there would be tax on future income. But in the meantime, the investor enjoyed fat tax breaks.

The Tax Reform Act of 1986 shot down these schemes by defining a new category of income and loss, "passive" income and loss. You can write off passive losses only against passive income. What's more, you can write off only amounts that are actually "at risk" in the activity. The days of huge writeoffs for borrowed money are over.

The main group of taxpayers who need to worry about these rules are those who invest in limited partnerships. For more information, see Chapter 9, Real Estate.

Nontaxable Income

Nontaxable income includes all sorts of receipts that taxpayers mistakenly report to the IRS. Make sure you're not lining government pockets with taxes on income you don't have to report. This includes:

- Gifts and inheritances (in some states there may be an inheritance tax, but there is no federal income tax on inheritances)
- Loans (if a loan is forgiven, the amount forgiven becomes taxable to the borrower the year it is forgiven)
- Life-insurance proceeds (death benefits are tax-free, although life-insurance settlement annuities may be partially taxable)
- Life-insurance dividends (dividends are tax-free until the total dividends you receive over time equals your contributions into the policy)
- Municipal-bond interest (interest from private activity bonds may trigger the AMT)
- IRA rollovers
- Capital gain on the sale of your home ($250,000 for single filers; $500,000 for joint filers)
- Property settlements between spouses in divorce or separation proceedings
- Child-support payments
- Lawsuit proceeds for personal injuries
- Workers' comp payments
- Disability-income-insurance payments from policies you pay for personally (if your employer pays the premiums, the disability income is taxable)

◆ Federal income-tax refunds
◆ State income-tax refunds if you don't itemize deductions for that year
◆ Home-rental income for 14 days or less of rental income
◆ Scholarships and fellowships used for tuition, fees, books, and course equipment

WHAT ARE ADJUSTMENTS TO INCOME?

❖ ❖ ❖

Adjustments to income are a group of specific tax deductions that cut your taxes by cutting your taxable income. These include:

◆ IRA contributions (subject to income limits)
◆ Moving expenses (subject to mileage and service requirements)
◆ One-half of self-employment tax paid
◆ Self-employed health insurance
◆ Self-employed Keogh and Simplified Employee Pension (SEP) retirement-plan contributions
◆ Penalty on early withdrawal of savings
◆ Alimony paid
◆ Student-loan interest during the first 60 months that interest payment is required (subject to income limits)

Once you've totaled your gross income, subtract adjustments to income to figure your adjusted gross income. This figure is important for two reasons. First, your personal exemptions and itemized deductions phase out as your adjusted gross income reaches certain levels. Personal exemptions shrink by 2% for each $2,500 or fraction over the threshold. Itemized deductions (except for medical expenses, investment interest, casualty or theft losses, and gambling losses) shrink by three cents for each dollar over the threshold (up to a maximum of 80% of total itemized deductions).

1998 PHASEOUT THRESHOLDS FOR EXEMPTIONS AND DEDUCTIONS

Filing Status	Personal Exemptions	Itemized Deductions
Single	$124,500	$124,500
Head of household	$155,650	$124,500
Married (joint)	$186,800	$124,500
Married (single)	$93,400	$62,250

Second, many itemized deductions, such as medical expenses and miscellaneous itemized deductions, are allowed only to the extent they exceed a certain percentage of adjusted gross income. For example, medical expenses are deductible only to the extent they exceed 7.5% of adjusted gross income. If your adjusted gross income is $50,000, you can deduct only those medical expenses greater than $3,750. If you have just $3,500 of deductible medical expenses, you're out of luck.

Clearly, it's important to keep adjusted gross income as low as possible to preserve the value of your personnel exemptions and itemized deductions. The chapters on investment income will be particularly helpful in accomplishing this. Most investments increase your total income, which naturally increases your adjusted gross income. But many tax-advantaged investments, such as municipal bonds, growth stocks, and life-insurance products, don't add to your current income, so they avoid increasing your adjusted gross income. These tax-advantaged investments are especially valuable if your income approaches the phaseout thresholds shown in the chart.

WHAT ARE DEDUCTIONS?

◆ ◆ ◆

Everyone loves tax deductions, or writeoffs. These are the little tax breaks Congress doles out to encourage and reward specific behavior. It shouldn't surprise you to learn that Congress uses the tax code to legislate certain behaviors even in cases where Congress can't legislate directly. Tax deductions give Congress the power to regulate financial choices through subtler incentives and penalties.

For example, Congress lets you deduct the interest you pay on your mortgage in order to encourage homeownership. The tax break brings down the actual cost of buying a house, which increases demand for houses, which supports the home-construction industry, which increases employment and economic activity, which generates more income for Congress to tax. Similarly, Congress lets you deduct investment expenses in order to encourage investing. When people invest more, they make more, which increases taxable income, which increases their taxes (unless they follow the advice in this book!).

Cynics might call tax deductions paybacks to powerful lobbies and contributors. While it's true that the housing industry, the insurance industry, and the oil and gas industries (all of which enjoy huge tax breaks), are some of Congress's most generous givers; this doesn't take away the fact that deductions are vastly popular. For example, some flat-tax advocates who propose scrapping all deductions and taxing income at a single rate have estimated that eliminating the mortgage-interest deduction could lower housing prices nationwide by an average of 15%. The popular outcry that this would trigger from America's homeowners assures that a continued mortgage-interest deduction will at least remain on the table.

Tax deductions grow more valuable as your income increases. If you're in the 15% tax bracket, every dollar you can deduct cuts your tax by 15 cents. If you're in the 39.6% tax bracket, that same deduction cuts your tax by 39.6 cents.

The starting point for every taxpayer is the standard deduction: $4,250 for single filers; $6,250 for heads of households; $7,100 for married couples filing jointly; and $3,550 for married couples filing separately (1998 estimates). If your actual itemized deductions are higher than the standard deduction, take your itemized total; if actual itemized deductions are lower, take the standard deduction. (Married couples filing separately must both itemize or both take the standard deduction; you can't have it both ways.) There's no magic to using tax deductions other than knowing what's available. The Dictionary of Tax Deductions at the end of this book gives you the most comprehensive list of tax deductions available anywhere. Before you take a look, consider this: You're reading a tax deduction right now.

Standard deductions are high enough that less than one-third of taxpayers itemize. Here are 1995 category averages for those that do. These aren't guidelines of any sort. They don't indicate how much the IRS will accept in any particular situation, and in an audit you must prove any deductions you do take. These are just average figures to give you a sense of how much deductions are worth.

AVERAGE ITEMIZED DEDUCTIONS BY INCOME RANGE

Adjusted Gross Income	Medical	Taxes	Interest	Charitable
$0–$15,000	$8,739	$2,555	$7,463	$1,097
$15,000–$30,000	$5,442	$3,112	$5,442	$1,338
$30,000–$50,000	$4,226	$3,112	$5,715	$1,465
$50,000–$75,000	$4,772	$4,429	$6,587	$1,768
$75,000–$100,000	$6,544	$6,171	$8,063	$2,286
$100,000–$200,000	$12,277	$9,758	$11,107	$3,433
$200,000 or more	$32,113	$36,076	$25,046	$16,882

Another way to look at deductions is to see how much they cost the government in taxes. The Congressional Joint Committee on Taxation publishes an annual report on "tax expenditures": the amount of tax the government loses from each deduction. (Yes, the government considers a $1 tax cut to be the same as $1 in direct spending. In other words, all of your money is the government's unless they let you keep it.) The committee reports that in 1996, total tax expenditures topped $455 billion. These include $43 billion for mortgage interest, $28.3 billion for state and local taxes, $15.2 billion for property taxes, and $18.1 billion for charitable gifts.

WHAT ARE TAX BRACKETS?

❖ ❖ ❖

Throughout this book you'll see the term "tax bracket." Your tax bracket is simply the percentage of tax you pay on your *last* dollar of income. If you're in the 15% bracket, every extra dollar of income costs you 15 cents in taxes. If you're in the 39.6% bracket, every extra dollar costs you 39.6 cents in taxes. Your tax bracket is the key to calculating your tax savings. If you're in the 15% tax bracket, each dollar you cut from your taxable income *saves* you 15 cents in taxes. If you're in the 39.6% bracket, each dollar you cut from taxable income *saves* you 39.6 cents in taxes. Tax brackets also control how much you pay on capital gains. Brackets are indexed for inflation so that rising wages over time don't necessarily push you into a higher bracket.

Many taxpayers mistakenly believe that their tax bracket is the percentage of income they pay on *every* dollar they earn. They believe that when they move up tax brackets, they pay the higher percentage on *all* of their taxable income. This isn't so, and you should never be afraid to earn more money just because it will push you into a higher tax bracket. The Internal Revenue Code uses a "progressive" system for determining your tax—the more you make, the greater percentage of income you owe. For example, married taxpayers pay 15% of the first $42,350; 28% of the next $59,950; 31% of the next $53,650; 36% of the next $122,450; and 39.6% of anything above (1998). If you're single, in the 28% tax bracket, you'll pay no income on the portion of your income equal to your personal exemptions and deductions; 15% on your taxable income up to $25,350; and 28% on the rest. Consequently, if you cut your taxable income by a dollar, you save 28 cents in taxes.

Many of the *Tax Planner*'s strategies require you to know your current tax bracket to figure how much you can save. If you don't already know your federal tax bracket, find a copy of last year's return and look it up in the chart:

1998 TAX BRACKETS

Single		Head of Household	
0–25,350	15%	0–33,950	15%
25,351–61,400	28%	33,951–87,700	28%
61,401–128,100	31%	87,701–142,000	31%
128,101–278,450	33%	142,001–278,450	36%
278,451 and up	39.6%	278,450 and up	39.6%
Married Filing Jointly		**Married Filing Separately**	
0–42,350	15%	0–21,175	15%
42,351–102,300	28%	21,175–51,150	28%
102,301–155,950	31%	51,151–77,975	31$
155,951–278,450	36%	77,976–139,225	36%
278,451 and up	39.6%	139,226 and up	39.6%

Finding your federal tax bracket is easy. But you're not done yet. Next you have to add in *state* taxes. These range from zero, in states without an income tax, up to as high as 12%.

If you itemize, you can deduct your state tax from your federal taxable income. Your combined rate is slightly less than the combined total of each individual rate. For simplicity's sake, you can simply add the two. To be more precise, add your federal rate plus [(1 minus your federal rate) × your state rate]. For example, if your federal rate is 28% and your state rate is 6%, your combined rate is [.28 + (1 − .28) × .06], or 32.32%.

People who live in states without an income tax might think they get off easy since they pay no state tax. But these states raise the bulk of their revenues from nondeductible sales tax. So people in those states actually come out worse than if they paid deductible income tax.

STATE TAX RATES

State	Top Rate	State	Top Rate
Alabama	5.0%	Montana	11.0%
Alaska	None	Nebraska	6.68%
Arizona	5.10%	Nevada	None
Arkansas	7.0%	New Hampshire	5.0%
California	9.3%	New Jersey	6.37%
Colorado	5.0%	New Mexico	8.2%
Connecticut	4.5%	New York	6.85%
Delaware	6.9%	North Carolina	7.75%
District of Columbia	9.5	North Dakota	12.0%
Florida	None	Ohio	6.799%
Georgia	6.0%	Oklahoma	7.0%
Hawaii	10.0%	Oregon	9.0%
Idaho	8.2%	Pennsylvania	2.8%
Illinois	3.0%	Rhode Island	27% of Federal Tax
Indiana	3.4%	South Carolina	7.0%
Iowa	8.98%	South Dakota	None
Kansas	6.45%	Tennessee	6.0%
Kentucky	6.0%	Texas	None
Louisiana	6.0%	Utah	7.0%
Maine	8.5%	Vermont	25% of Federal Tax
Maryland	4.875%	Virginia	5.75%
Massachusetts	5.95%	Washington	None
Michigan	4.4%	West Virginia	6.5%
Minnesota	8.5%	Wisconsin	6.77%
Mississippi	5.0%	Wyoming	None
Missouri	6.0%		

If your city or local government levies an income tax, add that too. If you itemize, you can deduct local taxes from your federal income.

Unfortunately, you're still not done. That's because many deductions and credits phase out or become taxable as your total income rises. If your income is at or near one of the thresholds for your deductions and credits, your true marginal rate can spike up like an EKG. The child-tax credit, for example, phases out by $50 for each $1,000 *or fraction* of adjusted gross income above $110,000. Earning a *single dollar* of income—say, from $111,000 to $111,001—can cost you *$50.28* in tax! This is a *5.028%* marginal tax rate that's probably unmatched in history. Here's another outrageous example. Social Security income is 85% taxable for "provisional incomes" above certain amounts. "Tax-free" municipal-bond income counts toward provisional income. So earning $1 of *tax-free* interest can actually boost your tax bill! What's more, you'll find different marginal rates for self-employment income, salary income, investments, and capital gains. If all this hasn't scared you off, here's how to figure your effective rate increase from disallowed exemptions, deductions, and credits:

$$\frac{\text{Top Bracket} \times \text{Disallowed Amount}}{\text{Excess Income over Threshold}}$$

Before the 1986 tax reform, there were 11 tax brackets ranging from 11% to 50%. The 1986 tax reform wiped out much of this confusion, cutting the number of brackets to two, with a third "phased-in" rate to eliminate the benefit of the lower bracket for

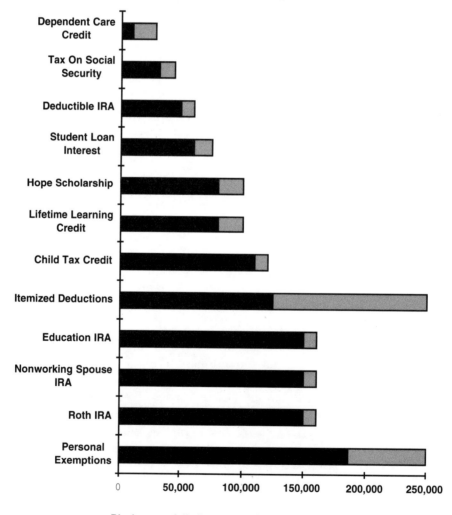

DEDUCTION/CREDIT PHASEOUTS
(JOINT FILERS)

Black area = full allowance   Gray area = partial allowance upper-income taxpayers. Since then, the number of brackets has crept back up. Now there are nine including special capital-gains and "recapture" rates.

Lots of long-range *Tax Planner* strategies call for you to estimate your future tax rate. If you're choosing between an ordinary IRA and a Roth IRA, for example, you'll need to know your future rate to know when the tax break will be more valuable. Similarly, if you're comparing a variable annuity against a mutual fund, you'll need to know how the ordinary rate you'll pay on annuity withdrawals compares with the capital-gains rate you'll pay on fund appreciation. Unfortunately, predicting your future tax rate is laughable, for several reasons:

- You don't know what your income will be when you get there.
- Congress will change the rates (several times!) by the time the future arrives.
- Even if your income is the same, your rate may be different. For example, your future income may be the same as your current income. But if your kids are grown and your house is paid off, your deductions will be lower and your rate can be higher.
- Future income may not all be taxed at your future marginal rate, but rather, at your average rate.

For lack of a better alternative, we'll use current rates when we make such comparisons. Still, you should understand their limits. And don't be overly swayed by computer programs purporting to predict the future. Plenty of these tax calculators pretend to tell you exactly what your results will be when choosing between IRAs or funds and annuities—down to the last dollar! These projections are only as good as their underlying assumptions. And we *know* that these assumptions are going to change. Comparisons such as this are useful when they reveal a *dramatic* difference. But in most cases they give a false sense of certainty where none is really appropriate.

WHAT ARE TAX CREDITS?

Tax credits are like turbocharged tax deductions, only better. Tax deductions cut your taxable income. Every dollar you deduct cuts your taxes by whatever percentage of that dollar equals your tax bracket. But tax credits cut your actual tax. Every dollar of credit you take cuts your actual tax by the full dollar.

Tax deductions grow more valuable as your taxable income rises. For someone in the 15% tax bracket, every dollar of deductions cuts actual tax by 15 cents; while for someone in the 39.6% bracket, every dollar of deductions cuts actual tax by 39.6 cents. But tax credits are proportionately more valuable for taxpayers in lower brackets. In the 39.6% bracket, you'd need $2,525.25 in deductions to get the same break as a $1,000 credit. In the 15% bracket, you'd need a whopping $6,666.66 in deductions to equal that $1,000 credit.

Most tax credits, such as those for dependent children and day-care expenses, are fairly straightforward and don't require a lot of explanation. But you can buy investments that pay you with tax credits. Low-income housing is one such investment, and low-income-housing tax credits may be the last true tax shelter left. If you qualify, and if real-estate deserves a place in your investments, low-income-housing tax credits can save you anywhere from $3,750 to $9,900 per year. For more information, see "Tax Credits for Real-Estate Investors," in Chapter 9.

What Is the Alternative Minimum Tax (AMT)?

The Alternative Minimum Tax (AMT) is one of the meanest and messiest parts of the Code. Imagine rolling a boulder up a hill. Once you're done, you're ready to relax with a cool drink (your refund, perhaps?). Now imagine the IRS sending you back down to roll a *bigger* boulder up the hill. That's what the AMT feels like.

Congress imposed the AMT to make sure high-income taxpayers pay at least some tax. But the AMT doesn't always succeed. The IRS reports that in 1996, 1,820 lucky individuals with incomes over $200,000 paid no taxes at all. What's more, the AMT is creeping down to the "middle class." This is because AMT exemptions aren't indexed for inflation. The tax trapped "just" 590,649 hapless victims in 1997. But it's likely to snare over nine million by 2009. Even taxpayers in the 15% bracket who take advantage of child and college-tuition tax credits could wind up paying AMT at 26% rates.

The AMT works a bit like the regular tax system in reverse. "Alternative minimum taxable income" (AMTI) equals regular taxable income plus a whole host of "add-backs": state and local taxes, the portion of medical deductions between 7.5% and 9% of adjusted gross income, miscellaneous itemized deductions, and others. Once you've figured your AMTI, subtract an exemption of $45,000 for a joint return, $33,750 for a single return, or $22,500 for a separate return. (These exemptions are cut by 25% of the amount by which AMTI exceeds $150,000 on a joint return, $112,500 on a single return, and $75,000 on a separate return.) The tax itself is 26% of AMTI up to $175,000 plus 28% of AMTI exceeding $175,000. If your AMT exceeds your regular tax, you pay the higher amount.

You're in danger of falling into the trap if you earn income from incentive stock options or private-activity municipal bonds, or you have especially high deductions and credits relative to your income. Fortunately, there are steps you can take now to ease that bite. For more information, see Chapter 14, Dictionary of Tax Deductions.

How to Hire Professional Help

If the thought of wading through this mess sends you to the medicine cabinet, help is all around you. Each year, about half of us hire professionals to prepare our tax returns. Tax-preparation fees range from a few dozen dollars for franchised storefront preparers to thousands of dollars for experienced tax attorneys. Nationally, tax-preparation fees reach nearly $8 billion per year. That's a lot of money to spend to learn how much you owe. How do you go about getting the best value for your money? And whom do you call to help you keep that total down over time?

There's no certification needed to hang out a shingle to prepare taxes. So naturally, there's a wide variety of help available. The list includes storefront tax preparers, enrolled agents, financial planners, accountants and CPAs, and attorneys. Each group presents individual strengths. Since anyone can call him or herself a tax preparer, it pays to investigate carefully.

Once you've decided which kind of help to hire, it's time to narrow your search. Look to friends or colleagues with similar financial pictures for recommendations. Also look to your other financial advisers. Who do they use? What do they pay? What kind of help do they get? Think of your tax adviser as an employee you hire for the part-time job of planning and preparing your taxes. Interview a prospective tax adviser just as you'd interview any prospective employee. Look for someone experienced with your business and your income level. Look for references from satisfied clients. Ask for a cost estimate. Ask if he or she will represent you, for an extra fee, in case of an audit. Finally, remember that even though the tax preparer signs at the bottom of the return, *you* are responsible for the final results.

In November 1996, *Money* magazine presented a hypothetical tax return to a group of 45 preparers. This was the seventh such tax-preparers test the magazine has conducted, and the results were, in *Money*'s word, "alarming." The group included CPAs, enrolled agents, and professional tax preparers. The report, published in the March 1997 issue, show just how important it is to pick the right preparer. The hypothetical return covered a family of four earning just over $133,000 and included a host of typical tax questions: salary and self-employment income; a qualified-plan inheritance and IRA rollovers; investment, inheritance, and stock-option income; a home refinancing; and parental support.

The 45 tax preparers spent anywhere from 4 to 47 hours on the return and charged from $300 to $4,950 (averaging $81 per hour). The final tax bills ranged from $36,322 all the way to $94,438. Not one preparer matched the magazine's own tally of $42,336. The three closest came within $100, which the magazine attributed to "ambiguities" and "varying interpretations of murky areas of tax law." The preparers' mistakes included counting IRA rollovers as income, miscalculating dividend income and tax credits, missing a cheaper way to calculate gain on a mutual-fund redemption, and fumbling a self-employment retirement-plan writeoff.

The three tax preparers closest to *Money*'s final figure were all CPAs. Still, there's no reason to rule out others as long as their skills and experience are appropriate for your return. Here is a comparison of the various types of preparers available.

1. Choose a Storefront Preparer for Low Cost

Storefront tax preparers, the kind that advertise on TV or hang out shingles at the local strip mall, can prepare most everyday returns. They're fine for holding nervous taxpayers' hands, or for those who just don't want to tackle the IRS forms. But they don't provide sophisticated tax planning, and they don't represent taxpayers before the IRS.

To qualify, most storefront tax preparers simply complete a course offered by the company. Storefront tax preparers are the least expensive professionals, charging anywhere from a few dozen to a few hundred dollars.

2. Consider Your Financial Planner

Many financial planners are now preparing clients' tax returns. Other planners are adding tax preparers to their staffs. This makes excellent sense if your planner knows how to do it right. Your planner already knows a great deal about your financial picture, and he or she can help integrate your tax planning into your other financial planning. Financial planners are usually more familiar with investments than are any other tax preparers, so if much of your taxes come from your investments, a financial planner may be particularly useful. However, financial planners don't represent taxpayers before the IRS, unless they also qualify as enrolled agents, CPAs, or attorneys.

To qualify as tax preparers, financial planners simply hang out a shingle. There's no formal qualification needed, so make sure your planner has the experience to prepare your return. Financial planners charge similar rates to CPAs: $50 per hour and up.

3. Choose an Enrolled Agent for IRS Experience

"Enrolled agents" are a special class of tax preparers licensed to represent taxpayers in disputes before the IRS. Most of them are former IRS agents. They know the ins and outs of the system and provide good value for their fees.

To qualify, an enrolled agent must have five years IRS experience or pass a special two-day exam administered by the IRS. Enrolled agents also must complete 72 hours of continuing education every three years. Enrolled agents generally charge from $50 to over $100 per hour.

4. CPAs Can Handle Almost Anything

Certified Public Accountants, or CPAs, are the workhorses of the tax-preparation business. Tax accountants prepare dozens or even hundreds of returns each year. CPAs can also represent taxpayers before the IRS. A good tax accountant can help coordinate all aspects of your tax picture, and many accounting firms have branched out into financial planning. Accounting firms range from "Big Five" firms, the national giants that audit the Academy Awards, to regional and local firms. Many firms "farm out" actual tax-prep work to independent contractors, then review their work.

To qualify, a CPA has to pass a tough three-day exam administered by the American Institute of Certified Public Accountants. (Some accountants may also have a Masters degree in Taxation.) CPAs also must complete 40 hours of continuing education per year. They generally charge from $50 to over $300 per hour.

5. Consider an Attorney for Sophisticated Planning

Tax attorneys can be the most expensive tax professionals. Most of them don't actually prepare many returns. But they're especially valuable for sophisticated tax planning. Attorneys can integrate your tax planning into your estate planning. They're the only professionals licensed to prepare wills, trusts, living trusts, incorporations, and other documents necessary to carry out your plans. Also, some conversations with your attorney may be "privileged": your attorney can't be forced to testify against you; any other tax preparer (except perhaps a priest!) can. (Conversations regarding ordinary tax preparation aren't privileged, but conversation in response to IRS legal action is.)

To qualify, a tax attorney needs to complete a three-year law degree and pass a state bar exam. There's no "major" in tax law required. In fact, most law schools offer just a handful of classes on tax law; most tax lawyers' knowledge comes from experience. (Some tax attorneys spend an additional year in school to earn a Master of Laws (LLM) degree in taxation; these tax LLMs have the most formal tax training available.) Attorneys also must complete continuing education programs administered according to state requirements. They generally charge from $100 to $500 an hour.

6. Computer Programs

There are several tax-preparation programs available at computer and software stores, office-supply stores, and even bookstores. You can also download tax-preparation "shareware" and "freeware" from various on-line services, although these programs aren't as complete as the popular commercial offerings.

Most of these programs lead you through some sort of "interview" to gather information. The interview will ask about your income and expenses, crunch the numbers, and offer pop-up screens with tax-saving tips and planning advice. You can experiment with filing jointly versus filing separately and play "what-if" scenarios to see how different choices affect your bottom line. The interview protects you from the actual tax forms until you print your return. Of course, the program also lets you enter information directly into the return. Some programs let you file your return electronically, for an additional fee. Others include IRS publications and texts of popular tax-planning books as well. One feature to look for is a state-tax module for your home state.

Tax-preparation programs can also help you find your true marginal tax rate in cases where additional income costs you deductions and credits. To do this, figure your tax as you normally would. Then add an extra $100 in income somewhere and see what it does to your taxes. If your extra income adds $30 dollars in tax, that means you've got a 30% marginal rate. You'll probably find that different kinds of income give you different marginal rates.

The programs are generally good at *preparing* your taxes. They'll help you organize your information and transfer it to the forms. They'll even help find possible deductions you might have missed. But they're not designed to *plan* your taxes. They don't look at your long-term picture, and they can't tailor advice to your own situation. What's more, the programs sometimes come with bugs. One popular program required buyers to order or download corrections two years in a row. They can't defend you if you get audited. Finally, they don't guarantee anything beyond penalties and interest assessed because of a calculation error on the program's part. Remember, just like with paid preparers, *you* are responsible for the final results.

One money-saving solution might be to prepare your return yourself using one of the software programs, then run it by your regular tax pro for review. Your pro won't be happy to learn you've replaced him or her with a machine, but you won't be the first.

7. Don't Forget Your Investment Adviser

If you use a financial planner, stockbroker, or money manager to help manage your investments, find out just how much he or she knows about taxes. You'll see later that your investments give you more control over your tax bill than any other part of your finances. Your investment adviser *must* know how your investments affect your taxes to help you earn the highest after-tax return, both today and tomorrow. Who cares how much you make on a hot stock tip if the windfall profit income costs you your deductions and personal exemptions? How valuable is municipal-bond interest if it eats away at your Social Security benefits?

Most investment advisers know the basic rules for different investments. The good ones respect *your* taxes and include them in their long-range plans. Choose a prospective investment adviser just as you'd choose a tax pro. How many clients does he have with similar tax pictures? What kind of advice does she give those clients? What specific suggestions does he make to cut their taxes? And how much time can she give you to help keep your taxes down? Remember, the proper goal is to earn the highest after-tax return possible.

There are several professional designations that indicate an adviser has taken specific training in taxes. These include the Certified Financial Planner, Chartered Life Underwriter, Chartered Financial Consultant, and Personal Financial Specialist programs. Also, CPAs and attorneys are entering the financial-planning field in increasing numbers:

- The Certified Financial Planner (CFP) designation is granted and monitored by the Denver-based CFP Board of Standards. The CFP is rapidly becoming an industry standard, and the International Association for Financial Planning, the industry's largest professional association, has recommended that all members obtain the designation. Prospective CFPs generally have to work in the business and complete self-study courses in insurance, investments, estate planning, retirement planning, taxes, and ethics. CFPs also have ongoing continuing education requirements.

- The Certified Life Underwriter (CLU) designation is granted and monitored by The American College, a Philadelphia-based life-insurance-industry arm. Prospective CLUs have to work in the industry plus complete self-study courses in life insurance, investments, estate planning, retirement planning, and taxes. CLU designees also have ongoing continuing education requirements.

- The Chartered Financial Consultant (ChFC) designation is also granted and monitored by the American College. The ChFC designation shares much of the same curriculum as the CLU program, with less focus on insurance and more emphasis on financial planning.

- The Personal Financial Specialist (PFS) designation is granted and monitored by the American Institute of Certified Public Accountants for CPAs who specialize in personal financial planning. PFS designees generally don't actually sell or manage investments. But their training qualifies them to advise clients on a wide range of financial-planning issues.

The stock-brokerage industry, with its traditional emphasis on securities sales and portfolio management, has not come up with a similar designation. Most brokerage firms are increasing their emphasis on financial planning, however, and stockbrokers are getting more training on tax-planning issues. Also, growing numbers of CPAs and attorneys are taking positions in the financial-planning field. These professionals can all provide solid long-term tax-planning help.

TWO

YOUR FAMILY

IN A VERY REAL SENSE, your family determines some of your most basic tax choices. Filing status, personal exemptions, and several valuable credits all depend on family status. Most of these choices are fairly straightforward. You qualify for certain rates, you get exemptions for your dependents, and you're eligible for credits or not. In these cases, all you need is to know the rules. But there are other strategies that require a bit more thought.

CLAIM THE RIGHT FILING STATUS

❖ ❖ ❖

Filing status is one of your most basic tax choices. It depends on your marital status at the end of the year. Your choice might seem obvious. But you can lose a ton of money over time if you make the wrong decisions. There are four categories of filers: (1) single; (2) head of household; (3) married filing jointly; and (4) married filing separately. Your status affects your tax bracket and rates, your standard deduction, your eligibility for certain deductions, credits, and other breaks. Here are the rules for choosing your status:

1. Single

You can file single if you were not married (or you were legally separated) as of December 31 of the tax year. Single filers get the lowest standard deduction, the highest rates at each income level, and the lowest phaseout thresholds for deductions, personal exemptions, and tax credits.

2. Head of Household

Heads of households with dependents get a special break even if they're not married. Heads of households get higher standard deductions and lower tax rates at each income level, plus higher phaseouts for deductions and personal exemptions.

You can file as head of household if you meet one of these tests:

♦ You pay more than one-half of the cost to maintain your house, which is the residence for more than one-half of the year of your child or relative who is your dependent; or

♦ You pay more than one-half of the cost of maintaining your parent's residence (not necessarily your own residence) if the parent is also your dependent; or

♦ You're married, but your spouse did not live with you the last six months of the year, and you pay more than one-half of the cost to maintain your home as the principal residence of your child.

3. Married Filing Jointly

You can file jointly if you are married as of December 31 of the tax year (unless you are legally separated). Joint filers get the lowest rates at any particular income, the highest standard deduction, and the highest phaseout thresholds for deductions, personal exemptions, and tax credits.

♦ You don't have to be married the entire year to file jointly. If you marry during the year, even on December 31, you can file jointly for the entire tax year.

♦ If your spouse dies during the year, you can file as a "qualifying widow(er)" and use joint rates for the following two years if you were eligible to file a joint return the year of your spouse's death and you claim a child, stepchild, adopted child, or foster child as a dependent.

♦ If your spouse dies while you own property jointly, be sure to recalculate your basis for figuring gain or loss on a sale. For example, if you buy a house jointly for $100,000, each of you has a $50,000 basis in the house. If your spouse dies when the house is worth $200,000, your spouse's basis "steps up" to $100,000, or half of the $200,000 value at death. Your gain when you sell the house will be just $50,000. For more information, see "Tax Breaks for Capital Gains" in Chapter 6.

♦ If you originally file separately, you can file an amended return and file jointly within three years of the original filing date. For more information, see "Find Gold in Old Returns," in Chapter 13.

The "marriage penalty" is a well-known trap for married couples that forces many of them to pay a higher tax than if they reported identical incomes as individuals. For more information on the marriage penalty, see "Marriage" on page 25.

4. Married Filing Separately

Even if you're married on December 31, you can continue to file apart from your spouse. This makes sense if one of you has particularly high deductions, such as extraordinary medical expenses, that would be limited by the higher floor on both earners' joint income. It can help one of you avoid the phaseout of itemized deductions and personal exemptions on separate income below the phaseout threshold. It also protects you if your spouse is cheating the IRS! However, married couples filing separately pay the highest rates at any particular income. Their dollar levels for moving up tax brackets are cut in half. Their phaseout thresholds for deductions, personal exemptions, and tax credits are also cut in half. What's more, they're completely ineligible for these tax breaks:

♦ IRA deductions for nonworking spouses

♦ Child and dependent-care credits

♦ The $25,000 rental real-estate loss allowance

♦ Low-income housing credits

Married couples in community-property states have to report income and deductions equally, except for deductions paid from separately owned property. Your opportunities to cut taxes by filing separately are even more limited in those states (Arizona, California, Idaho, Louisiana, Nevada, New Mexico, Texas, Washington, and Wisconsin).

Married couples filing separately have to either both itemize or both choose the standard deduction. You can't have it both ways, with one spouse taking all the deductions and the other taking a standard deduction.

Special Breaks for Senior Citizens, the Blind, and the Disabled

The tax code gives an extra break to senior citizens. Think of this as taxpayer "frequent flyer miles." The IRS says, in effect, "since you've been such a loyal taxpayer all these years, we'll give you a little break." Seniors get a higher standard deduction ($1,000 more for single, $800 for joint filers). Blind taxpayers get the same additional standard deduction. If you and your spouse are both 65 or older and blind, your standard deduction is $10,300—the standard $7,100, plus $800 each for age, plus $800 each for blindness.

There's also a special tax credit for senior citizens and disabled taxpayers with less than $7,500 in Social Security and federal-pension income. You qualify if you were 65 years old before the beginning of the tax year *or* you're retired because of permanent and total disability. Here's how it works:

- First, figure your "base amount": $5,000 for single filers and joint filers with one eligible spouse, $7,500 for joint filers with two eligible spouses, and $3,750 for married couples filing separately.

- Next, reduce the "base amount" by any nontaxable Social Security, railroad retirement, or veterans' administration pension benefits.

- Then, reduce the "base amount" by one-half of any adjusted gross income exceeding $7,500 if you are single, head of household, or qualifying widower.

- Finally, take a credit of 15% of any remaining "base amount."

To claim the credit, file Schedule R on your Form 1040.

CLAIM ALL YOUR PERSONAL EXEMPTIONS
◆ ◆ ◆

A dependent is someone who gets more than half of their support from you and meets certain other tests. You get one personal exemption for yourself, one for your spouse, and one for each dependent you can claim. Each personal exemption cuts your adjusted gross income by $2,700.

Dependents are defined as:

- Your child, stepchild, grandchild, parent or stepparent, sibling or stepsibling, in-law, aunt/uncle, niece/nephew, or anyone else not breaking state law by living with you (in some states, same-sex couples can declare each other as dependents)

- Earning less than $2,700 in taxable income (not including Social Security, tax-exempt interest, and so forth), except for children under age 19 or full-time students under age 24
- Who gets more than half of his or her support from you
- Is a U.S. citizen, U.S. resident, or resident of Canada or Mexico
- Who doesn't file a joint return with his or her spouse (except where each spouse's income is below the filing threshold and they file solely to claim a refund)

You'll need to provide a Social Security number for each dependent you claim. A dependent doesn't have to be alive for a full year to qualify for the full personal exemption. Children born during the year and people who die during the year qualify for personal exemptions. If you care for a foster child and you can show that actual expenses top the allowance you get from the state, claim the excess as an itemized deduction.

If your adjusted gross income tops the following thresholds, your personal exemptions phase out by 2% (4% if married filing separately) for each $2,500 or fraction over the threshold. Let's say you file singly and claim yourself as your sole exemption. Your taxable income is $130,000. Your income is $5,500 over the phaseout threshold. Your $2,700 deduction shrinks by $81, which equals 2% for each $2,500 over the threshold plus another 2% for the extra $500 fraction.

1998 PHASEOUT THRESHOLDS FOR PERSONAL EXEMPTIONS

Single	Head of Household	Married (Joint)	Married (Separate)
$124,500	$155,650	$186,800	$93,400

Multiple-Support Declaration

If you share in supporting someone, you can still claim him or her as a dependent, even if you don't provide more than one-half of the person's support, with a Multiple Support Declaration, Form 2120. This is a smart strategy when two or more siblings help support a parent. Here's how it works:

- You have to provide more than 10% of the person's support.
- You and the other contributors jointly have to provide more than one-half of the person's support.
- Each of the other contributors has to be eligible to claim the person as a dependent, except that each of them did not provide more than one-half of the support.
- Each of the other contributors has to sign the Multiple Support Declaration allowing you to take the exemption.

Form 2120
(Rev. January 1997)

Department of the Treasury
Internal Revenue Service

Multiple Support Declaration

▶ Attach to Form 1040 or Form 1040A of person claiming the dependent.

OMB No. 1545-0071

Attachment
Sequence No. **50**

Name of person claiming the dependent

Social security number

During the calendar year 19 ...., I paid over 10% of the support of

Name of person

I could have claimed this person as a dependent except that I did not pay over half of his or her support. I understand that the person named above is being claimed as a dependent on the income tax return of

Name

Address

I agree not to claim this person as a dependent on my Federal income tax return for any tax year that began in this calendar year.

Your signature

Your social security number

Address (number, street, apt. no.)

Date

City, state, and ZIP code

Instructions

Paperwork Reduction Act Notice

We ask for the information on this form to carry out the Internal Revenue laws of the United States. You are required to give us the information. We need it to ensure that you are complying with these laws and to allow us to figure and collect the right amount of tax.

You are not required to provide the information requested on a form that is subject to the Paperwork Reduction Act unless the form displays a valid OMB control number. Books or records relating to a form or its instructions must be retained as long as their contents may become material in the administration of any Internal Revenue law. Generally, tax returns and return information are confidential, as required by Internal Revenue Code section 6103.

The time needed to complete and file this form will vary depending on individual circumstances. The estimated average time is: **Recordkeeping,** 7 minutes; **Learning about the law or the form,** 3 minutes; **Preparing the form,** 7 minutes; and **Copying, assembling, and sending the form to the IRS,** 10 minutes.

If you have comments concerning the accuracy of these time estimates or suggestions for making this form simpler, we would be happy to hear from you. See the instructions for the tax return with which this form is filed.

Purpose of Form

When two or more persons together pay over half of another person's support, only one of them can claim the person they support as a dependent for tax purposes.

Each person who does not claim the dependent completes and signs a Form 2120 (or similar statement containing the same information required by the form) and gives the form (or statement) to the person claiming the dependent. That person attaches all the forms or statements to his or her tax return. See **How To File** on this page.

Who Can Claim the Dependent

Generally, to claim someone as a dependent, you must pay over half of that person's living expenses (support). However, even if you did not meet this support test, you might still be able to claim him or her as a dependent if **all five** of the following apply:

1. You and one or more other eligible person(s) (see below) together paid over half of another person's support.

2. You paid over 10% of the support.

3. No one alone paid over half of the person's support.

4. The other four dependency tests are met. See **Dependents** in the Form 1040 or Form 1040A instructions.

5. Each other eligible person who paid over 10% of the support agrees not to claim the dependent by completing a **Form 2120** or similar statement.

An **eligible person** is someone who could have claimed another person as a dependent except that he or she did not pay over half of that person's support.

How To File

The person claiming the dependent must attach all the completed and signed Form(s) 2120 or similar statement(s) to his or her tax return. The name and social security number of the person claiming the dependent must be at the top of each Form 2120 or similar statement.

Additional Information

See **Pub. 501,** Exemptions, Standard Deduction, and Filing Information, for details.

 Printed on recycled paper

MARRIAGE

❖ ❖ ❖

Congratulations! You've found "the one." As you begin your married life, you'll feel an extra glow knowing the IRS shares your joy. Why? Because if you both work, the IRS will probably collect more tax. The "marriage penalty" is a quirk in the tax law that two-income couples have criticized for years. Married couples don't pay the same amount of tax that they would if they filed the same returns as individuals.

The Congressional Budget Office reported in 1997 that 42% of couples paid a "marriage penalty" averaging $1,400 more than if they had filed as singles. Generally, the marriage penalty hits two-income couples whose combined incomes are split more evenly than 70/30. The average penalty was $770 for couples with adjusted gross income under $20,000; $1,190 for couples with adjusted gross income between $20,000 and $50,000; $1,240 for couples with adjusted gross income between $50,000 and $100,000; and $2,640 for couples with adjusted gross income over $100,000. In contrast, 51% of married couples got a "marriage bonus" averaging $1,300 less than they would if they had filed as singles. The marriage bonus rewards couples with just one income, or one income much higher than the other.

There are three reasons for the marriage penalty.

◆ When both spouses work, the first spouse's income uses up the couple's combined deductions and personal exemptions, plus the benefit of moving up through tax brackets. The couple's second income piles on top of the first and is taxed more at the couple's highest rates.

   ▶ **Example:**   You and your fiancé each make $50,000 per year, and each take the standard deduction. Your taxable incomes are $43,050 ($50,000 minus the $2,700 personal exemption and the $4,250 standard deduction). You each pay $8,758.50 (15% of the first $25,350, plus 28% of the remaining $17,700).

   When you marry, your new taxable income is $87,500 ($100,000 minus two $2,700 personal exemptions and the $7,100 standard deduction). That's $1,400 higher than your combined taxable incomes as singles. You get the same deduction and exemptions whether you both work or not. So you pay 15% on your entire $37,500. Your new spouse pays 15% on just $4,850 of income, then 28% of the remaining $45,150. Your total tax bill is $18,994.50, a full $2,406 higher than if you had filed as singles.

   ◆ The standard deduction for married couples isn't twice the standard deduction for individuals.
   ◆ Finally, tax brackets for married couples don't rise at precisely twice the amount for single individuals.

   Having said all that, here are some tips for cutting your taxes at marriage.

TAX-BRACKET INCREASES—SINGLE VS. MARRIED

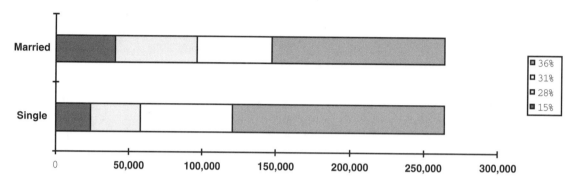

- ◆ Are you planning a year-end wedding? It might pay to wait a few weeks or months to avoid a marriage penalty (or even jump the gun to claim a marriage bonus!). If you can, take a "dry run" at estimating your taxes both ways, married and single, to see which costs least. Then, if it's not too disruptive, choose a date that lets the IRS help pay for the honeymoon.

- ◆ File a new Form W-4 with your employer (or start adjusting your quarterly estimates) as soon as possible in the year you marry. If your joint tax bill goes up, you'll avoid penalties for underwithholding. If your bill goes down, you'll start seeing savings as soon as the new W-4 takes effect.

The Myth of the Second Income

The "marriage penalty" is just one cost that eats away at two-income families. In fact, economists now realize that many "two-income families," particularly those with young children, don't take home two incomes at all.

Let's look at a typical second paycheck to see how this happens:

- ◆ We've already seen how the second earner pays tax at the couple's highest rates. For most two-income families this is 28% of the second check. It's even higher if the extra income phases out your deductions and credits.

- ◆ Next, add in Social Security and Medicare. This is 7.65% of the second paycheck up to the Social Security wage base (currently $72,600), plus 1.45% of anything more. If the second earner is self-employed, the self-employment bite is 15.3% of the first $72,600 plus 2.9% of anything more.

- ◆ Add in state and local taxes. Taxes alone can eat up nearly half of the second paycheck.

- ◆ Next, add in child-care costs. These can range up to hundreds of dollars a month.

- ◆ Next, add in the cost of keeping a job. This includes commuting; lunches, snacks, and coffee; buying and maintaining a professional wardrobe; and the usual charitable gifts you make at the office.

- ◆ Finally, add in the "extra" costs of running a family on top of your jobs. You'll eat out more and buy more convenience foods. You might pay a maid or lawn-care service to take care of jobs that you're too tired to do.

By the time you're all finished, you might find the "costs" of the second job eat up the entire second paycheck. In fact, one study concluded that a typical two-income family, with one spouse earning $60,000 and the other earning $30,000, would take home just as much as a single spouse earning just $64,000. Of course, there are still reasons to keep the second job even if the after-tax pay nets out pennies on the dollar. You'll keep pace with your peers as you climb the corporate ladder, and you'll protect your retirement plan and other benefits.

DIVORCE

❖ ❖ ❖

Divorce is never easy, and rarely cheap. You're not just breaking up a marriage—you're breaking up a taxpayer. Fortunately, there are tax strategies you can use to ease the financial bite. These include timing your divorce to take advantage of a final year of joint-filing status, structuring settlements to shift the tax burden to the lower-bracket spouse, and favoring deductible alimony over nondeductible child support. If you and your spouse can agree to continue considering yourselves as a single economic unit, you can wring some real tax savings out of the whole messy process.

Time Your Divorce for Tax Savings

Remember the marriage penalty? Spouses with roughly equal incomes pay more tax than if they had filed apart. Divorce can reverse this penalty, or it can eliminate the "marriage bonus" for spouses with unequal incomes. If you time your divorce right, you can squeeze an extra year of savings out to help pay the lawyers' bills.

Filing status depends on whether you're married December 31. If you're married, you can choose to file jointly. If you're divorced or separated under a final decree of separate maintenance, you can't. "Closing" a bad marriage is probably more important than saving taxes. But if your case comes due near the end of the year, time your divorce to take advantage of one last year's marriage bonus, or eliminate the final year's marriage penalty.

Shift Property to the Lower-Bracket Spouse

Property settlements generally don't trigger tax at the time of the transfer. This is true even when one spouse gets cash or assumes liabilities as part of the settlement. (The exceptions are transfers to nonresident aliens, trust transfers of mortgaged property, and, of all things, transfers of U.S. Savings Bonds.) Instead, the spouse getting property pays tax when he or she sells it down the road. The basis for figuring gain or loss is the same as it was at the time of the transfer. So consider the future tax burden before you transfer property. The spouse who will pay tax on built-in gain may want to get more property or alimony.

If you have more than $250,000 gain in the marital residence, consider selling it before the divorce to exclude the full $500,000 for married couples filing jointly. This lets you protect more gain than either spouse could protect alone. If this can't work, the $250,000 exclusion is worth more to the spouse with the higher tax rate.

You can transfer money from your employer-retirement plan or IRA to your former spouse. This is done through a qualified domestic relations order, a court order that assigns a spouse's right to receive payments under the plan. The recipient will owe tax on that distribution unless he or she rolls it over to an IRA or to his or her own employer-retirement plan.

Favor Alimony over Child Support

This strategy uses the same principle as the last. Alimony is usually taxable to the one who gets it, generally in a lower tax bracket than the one who pays it. Child support is taxable to the one who pays it. Favoring alimony over child support ensures that the income used to provide the payment is taxed at the divorced couple's lower tax rate. Here's how to qualify the payments for this treatment:

- The payments have to be made in cash to a separated or divorced spouse.
- The payments have to be ordered by a decree of divorce, legal-separation agreement, decree of support, or decree of annulment.
- The paying spouse's obligation has to end at the death of the one receiving it.
- The spouse who gets the alimony can deduct the cost of legal fees related to arranging it. These fees are a miscellaneous itemized deduction subject to the 2% floor.

You can schedule payments to fall over time. But don't cut them by more than $15,000 the second and third year. If you do, the spouse who pays will have to "recapture" the excess first and second years' payments and report them as taxable income. The purpose of this rule is to keep you from disguising property settlements as alimony. Just looking at the following math should convince you not to make this mistake. Here's how it works:

- If your payment in year two is more than $15,000 higher than the payment in year three, you'll have to recapture as much of the second year's payment that tops the payment in year three plus the $15,000 allowance.
- If your payment in year one is more than $15,000 higher than the average of the payments you make in years two and three (minus any recapture from year two), you'll have to recapture as much of the first year's payment that tops the average payment in years two and three plus the $15,000 allowance.
- These rules don't apply to payments you make under a continuing liability to pay a fixed portion of your income from employment or investments, or to payments that stop because of death or remarriage.

▶ **Example:** You pay your spouse $60,000 in year one, $25,000 in year two, and $5,000 in year three. In year four, you'll report $37,500 as taxable income:

ALIMONY RECAPTURE

Recapture from Year Two:

Payment from year two	$25,000
minus payment from year three	$ 5,000
minus allowance	<u>$15,000</u>
Recapture	$ 5,000

Recapture from year one

Payments from years two and three	$30,000
minus recapture from year two	<u>$ 5,000</u>
Average payment years two and three	$12,500
Payment from year one	$60,000
minus average	$12,500
minus allowance	<u>$15,000</u>
Recapture	$32,500

Report recapture on Form 1040, line 11. Where it says "alimony received," cross out "received" and write "recapture."

Tax Breaks for Your Kids

❖ ❖ ❖

Kids are a great way to cut your tax bill. The more you have, the more you save. Every one of them gives one more personal exemption. Of course, if you're a parent, you really need the help—you don't have money left over to pay tax in the first place.

The tax code rewards parents in all sorts of ways, and the politicians who write the tax code trip over each other trying to cook up new ones. Tax breaks for children include the personal exemption for each eligible dependent, the new child-tax credit, and the child and dependent-care credit. You can also shift investments to your children using trusts and custodial accounts.

1. Claim the New Child-Tax Credit

You can claim a child-tax credit for each child, grandchild, stepchild, or foster child under age 17 who is your dependent. The child-tax credit is $500 for 1999 and thereafter.

As with most credits, this one phases out as adjusted gross income rises. The child credit shrinks by $50 for each $1,000 or fraction that adjusted gross income tops the following thresholds. A dollar here can be the most expensive dollar you ever earn. Just one extra dollar in income can cost you $50 in tax.

PHASEOUTS FOR CHILD TAX CREDITS

Single	Head of Household	Married (Joint)	Married (Separate)
$75,000	$75,000	$110,000	$55,000

▶ **Example:** You're a married couple with one child, and your adjusted gross income is $116,100. Your credit is cut by $350 ($50 for each of the six thousand above the threshold plus $50 more for the final $100).

The credit phases out completely for married filers at $119,001 (1999 and later) and single filers at $84,001.

2. Claim the Dependent-Care Credit

The dependent-care credit gives you a break for day-care expenses that let you (or both you and your spouse) work. This includes an in-home nanny or babysitter as well as outside day-care costs. Here's how to claim the credit:

- The credit is available for these "qualifying persons": a child under age 13, your incapacitated spouse, or any other incapacitated dependent. If the incapacitated person has gross income of $2,700 or more, so that he or she doesn't qualify as a dependent, you can still claim the credit for the cost of his or her care.

- Expenses outside the home include a day-care center, day camp, nursery school, or care in the home of a babysitter. Expenses inside the home include ordinary domestic services such as laundry, cleaning, and cooking, plus Social Security, Medicare, and unemployment taxes on household employees.

- Your day-care provider can't be your child, your spouse, or anyone else you can claim as a dependent.

- The credit is available for any dependent, including adults and parents as well as children.

- The credit itself equals 20% to 30% of qualifying expenses up to a base of $2,400 (one dependent) or $4,800 (two or more dependents). If you're married and one spouse's income is below the base, the base is limited to the lower-paid spouse's income.

If your employer offers a dependent-care flexible-spending account (FSA), any reimbursement you claim from the account cuts your $2,400 or $4,800 base amount. If you have a choice, simply figure which strategy saves you more. Generally, as your tax bracket rises, the flexible-spending account grows more valuable. Let's say your adjusted gross income is $25,000 and you're in the 15% bracket. If you put $4,800 into a dependent-care FSA, you'll save just $720, $336 less than the maximum $1,056 credit. Now let's say your adjusted gross income is $80,000 and you're in the 28% bracket. If

CHILD AND DEPENDENT-CARE CREDIT

Adjusted Gross Income	Credit Percentage	Maximum Credit One Dependent	Maximum Credit Two+ Dependents
$10,000 or less	30%	$720	$1,440
$10,001–$12,000	29%	$696	$1,392
$12,001–$14,000	28%	$672	$1,344
$14,001–$16,000	27%	$648	$1,296
$16,001–$18,000	26%	$624	$1,248
$18,001–$20,000	25%	$600	$1,200
$20,001–$22,000	24%	$576	$1,152
$22,001–$24,000	23%	$552	$1,104
$24,001–$26,000	22%	$528	$1,056
$26,001–$28,000	21%	$504	$1,008
$28,001 or more	20%	$480	$960

you put the same $4,800 into a dependent-care FSA, you'll save $1,344, $384 more than the maximum credit. For more information on dependent-care FSAs, see Chapter 4, Your Job and Your Business.

Figure the credit on Form 2441 and carry the amount to Form 1040.

3. Claim the Adoption Credit

The adoption credit eases the cost of adopting a child. Here's how it works:

- You can claim a credit of up to $5,000 for "qualified adoption expenses."
- The credit is $6,000 for a special-needs child, one who's physically or mentally incapable of caring for himself or herself.
- Qualified adoption expenses include reasonable and necessary adoption fees, court costs, attorney fees, and other expenses.
- The credit phases out for adjusted gross income between $75,000 and $115,000.
- If your employer gives you tax-free adoption assistance, you can still claim the credit for any amounts above your employer reimbursement.
- Generally, if you adopt a U.S. citizen or resident, you can claim the credit the year the adoption becomes final. If you pay expenses in any year before the adoption becomes final, you can claim the credit in the year after the year you pay the expenses. If you adopt a foreign child, you can claim the credit only in the year the adoption becomes final.
- You can claim as much of the credit as you need to wipe out an entire year's tax bill, minus any credits for child and dependent-care expenses, the credit for the elderly or disabled, and any tentative alternative minimum tax. If the credit in a

---

Form **2441**	**Child and Dependent Care Expenses**	OMB No. 1545-0068
Department of the Treasury Internal Revenue Service (U)	▶ **Attach to Form 1040.** ▶ **See separate instructions.**	19**98** Attachment Sequence No. **21**

Name(s) shown on Form 1040	Your social security number

Before you begin, you need to understand the following terms. See **Definitions** on page 1 of the instructions.

- **Dependent Care Benefits**
- **Qualifying Person(s)**
- **Qualified Expenses**
- **Earned Income**

Part I **Persons or Organizations Who Provided the Care—**You **must** complete this part.
(If you need more space, use the bottom of page 2.)

1	**(a)** Care provider's name	**(b)** Address (number, street, apt. no., city, state, and ZIP code)	**(c)** Identifying number (SSN or EIN)	**(d)** Amount paid (see instructions)

Did you receive **dependent care benefits?**	**No** ——▶ Complete only Part II below.
	Yes ——▶ Complete Part III on the back next.

Caution: *If the care was provided in your home, you may owe employment taxes. See the instructions for Form 1040, line 55.*

Part II **Credit for Child and Dependent Care Expenses**

2 Information about your **qualifying person(s).** If you have more than two qualifying persons, see the instructions.

(a) Qualifying person's name		**(b)** Qualifying person's social security number	**(c)** Qualified expenses you incurred and paid in 1998 for the person listed in column (a)
First	Last		

3	Add the amounts in column (c) of line 2. DO NOT enter more than $2,400 for one qualifying person or $4,800 for two or more persons. If you completed Part III, enter the amount from line 24	**3**
4	Enter YOUR **earned income**	**4**
5	If married filing a joint return, enter YOUR SPOUSE'S earned income (if your spouse was a student or was disabled, see the instructions); **all others,** enter the amount from line 4	**5**
6	Enter the **smallest** of line 3, 4, or 5	**6**
7	Enter the amount from Form 1040, line 34 . . . . **7**	

8 Enter on line 8 the decimal amount shown below that applies to the amount on line 7

If line 7 is—		Decimal amount is	If line 7 is—		Decimal amount is
Over	But not over		Over	But not over	
$0—10,000		.30	$20,000—22,000		.24
10,000—12,000		.29	22,000—24,000		.23
12,000—14,000		.28	24,000—26,000		.22
14,000—16,000		.27	26,000—28,000		.21
16,000—18,000		.26	28,000—No limit		.20
18,000—20,000		.25			

8	× .

9 Multiply **line 6** by the decimal amount on line 8. Enter the result. Then, see the instructions for the amount of credit to enter on Form 1040, line 41 . . . . **9**

For Paperwork Reduction Act Notice, see page 3 of the instructions.   Cat. No. 24558B   Form **2441** (1998)

Form 2441 (1998)　　　　　　　　　　　　　　　　　　　　　　　　　　　　　Page **2**

Part III　**Dependent Care Benefits**

10　Enter the total amount of **dependent care benefits** you received for 1998. This amount should be shown in box 10 of your W-2 form(s). DO NOT include amounts that were reported to you as wages in box 1 of Form(s) W-2	**10**	
11　Enter the amount forfeited, if any. See the instructions	**11**	
12　Subtract line 11 from line 10	**12**	

13　Enter the total amount of **qualified expenses** incurred in 1998 for the care of the **qualifying person(s)** . . . **13** ___

14　Enter the **smaller** of line 12 or 13 . . . . **14** ___

15　Enter YOUR **earned income** . . . . **15** ___

16　If married filing a joint return, enter YOUR SPOUSE'S earned income (if your spouse was a student or was disabled, see the instructions for line 5); if married filing a separate return, see the instructions for the amount to enter; **all others,** enter the amount from line 15 . . . **16** ___

17　Enter the **smallest** of line 14, 15, or 16 . . . . . **17** ___

18　**Excluded benefits.** Enter here the **smaller** of the following:

- The amount from line 17, or
- $5,000 ($2,500 if married filing a separate return **and** you were required to enter your spouse's earned income on line 16).　. . . . . **18** ___

19　**Taxable benefits.** Subtract line 18 from line 12. Also, include this amount on Form 1040, line 7. On the dotted line next to line 7, enter "DCB" . . . . **19** ___

To claim the child and dependent care
credit, complete lines 20–24 below.

20　Enter $2,400 ($4,800 if two or more qualifying persons) . . . . **20** ___

21　Enter the amount from line 18 . . . . **21** ___

22　Subtract line 21 from line 20. If zero or less, **STOP.** You cannot take the credit. **Exception.** If you paid 1997 expenses in 1998, see the instructions for line 9 . . . . **22** ___

23　Complete line 2 on the front of this form. DO NOT include in column (c) any excluded benefits shown on line 18 above. Then, add the amounts in column (c) and enter the total here . . . . **23** ___

24　Enter the **smaller** of line 22 or 23. Also, enter this amount on line 3 on the front of this form and complete lines 4–9 . . . . **24** ___

✪ *Printed on recycled paper*

single year is larger than that amount, you can carry the rest of the balance for the next five years.

♦ Beginning in 2002, you can claim the credit only if you adopt a special-needs child. Claim the credit on Form 8839 and carry the balance to Form 1040.

4. Claim the Earned-Income Tax Credit

The Earned Income Tax Credit (EIC) is a *refundable* tax credit for working families with dependent children and, in some cases, childless workers. That means if the credit exceeds your actual tax, the government will pay you the difference. You can claim it when you file your return, or you can take it throughout the year in the form of "advance EIC" payments. Here's how it works:

♦ You can claim the EIC if you have earned income from wages, salaries, tips, and self-employment income, with "modified adjusted gross income" under $26,450 (with one qualifying child) or $30,095 (with two or more qualifying children). A "qualifying child" is your child, adopted child, grandchild, stepchild, or foster child living with you for more than six months of the year and under age 19 (age 24 if a full-time student).

♦ You can also claim the credit with no children if your earned income and modified adjusted gross income are both under $10,000. (These figures are for the 1998 tax year and are adjusted for inflation.)

♦ "Modified adjusted gross income" equals adjusted gross income, but doesn't include certain losses from capital losses, trusts and estates, and certain businesses.

♦ You can't claim the credit if you have more than $2,250 in interest, dividends, net rent or royalty income, capital gains, or passive income.

♦ The IRS publishes a table each year (included with your Form 1040) telling you what credit to take.

♦ If you know that you'll qualify for the credit, you can file a Form W-5 with your employer to get a part of the credit paid with each paycheck. You have to include these payments as income when you file your return, and you may have to refund a part of the advance EIC if you get too much during the year.

The IRS has begun cracking down on people who file for advance EIC payments they don't deserve and is penalizing them by denying them the credit for future years. So if you choose this strategy, make sure to figure it properly. Most low-income taxpayers who use professional tax preparers do so to calculate the EIC.

5. Shift Investments and Income to Your Children

Putting investments in your children's names, so that the income will be taxed at their lower rate, is a classic strategy for cutting taxes on your investments. The Tax Reform Act of 1986 clamped down by imposing a "kiddie tax" equal to the parents' highest rate on unearned income over $1,400 (indexed for inflation) for children under age 14. But shifting income remains a valuable strategy for cutting your own tax while building up your family's fortunes.

Here's how to figure the tax on your child's income:

- If your child has less than $700 of gross income, there's no need to file a return.

- If the child has investment income, file a return once the child's total income tops $700.

- If the child has earned income but no investment income, file a return once the child's earned income tops $4,150.

- Once your child's net investment income tops $1,400, the kiddie tax kicks in. If your child itemizes deductions (!) and has more than $700 in deductible investment expenses (!), the floor is $700 plus the deductible investment expenses.

- To figure the actual kiddie tax, first figure your own tax. Then figure how much your children's income subject to the tax increases your tax. Finally, allocate the extra tax to each child in proportion to each child's income subject to the tax.

- Figure the kiddie tax on Form 8615. You can attach it to the child's return or to your own.

- If you're married filing separately, use the larger separate taxable income to figure the kiddie tax. If you're divorced, use the income of the parent who has custody for the greatest part of the year. Your child's income does not add to your adjusted gross income for purposes of figuring limits on deductions or credits. For example, your child's income does not affect your ability to contribute to an IRA.

If your child's income is solely from interest and dividends, you can report it all on your own return with Form 8814. You'll pay $105 plus 15% of the child's income over $700, plus whatever kiddie tax is due. This saves you the trouble of filing your child's own return. However, this choice will increase your adjusted gross income for purposes of figuring limits on deductions or credits.

Just how much can you save by putting investments in your child's name? The fact is, you can invest a substantial amount of money without cracking that $1,400 limit. A stock index fund paying a 2% dividend can grow to $70,000 before the income tops $1,400. The tax on 2% of $70,000 will be just $105. If you're in the 28% bracket, you'd pay $392; in the 39.6% bracket you'd pay $554.40.

Children under the age of majority can't hold investment property in their own name. Some sort of trust or custodial account is necessary. Custodial accounts are the most common because they require less paperwork (and no legal fees) to establish. Each state has a Uniform Gifts to Minors (UGMA) or Uniform Transfers to Minors (UTMA) statute governing these accounts. Here's how they work:

- Generally, you establish an account with an adult as "custodian' to hold the investments for the benefit of the beneficiary child.

- You can use funds from the account for the benefit of the child. But you can't use the child's funds to cover your parental responsibilities.

Form **8615**	**Tax for Children Under Age 14** **Who Have Investment Income of More Than $1,400**	OMB No. 1545-0998 **1998**

Department of the Treasury
Internal Revenue Service (O)

▶ **Attach ONLY to the child's Form 1040, Form 1040A, or Form 1040NR.**

Attachment
Sequence No. **33**

Child's name shown on return | Child's social security number

A Parent's name (first, initial, and last). *Caution: See instructions on back before completing.* | **B** Parent's social security number

C Parent's filing status (check one):

☐ Single ☐ Married filing jointly ☐ Married filing separately ☐ Head of household ☐ Qualifying widow(er)

Part I **Child's Net Investment Income**

1	Enter the child's investment income, such as taxable interest and dividends. See instructions. If this amount is $1,400 or less, **stop;** do not file this form	**1**	
2	If the child **did not** itemize deductions on **Schedule A** (Form 1040 or Form 1040NR), enter $1,400. If the child **did** itemize deductions, see instructions	**2**	
3	Subtract line 2 from line 1. If the result is zero or less, **stop;** do not complete the rest of this form but **do** attach it to the child's return	**3**	
4	Enter the child's **taxable income** from Form 1040, line 39; Form 1040A, line 24; or Form 1040NR, line 38 . . . . ▶	**4**	
5	Enter the **smaller** of line 3 or line 4 . . . . ▶	**5**	

Part II **Tentative Tax Based on the Tax Rate of the Parent Listed on Line A**

6	Enter the parent's **taxable income** from Form 1040, line 39; Form 1040A, line 24; Form 1040EZ, line 6; TeleFile Tax Record, line J; Form 1040NR, line 38; or Form 1040NR-EZ, line 14. If less than zero, enter -0-	**6**	
7	Enter the total net investment income, if any, from Forms 8615, line 5, of **all other** children of the parent identified above. **Do not** include the amount from line 5 above	**7**	
8	Add lines 5, 6, and 7	**8**	
9	Enter the tax on line 8 based on the **parent's** filing status. See instructions. If **Schedule D** or **J** (Form 1040) is used to figure the tax, check here . . . . ▶ ☐	**9**	
10	Enter the parent's tax from Form 1040, line 40; Form 1040A, line 25; Form 1040EZ, line 10; TeleFile Tax Record, line J; Form 1040NR, line 39; or Form 1040NR-EZ, line 15. If any tax is from **Form 4972 or 8814,** see instructions. If **Schedule D** or **J** (Form 1040) was used to figure the tax, check here . . . . ▶ ☐	**10**	
11	Subtract line 10 from line 9 and enter the result. If line 7 is blank, enter on line 13 the amount from line 11 and go to **Part III**	**11**	
12a	Add lines 5 and 7 . . . . **12a**		
b	Divide line 5 by line 12a. Enter the result as a decimal (rounded to at least three places) . .	**12b**	✕ .
13	Multiply line 11 by line 12b . . . . ▶	**13**	

Part III **Child's Tax**—If lines 4 and 5 above are the same, enter -0- on line 15 and go to line 16.

14	Subtract line 5 from line 4 . . . . **14**		
15	Enter the tax on line 14 based on the **child's** filing status. See instructions. If **Schedule D** or **J** (Form 1040) is used to figure the tax, check here . . . . ▶ ☐	**15**	
16	Add lines 13 and 15	**16**	
17	Enter the tax on line 4 based on the **child's** filing status. See instructions. If **Schedule D** or **J** (Form 1040) is used to figure the tax, check here . . . . ▶ ☐	**17**	
18	Enter the **larger** of line 16 or line 17 here and on Form 1040, line 40; Form 1040A, line 25; or Form 1040NR, line 39 . . . . ▶	**18**	

General Instructions

Purpose of Form

For children under age 14, investment income over $1,400 is taxed at the parent's rate if the parent's rate is higher than the child's rate. If the child's investment income is more than $1,400, use this form to figure the child's tax.

TIP: See Pub. 929, Tax Rules for Children and Dependents, if the child, the parent, or any of the parent's other children under age 14 received capital gain distributions or farm income. It has information on how

to figure the tax using **Schedule D** or **J,** which may result in less tax.

Investment Income

As used on this form, "investment income" includes all taxable income other than earned income as defined on page 2. It includes taxable interest, dividends, capital gains, rents, royalties, etc. It also includes pension and annuity income and income (other than earned income) received as the beneficiary of a trust.

Who Must File

Generally, Form 8615 must be filed for any child who was under age 14 on January 1,

1999, had more than $1,400 of investment income, and is required to file a tax return. But if neither parent was alive on December 31, 1998, do not use Form 8615. Instead, figure the child's tax in the normal manner.

Note: *The parent may be able to elect to report the child's interest and dividends on his or her return. If the parent makes this election, the child will not have to file a return or Form 8615. However, the Federal income tax on the child's income, including capital gain distributions, may be higher if this election is made. For more details, see* **Form 8814,** *Parents' Election To Report Child's Interest and Dividends.*

For Paperwork Reduction Act Notice, see back of form.   Cat. No. 64113U   Form **8615** (1998)

Additional Information

For more details, see Pub. 929.

Incomplete Information for Parent or Other Children

If the parent's taxable income or filing status or the net investment income of the parent's other children is not known by the due date of the child's return, reasonable estimates may be used. Write "Estimated" on the appropriate line(s) of Form 8615. For more details, see Pub. 929.

Amended Return

If after the child's return is filed the parent's taxable income changes or the net investment income of any of the parent's other children changes, the child's tax must be refigured using the adjusted amounts. If the child's tax changes, file **Form 1040X,** Amended U.S. Individual Income Tax Return, to correct the child's tax.

Alternative Minimum Tax

A child whose tax is figured on Form 8615 may owe the alternative minimum tax. For details, see **Form 6251,** Alternative Minimum Tax—Individuals, and its instructions.

Line Instructions

Lines A and B

If the child's parents were married to each other and filed a joint return, enter the name and social security number (SSN) of the parent who is listed first on the joint return.

If the parents were married but filed separate returns, enter the name and SSN of the parent who had the **higher** taxable income. If you do not know which parent had the higher taxable income, see Pub. 929.

If the parents were unmarried, treated as unmarried for Federal income tax purposes, or separated either by a divorce or separate maintenance decree, enter the name and SSN of the parent who had custody of the child for most of the year (the custodial parent).

Exception. If the custodial parent remarried and filed a joint return with his or her new spouse, enter the name and SSN of the person listed first on the joint return, even if that person is not the child's parent. If the custodial parent and his or her new spouse filed separate returns, enter the name and SSN of the person with the **higher** taxable income, even if that person is not the child's parent.

Note: *If the parents were unmarried but lived together during the year with the child, enter the name and SSN of the parent who had the **higher** taxable income.*

Child's Investment Income Worksheet—Line 1 (keep a copy for your records)

1. Enter the amount from the child's Form 1040, line 22; Form 1040A, line 14; or Form 1040NR, line 23, whichever applies . . . . . .   1. _____

2. Enter the child's **earned income** (defined on this page) plus any deduction the child claims on Form 1040, line 30, or Form 1040NR, line 30, whichever applies . . . .   2. _____

3. Subtract line 2 from line 1. Enter the result here and on Form 8615, line 1 . . . .   3. _____

Line 1

If the child had no earned income (defined later), enter the child's adjusted gross income from Form 1040, line 34; Form 1040A, line 19; or Form 1040NR, line 34.

If the child had earned income, use the worksheet on this page to figure the amount to enter on line 1. But if the child files **Form 2555 or 2555-EZ** (relating to foreign earned income), has a net loss from self-employment, or claims a net operating loss deduction, you **must** use the worksheet in Pub. 929 instead.

Earned income includes wages, tips, and other payments received for personal services performed. Generally, it is the total of the amounts reported on Form 1040, lines 7, 12, and 18; Form 1040A, line 7; or Form 1040NR, lines 8, 13, and 19.

Line 2

If the child itemized deductions, enter the **greater** of:

● $1,400, **or**

● $700 plus the portion of the amount on **Schedule A** (Form 1040), line 28, or **Schedule A** (Form 1040NR), line 17, that is directly connected with the production of the investment income on Form 8615, line 1.

Line 6

If the parent filed a joint return, enter the taxable income shown on that return even if the parent's spouse is not the child's parent.

Line 9

Figure the tax using the Tax Table, Tax Rate Schedules, or **Schedule D or J** (Form 1040), whichever applies. If any net capital gain is included on line 5, 6, or 7, Part IV of Schedule D must be used to figure the tax on the amount on line 8, unless Schedule J may be used. See Pub. 929 for details on how to figure the net capital gain included on line 8. If any farm income is included on line 5, 6, or 7, the tax may be less if you use Schedule J.

Line 10

If the parent filed a joint return, enter the tax shown on that return even if the parent's spouse is not the child's parent. If the parent filed **Form 4972, do not** include

any tax from that form on line 10. If the parent filed **Form 8814,** enter "Form 8814" and the total tax from line 9 of Form(s) 8814 on the dotted line next to line 10 of Form 8615.

Line 15

Figure the tax using the Tax Table, Tax Rate Schedule X, or Schedule D or J, whichever applies. If line 14 includes any net capital gain, use Schedule D to figure the tax. See Pub. 929 for details on how to figure the net capital gain included on line 14. If any farm income is included on line 14, the tax may be less if you use Schedule J.

Line 17

Figure the tax as if these rules did not apply. For example, if the child has a net capital gain, use Schedule D to figure his or her tax.

◆ Income from the account is reported under the child's Social Security number and taxed under the above rules.

◆ When the child reaches majority, generally at age 21, the assets in the account revert to the child alone. Many parents are reluctant to commit large sums to custodial accounts, fearing an irresponsible child will blow the money on irresponsible or frivolous purchases. But there are ways to invest that "lock up" the money away from the reach of a spendthrift heir. For example, you can use funds to buy a minority interest in your own house, or minority interests in a family limited partnership.

◆ Before committing substantial sums into your child's name, consider that if you apply for college financial aid, the school will expect the child to use a greater percentage of that money for tuition than if you had held the funds yourself. (For more information, see Chapter 11, Investing for College.

◆ Many parents fund custodial accounts with annual gifts. You can give $10,000 per year to as many people as you want without paying gift tax. If your spouse joins you, you can give $20,000 per year to as many people as you want. This amount is the gift tax annual exclusion. If your gifts to any person top $10,000 in a year, you'll owe gift tax on the amount over $10,000. You don't actually pay tax until your combined taxable gifts exceed the estate tax unified credit exemption equivalent—$625,000 for 1998. This involves some estate planning issues. Just be aware that you're safe in making gifts up to $10,000.

TAX BREAKS FOR SUPPORTING YOUR PARENTS

◆ ◆ ◆

More and more taxpayers find themselves "sandwiched" between generations: caring for parents as well as for their teenage and college-bound kids. Fortunately, there are tax breaks to ease the load. These include claiming your parent or parents as dependents; filing a Multiple Support Declaration to claim personal exemptions for your parents even if you don't otherwise qualify; and several strategies for shifting income and deductions to benefit the generation with the highest tax burden.

Claim Your Parent as a Dependent

You can claim your parents as dependents if you furnish more than 50% of their support, and their adjusted gross income (not counting Social Security) is $2,700 or less. If you can, claim them as dependents to cut your own tax without costing them anything.

File a Multiple Support Agreement

A Multiple Support Agreement, IRS Form 2441, lets you claim a personal exemption for a parent you couldn't otherwise claim. For more information, see "Claim All Your Personal Exemptions, page 22."

Pay Medical Expenses for Your Parents

If you pay your dependent parents' medical expenses directly to their health-care provider (rather than giving them money to pay the expenses themselves), you can deduct the expenses directly on your own return. This works even if you pay the expenses with money your parents give to you.

Shift Investment Losses Between Generations

When it comes to investing, nobody's perfect. Some day all of us will have to take a loss. However, you can use a lower-bracket relative to shelter eventual gains if the investment value returns.

A sale to a related party—a parent, grandparent, child, grandchild, sibling, or corporation more than 50% owned by the seller—doesn't qualify as a completed sale. If you or a family member are in a low tax bracket and can't take advantage of a loss, sell the asset to a related party. The loss isn't deductible then. But if the related party sells the asset at a profit, they'll owe tax on just the gain that tops the original owner's loss.

> ◗ **Example:** Your retired father bought units in a limited partnership for $10,000. It's worth just $5,000 now, but his low 15% bracket limits the value of the loss. If you're in a higher bracket, buy the partnership units from him. You'll owe no tax on any sale up to $10,000.

If you'd like to take a loss but keep the property in the family, sell to an in-law. You'll get your deduction for the loss. But in-laws don't count as related parties, so use them to have your cake and eat it, too.

Rent a Home to Your Parents

This is a powerful strategy for claiming deductions your parents can't. Many retired parents have paid off their houses and can't claim a mortgage-interest deduction. What's more, without that mortgage-interest deduction (and with their higher standard deduction), many don't itemize at all. So there's not even a deduction for property taxes.

If you buy your parents' home and rent it back, with a lease for a period of years or even for life, you can create tax deductions without paying anything out of your own pocket. Interested? Here's how it works:

- First, buy the house from your parents at a fair-market price. You can put down as much or as little as you like. You can finance it through a bank or have them take back a mortgage at a fair-market rate.
- Next, lease the house to your parents for whatever term you choose. The lease can be for a term of years or a lifetime if you choose. If you'd like, the rent can equal your actual carrying costs: the mortgages, the taxes, and the homeowners' insurance. No actual cash has to change hands except for payments to third parties: taxes, insurance, and maintenance.

◆ Treat the house as rental property. Your payments for the mortgage, taxes, and insurance cancel out your rental income. You can also depreciate the house and claim the rental real-estate loss allowance if your adjusted gross income is under $150,000. (For more information, see Chapter 9, Real Estate.)

This strategy also helps shelter assets for Medicaid planning. Medicaid planning is a controversial strategy of artificially impoverishing yourself in order to qualify for Medicaid nursing-home financing. The federal government has recently cracked down on this process and has even passed a "Grandma's Going to Jail" law that makes it a felony for attorneys and financial advisers to advise clients to transfer assets to qualify for Medicaid. Renting a home to your parents takes the property off their books for value received. What's more, you get any gain in value. Your parents retain an asset—the mortgage—but one with a fixed value, not an increasing value. If the state comes back to claim reimbursement, at least the gain stays in the family.

THREE

BUYING, OWNING, AND SELLING YOUR HOME

YOUR HOME IS LIKELY your biggest single investment. It can also be your biggest tax shelter if you use it right. There's no question that the tax code favors homeowners. Homeowners can write off their mortgage-interest payments and property taxes. They can tap their equity to convert nondeductible personal interest into deductible home-equity debt. Their equity grows tax-deferred until they sell their house. And even then, they can exclude up to $500,000 of gain from their income.

If you don't yet own a home, this chapter can help you figure how much tax you'll save by buying. You also learn how the tax code can help you build a down-payment fund. If you do own a home, this chapter shows you how to use it to convert nondeductible personal interest—car loans, student loans, and credit cards—into tax-deductible home-equity interest. You learn how to cut your tax when you sell your home. Finally, you learn how to make the most of your vacation home.

BUY A HOME FOR TAX SAVINGS AND MORE

◆ ◆ ◆

Buying a home is one of your biggest financial decisions. You shouldn't do it just for tax savings: as you'll see, you might not save as much as you think. But tax savings are an important part of the total picture. When you rent, you get to live in your home and collect worthless rent receipts. When you buy, you build equity *and* get a deduction for mortgage interest.

Here are the basic rules for deducting mortgage interest:

- ◆ You can write off interest on up to $1 million of "acquisition indebtedness" you use to buy your primary residence and one additional residence. Loans you use to substantially improve your home also qualify as acquisition indebtedness.

- ◆ You can deduct interest on up to $1 million of home-construction loans for 24 months from the time construction begins. Interest before and after this period is nondeductible personal interest.

- ◆ Your lender will report the interest you pay on Form 1098. This form also goes to the IRS. Check the amount your lender reports to make sure it's correct. If not, contact your lender and have him or her issue a revised form. If the amounts that you and your lender report don't agree, the IRS may question your return.

- ◆ You can deduct points you pay to buy or improve your primary residence if charging points is an established practice in your geographical area and the points charged don't exceed the points generally charged in the area. The amount has to be figured as a percentage of the loan amount and specifically itemized as points, loan-origination fee, or loan-discount fee. Finally, points have to be paid directly to the lender. If your points don't meet these tests, you can still amortize them over the life of the loan. Your lender will report the deductible amount on Form 1098.

◆ If you miss a payment and pay a late fee, your late fee is tax-deductible. Prepayment penalties are also tax-deductible.

Leverage Multiplies Your Investment Gain

Buying a home does more than just cut your tax: It leverages your investment. Leverage is using borrowed money to boost your return, sometimes referred to as "other people's money," or OPM. Depending on your down payment, your mortgage can leverage you five, ten, or even twenty times your initial investment. There's no other investment that lets the average taxpayer put down so little money to control so much appreciation. This leverage is the key to profiting from your home. Over the long run, residential real estate values generally keep up with inflation. It's the leverage, and not the mere appreciation, that multiplies the gain and makes most homes their owner's best investment.

> ▶ **Example:** You put $10,000 down to buy a $100,000 house. A year later, the house is worth $104,000. The house itself appreciates just $4,000, or 4%. But your $10,000 equity appreciates the same $4,000, for a whopping 40% gain.

Nearly all your payments in the early years go to interest. So, nearly all your payments in the early years are deductible. This also means your leverage is greatest in the early years.

> ▶ **Example:** You take out a 30-year mortgage for $100,000 at 8%. Your monthly payment is $733.76. Just $67.09 of your first payment goes toward repaying principal. The remaining $666.67 is deductible interest. Three years later, just $78.69 of your thirty-seventh payment goes toward repaying principal. The remaining $655.07 is deductible interest.

As the years go by, your equity grows, your principal payments grow, and your interest payments shrink, cutting your deduction. Of course, as your equity grows, you increase the amount you can borrow with a home-equity loan or line of credit.

How Much House Can You Buy?

Obviously, your tax break depends on how much you borrow. Mortgage lenders use various ratios to figure this amount. "Debt-to-income" ratios measure what percentage of your income you can pay for housing and monthly installment expenses. "Loan-to-value" ratios tell you what percentage of your home's purchase price you can borrow and how much cash you have to put down. The conventional formula for mortgages up to $240,000 (the 1999 limit for resale on the secondary market) uses what's called a "28/36" limit:

◆ Total housing expenses, including principal payments, interest, taxes, and insurance, should total no more than 28% of your gross income.

HOW MUCH HOUSE PAYMENT CAN YOU AFFORD?

1. Monthly Gross Income _____

    Include salary, wages, self-employment income,
    alimony and child support, plus any additional income

2. Debt-to-income ratio _____

    Multiply Line 1 by .36 (or your lender's ratio, if higher)

3. Nonhousing debt _____

    Include all debts not scheduled to be paid off within
    ten months; include car loans or lease payments,
    student loans, and credit-card payments

4. Income available for housing _____

    Subtract Line 3 from Line 2

5. Housing expense _____

    Multiply Line 1 by .28 (or your lender's ratio, if higher)

6. Maximum housing expense _____

    Enter the lesser of Line 4 or Line 5; this is the maximum
    available for mortgage, property tax, homeowners'
    insurance, plus PMI.

- ◆ Total debt payments, including mortgage, car loans, student loans, and credit cards, should total no more than 36% of your gross income. (Most lenders let you exclude payments scheduled to end within ten months.)

FHA-insured loans may stretch these limits to 29/41. Portfolio lenders (those who keep and service their own loans), jumbo lenders (those who lend above the $214,600 resale limit), and "B," "C," and "D" lenders (those who make loans to poor-credit risks) may stretch them even higher. Some lenders will accept debt-to-income ratios up to 55% of gross income. At that point you'll probably find it tough to buy groceries.

If your down payment is less than 20%, you'll generally have to make an additional monthly payment for private mortgage insurance (PMI). The annual cost is usually 0.65% of the mortgage balance. Some lenders now fold the insurance premium into the loan itself. This makes your PMI tax-deductible as well.

Once you've figured how much you can borrow, add your down payment to figure how much house you can afford.

Buying a house might not give you the instant tax cut you expect. That's because your total itemized deductions, including interest income, don't really cut your tax until they exceed your standard deduction. For 1998, single filers get a "free" $4,250 deduction; heads of households get $6,250; married couples filing jointly get $7,100; and married couples filing separately get $3,550. If you're married renters, filing jointly, and your state and local taxes, charitable contributions, and other deductions add up to just $2,000, you get to deduct the full $7,100. If you buy a house and pay $4,000 in interest the first year, you don't get any benefit from the interest deduction because your total itemized deductions don't top the "free" $7,100 standard deduction. Maybe next year you'll pay $8,000 in interest for a total of $10,000 in itemized deductions. That's better, but it's still just $2,900 more than the standard deduction. You don't get the full benefit of the $8,000 deductible interest.

Of course, you can deduct your property taxes as well. You may also be able to write off any points you pay up front on the loan and any interest and partial-year property taxes you pay with your closing costs. These taxes and points may help you squeeze out a full year's deduction even if you buy your home near the end of the year.

Which Mortgage Is Best?

Before discussing which mortgage is best for you, it's important to realize what makes a mortgage good—namely, a low after-tax cost. Remember, the point isn't just to give yourself a tax deduction. The proper goal is to use the tax law to cut your cost of borrowing. Taxes are just one part of your overall financial picture.

Your deduction depends primarily on your interest rate. Higher rates obviously give you a bigger deduction, but cost you more out of pocket. Generally, 30-year fixed mortgages carry the highest rate. Fifteen-year fixed mortgages have lower rates but higher payments since each payment includes more principal. Finally, adjustable-rate mortgages offer the lowest initial rates of all. If you choose a lower adjustable rate, your initial monthly payments, and tax deduction, will be lower than if you choose a fixed rate. For example, if you take a $100,000 for 30 years with a fixed rate of 8%, your first payment will be $733.76, including $666.67 of interest. If you take the same $100,000 loan for 30

MORTGAGE-INTEREST TAX SAVINGS

This worksheet will calculate your tax savings the year you buy your home, (including as many months of mortgage payments as appropriate) plus future years including 12 full months of mortgage payments.

	First Year	*Future Years*
1. Current Itemized Deductions (medical expenses, state and local taxes, charitable, miscellaneous, etc.)	_____	_____
2. Mortgage Interest	_____	_____
If unavailable, estimate 90% of the payment for a 30-year loan or 70% for a 15-year		
3. Property Taxes	_____	_____
4. "Points"	_____	_____
5. Total Itemized Deductions Add Lines 1–4	_____	_____
6. Standard Deduction	_____	_____
Single:	$4,250	
Head of household:	$6,250	
Married filing jointly:	$7,100	
Married filing separately:	$3,550	
7. "Excess" Itemized Deductions Subtract 6 from 5	_____	_____
8. Tax Bracket	_____	_____
9. Tax Savings Multiply 7 by 8	_____	_____

years with an adjustable rate starting at 6%, your first payment will be $599.55, including just $500 of interest. Over the course of the first year, you'll pay nearly $2,000 less interest. If the adjustable loan makes sense on its own merits, $2,000 in your pocket is clearly better than a $2,000 tax deduction. Just be aware how the lower rate cuts your tax advantage.

You can shop for a mortgage yourself, or you can use a mortgage broker. The U.S. Department of Housing and Urban Development reports that in 1996, mortgage brokers were involved in half of the nation's three million mortgage originations. Independent mortgage brokers represent up to dozens of lenders. They can advise you which mortgage makes the most sense for you. They can shop across the country for the lowest rates. And they can make sure your application is complete and correct before you submit it, saving time and aggravation. The faster you close on your home, the faster you convert those worthless rent receipts into valuable tax deductions.

CONSIDER RETIREMENT SAVINGS FOR EXTRA DOWN-PAYMENT HELP

❖ ❖ ❖

The Taxpayer Relief Act of 1997 threw homebuyers a bone. Now you can withdraw up to a $10,000 lifetime limit from your IRA (or even someone else's), without the usual 10% penalty for withdrawals before age 59½, to pay "qualified acquisition costs" of a "primary residence" of a "first-time homebuyer." In most cases, this won't harness much value from the IRA's tax-deferred compounding. The real value is letting you off the hook for the 10% penalty.

Here are the rules:

♦ "Qualified acquisition costs" include the cost of buying, building, or renovating a residence, including any reasonable or usual settlement, financing, or closing costs.

♦ A "first-time homebuyer" is an IRA owner (or spouse, child, grandchild, or ancestor of the individual) who has not owned a home (and whose spouse has not owned a home) in the two-year period ending on the date of acquisition of the home. (In fact, a "first-time homebuyer" doesn't have to be a first-time homebuyer at all.)

♦ You have to use the money within 120 days of taking it from the IRA.

♦ If you take the money from a regular IRA or a spousal IRA, you still owe regular tax on the money you withdraw.

♦ If you take the money from a Roth IRA within five tax years of the period beginning with the first tax year you contribute to the account, you'll pay ordinary income tax on any portion of the withdrawal exceeding your contributions to the account (for more information on the five-year rule, see the discussion of Roth IRAs in Chapter 12).

If you participate in an employer retirement plan, you may be able to borrow from your account to buy a home. The law lets you borrow up to $50,000 or 50% of your vested account balance, whichever is lower, and take up to 20 years to pay back the loan. For more information, see your plan administrator.

If you contribute to a 401(k) or 403(b) plan, you might also be able to take a "hardship" withdrawal for an immediate and heavy financial need. This can include the purchase of a home (excluding mortgage payments) and payment of any amounts necessary to prevent foreclosure on your mortgage. Hardship withdrawals are limited to your original contributions. Also, you can't make new contributions for 12 months after taking a hardship distribution.

How valuable is the new IRA opportunity? Let's consider it first as an investment question, then look at the tax picture. If you're saving to buy a house, you probably have a clear time frame—say, three years—that rules out stocks. (Most investment advisers recommend avoiding stocks unless you have a three-to-five-year time frame). You also don't want volatile investments that could drop right before you need the money. This usually indicates money markets or short-term bond funds.

Having picked your investment, how much help do you get with your taxes? The IRA rules really don't save a lot for short-term accumulations such as down-payment funds. Tax deferral boosts your returns, but not by much.

> ▶ **Example:**   You're in the 28% bracket and you have $150 per month, before tax, to save for a house in three years. You've chosen a short-term bond fund paying 8%.

- ◆ In an IRA, you can save the full $150 per month. After 36 months, you'll amass $6,121. After you pay taxes on your withdrawal, you'll have $4,407.
- ◆ In a taxable account, you can save $108 per month ($150 minus $42 in tax). After 36 months, you'll have $4,253, just $154, or 3 1/2% less, than in the IRA.

Having said all this, the tax law still can help you buy a house. Find out whether your employer-retirement plan lets you withdraw cash to buy a house. If so, contribute as much as you can, knowing you can tap the money for a house as well as retirement. If you don't have a plan, or your plan doesn't let you withdraw cash to buy a house, fund an IRA, knowing you can tap the money for a house as well as retirement.

WHEN SHOULD YOU PAY OFF YOUR MORTGAGE?

❖ ❖ ❖

Lots of homeowners, and financial advisers, prefer to pay mortgages faster than scheduled. This gives you several advantages. Your equity and net worth grow faster. You pay no tax on your equity growth (if you pay any at all), until you sell your house. Your additional home equity doesn't count against you when you apply for college financial aid. And in some states, such as Florida, your equity is protected from creditors. This is particularly valuable for doctors, lawyers, and other high-risk professionals.

One of the most common prepayment plans is the biweekly plan, in which you split your payment in half and make a payment every two weeks. Over the course of a year, you make 26 biweekly payments, equaling one extra monthly payment. You can also add one-twelfth of your regular payment to your check each month, or make an extra lump-sum payment every year. All these can cut years off your mortgage if you start early enough. While it sounds like a miracle, it's just compound interest at work. The net result is the same as investing one monthly payment per year in an account earning the same rate as your mortgage. So, if your mortgage interest rate is higher than what you can earn in a side investment, consider prepaying your mortgage as an investment alternative.

Some homeowners worry that these plans will cost them their tax deductions. This is a false worry for two reasons. First, most of your payments in the early years go to interest, not principal. This is true even if you begin prepayments immediately after taking out the mortgage. So the effect on your tax deduction is tiny at first. Second, by cutting your interest payments, mortgage prepayments cut your real, after-tax cost of borrowing, even though they cut your tax deduction. If you're smart enough to shop for the best mortgage, you know that your real goal is the lowest after-tax cost of borrowing, not just the biggest tax deduction.

Beware of "consultants" who offer to sell you biweekly payment plans. These plans generally charge a one-time setup fee of $195 to $395, plus a debit fee $2 to $3 for each biweekly payment. They promise to cut your mortgage payments by up to 40%, which is true enough. The problem is, their fees equal an unconscionably high "load," or commission, you would never pay on a comparable investment. Let's say you have a $100,000 mortgage at 8%, with a monthly payment of $733.76. If you sign up for a biweekly payment plan with a $2.50 debit fee, you'll effectively "invest" one $733.76 payment per year at a guaranteed rate of 8%. So far, so good. But you'll pay biweekly debit fees of $65 for the privilege. Those fees alone equal an 8.9% "load." And that's not including the setup fee, which can top 50% of your first year's prepayment. These programs are fine if you don't have the discipline to make the prepayments yourself. But make sure the fees don't devour your savings before you enroll.

Some advisers recommend not paying your mortgage at all. In fact, some say you should take out the biggest mortgage you can and stretch it for as long as you can. Their reason is that you should be able to earn more, after tax, with stocks or other investments than you can by paying off your loan. This is leverage, plain and simple, making money on the spread between the interest you pay on the loan and what you can earn on the outstanding balance. Of course, this is one of those cases where the pure numbers might not make sense. If you don't feel comfortable with a large mortgage debt, then by all means pay it down. Your tax savings might not make up for the peace of mind you lose with the debt.

"Interest only" mortgages let you maximize your leverage and tax deduction, avoid liquidating investments to make a down payment, and give you flexibility if your income fluctuates. These are mostly adjustable-rate loans that charge only interest for the first ten years. At that point, you begin repaying principal as with any other mortgage, generally over one 20-year period. Or, you can refinance for another interest-only period. Payments are lower than with a standard mortgage since nothing goes toward principal. If you can invest your monthly savings at a higher rate than the cost of the loan, you profit more than if you "invest" it in paying down your principal. Several innovative programs offer 100% financing secured by the house itself and a portfolio of securities equal to perhaps a third of the purchase price. These give you the ultimate in leverage—you capture 100% of the property's appreciation without putting down a dime—and let you use appreciated securities to finance your down payment without having to sell them and pay tax on capital gains.

CUT YOUR TAXES
WITH HOME-EQUITY DEBT

◆ ◆ ◆

You can deduct the interest you pay on up to $100,000 of loans or lines of credit secured by your primary residence and one additional residence. Sure, you can use it to add a room, or turn your master bath into whirlpool nirvana. You can also use it to pay off car loans, student loans, and any other nondeductible debt. This lets you convert nondeductible personal interest into deductible home-equity debt.

Your home-equity indebtedness doesn't have to be an actual second mortgage. A single mortgage can include both acquisition indebtedness and home-equity indebtedness. If you refinance an existing mortgage and take out equity (finance the new loan for more than the old loan balance), you can deduct the interest on the original balance plus whatever you use to substantially improve your residence as acquisition indebtedness and interest on up to $100,000 more as home-equity indebtedness.

> ▶ **Example:**   You originally take out a mortgage for $150,000 and eventually pay down the mortgage to $120,000. Now you take out a new mortgage for $180,000. Interest on $120,000 of the new mortgage qualifies as acquisition indebtedness; interest on the remaining $60,000 of the new mortgage qualifies as home-equity indebtedness.

Here are some important considerations with this strategy:

◆ Obviously, it's important to compare rates before doing this. If you buy a car with a special 2.9% interest rate, for example, there's no way the tax deduction for home-equity interest can make up for losing the special car rate. Remember, the point is to use tax planning to cut your after-tax cost of borrowing.

◆ Many credit cards come with low "teaser" rates the first year, before jumping to 12–18%. Before you use a home-equity loan to pay off credit cards, make sure the after-tax rate you'll pay is *lower* than the credit-card rate. It might also be less expensive to transfer your balance to a new card with a lower rate.

◆ Home equity is a great way to deduct otherwise nondeductible student loans. But avoid paying off loans while the student is still in college or qualifies for the student-loan-interest deduction. With many loan programs, the federal government pays or waives the interest while the student is still in school. It doesn't pay to use home-equity interest to pay when no interest is due to begin with.

◆ This strategy doesn't work if you use the home-equity debt to buy life insurance or annuities. Since life-insurance and annuity income is tax-deferred, the life-insurance and annuity rules override the home-equity rules.

◆ If you pay points on a home-equity loan, don't deduct the total up front. Instead, pay them proportionately over the term of the loan. If you pay off the loan early, deduct any remaining amount in the final year of the loan.

Choose the Right Home-Equity Loan

Today there is an enormous variety of home-equity lending programs available. You probably learned this just by reviewing your junk mail after you bought your home. Make sure you choose the one that's right for you. Lenders are making millions of dollars available for loans, and there's lots of competition. Be sure to comparison shop on features such as rates, appraisal fees, and origination fees or points.

Lenders will use the same sort of loan-to-value and debt-to-income ratios to qualify you as with first mortgages, but the limits are higher with home-equity debt. Loan-to-value ratios can range as high as 135% of the property value (only the interest secured by the actual property value is deductible), and debt-to-income ratios can range as high as 55%.

A home-equity loan is a traditional second mortgage with a fixed or variable interest rate for a set payoff schedule, amortized just like a mortgage. Loan advantages include fixed payments and a predetermined payoff date.

A home-equity line of credit is a revolving line of credit, much like a credit card, with a fixed or variable interest rate. Your monthly payments will vary depending on your balance. Rates are usually lower than an unsecured line of credit because the line of credit is secured by your home. Lines of credit give you more flexibility with payments. They're also less likely to require an up-front origination fee or points.

AVOID TAX WHEN YOU SELL YOUR HOME

◆ ◆ ◆

Most homeowners will never pay tax on the profit they make on their home. The Taxpayer Relief Act of 1997 replaced a complicated system that required you to "roll" your gains on one house into another to escape taxes and gave you a one-time $125,000 exclusion for sales after age 55. The new system simply excludes up to $250,000 of gain on the sale of your primary residence every two years ($500,000 for joint filers). The Congressional Joint Committee on Taxation reports that in 1996 the old system would save taxpayers a total of $20.1 billion in tax. The new system with the larger exclusion should save taxpayers even more.

Here's how the new system works. Your "basis" in your home, for purposes of figuring capital gains, is equal to your purchase price, plus any expenses of acquiring the home (closing costs, and so forth), plus any improvements you make. Improvements include upgrades, additions, and similar costs, but not maintenance, such as painting or a new roof. Your "adjusted sale price" is the price you get for the house, minus the cost of selling it (real-estate commissions, advertising, and fix-up expenses, and the like). Your profit is your adjusted sale price minus your basis.

Fortunately, you pay tax only if the profit is more than $250,000 ($500,000 for joint filers). Here are the rules for escaping tax on the sale of your home:

◆ You can sell your primary residence and exclude up to $250,000 of gain ($500,000 for joint filers) from your income.

◆ You can do this every two years.

- ◆ If you have to sell your house before the end of the two-year period, you can exclude a pro-rata share of the $250,000 depending on how long you occupy the house. For example, if you occupy it for a year, you can exclude up to $125,000 of gain, or $250,000 for joint filers.

- ◆ If a single taxpayer marries someone who's used the exclusion within two years of the marriage, the newly married couple can exclude up to $250,000. Once two years has passed since either spouse has used the exclusion, the couple can exclude the full $500,000 on their next, combined, sale.

- ◆ If one spouse has died and the couple owned the house jointly, the deceased spouse's basis is "stepped up" to fair-market value on the date of the spouse's death. Let's say you and your spouse buy a house for $80,000. The house is now worth $280,000 and your spouse dies. Your gain before the death would have been $200,000. However, your spouse's basis is stepped up to $140,000, or half of the fair-market value. Your new basis in the house is now $180,000—your half of the $80,000 purchase price, plus your spouse's half of the $280,000 fair-market value at the time of your spouse's death.

There's no break for selling a home at a loss.

The new system offers a break for homeowners who sold a home and paid a tax before the July 7, 1997, transition date. If you buy a new primary residence for at least as much money as you got for the old one, no more than two years after the original sale, you can file an amended return and claim a refund of the tax you paid on the sale of the home. When you later sell the new home, you can exclude $250,000 or $500,000 of total gain on your series of homes. If you can still buy a replacement home in time to satisfy the two-year rule, you can rescue the tax you paid on up to $500,000 in gain. This can save you over $100,000 in tax.

If you and your spouse bought your house before January 1, 1977, you may be able to shelter all the gain after the first spouse's death. How? Include the entire value of the house in the first spouse's estate tax return. As long as the deceased spouse leaves the house to the survivor, there will be no actual estate tax due on the transfer. If the survivor sells the house, the survivor pays tax only on the gain after the first spouse's death. This is a gray area, so check with your tax adviser for more information.

CONSIDER A REVERSE MORTGAGE FOR EXTRA RETIREMENT INCOME

◆ ◆ ◆

A reverse mortgage lets you borrow against your home's equity without making repayments until your death. The "lender" advances you money, in a lump sum or a series of payments, for a term of years or a lifetime. At your death, the lender collects the house and returns any equity not needed to repay the income you take out over your life. Since the money comes in the form of a nontaxable loan, there's no tax to pay on amounts you receive from the arrangement.

You already get a $250,000 tax exclusion when you sell your home ($500,000 for married couples). Any further appreciation escapes tax at your death. The reverse mortgage lets you tap this tax-free growth without having to sell the family homestead.

MAKE THE MOST OF YOUR SECOND HOME

❖ ❖ ❖

Now that the baby boomers have settled into their suburban trophy houses, the market for second homes is heating up. Many second-home buyers are looking for vacation destinations. Others are buying a future retirement home. As the baby boomers accumulate wealth and move toward retirement, many real-estate experts predict that year-round resort communities suitable for retirement living, such as Hilton Head, South Carolina, and Scottsdale, Arizona, will post the healthiest price gains in years to come.

Tax rules for second homes are generally the same as for primary homes, with these differences:

◆ You can deduct the interest you pay on up to $1 million of acquisition indebtedness to buy your primary residence and *one* additional residence. This means you can deduct the interest you use to buy a second home so long as the total debt on your primary residence and second home does not top $1 million. If the total tops $1 million, you can still deduct the interest you pay on the first $1 million of acquisition indebtedness. Obviously, you'd want to write off the highest-rate mortgage first to maximize your break.

◆ You don't actually have to buy a *house,* or even a condominium, to enjoy a second-home tax break. You can deduct the interest you pay on a loan secured by a time-share, boat, or camper so long as it includes sleeping, cooking, and toilet facilities. In fact, you can write off the interest you pay on such a "residence" even if your primary residence is a rental.

◆ You can deduct property taxes on an unlimited number of vacation homes. You lucky devil.

Vacation homes give you two specific tax opportunities. First, you can convert your vacation home into your primary residence to shelter up to $500,000 gain in *both* residences, not just one. Second, you can rent your vacation home for partially or fully tax-free income.

Shelter *Two* Home Sales from Tax

Current law lets you shelter $250,000 of gain ($500,000 for joint filers) when you sell your *primary* residence. This would seem to rule out vacation-home sales. But nothing prevents you from selling your primary residence, converting a vacation home into a primary residence, then later selling the "converted" residence with the same tax break. This is a real windfall for retirees planning to make their vacation home a permanent retirement residence.

Vacation-Home Rental-Income Rules

A recent survey by Chase Manhattan Bank shows that 28% of second-home owners rent their homes. You can use your vacation-home expenses to shelter rental income depending on whether you use it yourself, rent it out, or both. If you use it yourself, you can deduct your mortgage-interest and property taxes just as you would do with your primary home. If you rent it out, you can probably take advantage of these same expenses to shelter some or all of your income. This is true whether you rent it occasionally, or even for a period of years before retirement. This quick test will help you figure your specific vacation-home tax rules.

First, you'll need to figure out how many days of "personal use" you take. Personal use includes days your family uses the house and any days you rent the house for below-market rates. It includes days you trade the use of your home for someplace else. It also includes time you donate to charities, to offer at auction or as prizes. (These donations don't qualify for charitable gift deductions. This is no problem if you use the home enough to treat it as a personal residence. But if you're trying to hold down personal use to treat your home as rental property, it's best to avoid donating use of the home.) Finally, personal use doesn't include time you spend making repairs or getting the property ready for tenants.

VACATION HOME TAX RULES

If you rent your home for 14 days or less, go to 1, following.

If you rent your home for more than 14 days *and* use it personally for more than the greater of 14 days or 10% of the rental days, go to 2, following.

If you rent your home for more than 14 days *and* use it personally for less than the greater of 14 days or 10% of the rental days, go to 3, following.

1. Pocket Tax-Free Income

This is the simplest and happiest case. If you rent out your vacation home for 14 days or less, pocket the rental income, tax-free. You can still deduct your mortgage interest (so long as your total acquisition indebtedness falls under $1 million) and property tax, just as you would with your primary residence. This strategy also works with your primary residence. Plenty of Atlanta and Los Angeles residents pocketed handsome tax-free windfalls renting their homes to Olympics spectators.

2. Treat Your Home as Residential Property

This is the messiest case. If you use your vacation home for the greater of 14 days *or* 10% of the rental days, you have to report the income, but you should be able to write off enough expenses to avoid paying tax on the income. Here's how it works:

◆ Report your rental income on Schedule E.

◆ Deduct your rental expenses against rental income on Schedule E.

◆ Finally, deduct the personal portion of your property taxes and mortgage interest as itemized deductions on Schedule A.

To figure the rental portion of your mortgage-interest and property taxes, divide the number of days of fair rental by the number of days of total use. Personal use for figuring this amount includes days the house stands empty. So you can actually divide the number of days of fair rental into the number of days of the year. That percentage of mortgage-interest and property tax is deductible as a rental expense on Schedule E.

To figure the rental portion of your maintenance and utilities, divide the number of days of fair rental by the number of days of total use (including fair rental and personal use). Personal use here doesn't include days the house sits empty. So the rental portion of maintenance, supplies, and utilities will be a higher percentage of the total expense. That portion of maintenance and utilities is also deductible as a rental expense on Schedule E.

If the rental portions of your mortgage interest and maintenance and utilities aren't enough to shelter your rental income, you can also deduct the cost of renting the house. This includes advertising, commissions to rental agents, and any costs of travel to prepare the house for rental. Any operating expenses you can't deduct are carried forward to future years.

> ▶ **Example:** In 1998, you used your ski condo for 21 days and rented it out for 21 days at $100 per day. You spent a total of $14,000 on mortgage-interest and property tax, $6,000 on maintenance and utilities, and $200 to advertise the rental. You reported $2,100 as rental income. You deducted $805 worth of mortgage-interest and property tax (21 days of rental divided into 365 days, times $14,000 in mortgage interest and taxes), $3,000 of maintenance and utilities (21 days of rental use divided by 42 days of total use, times $6,000 of maintenance and utilities), plus $200 of advertising expense, for a total of $4,005. Your expenses sheltered your $2,100 of income. You got no current deduction for the $1,905 "loss" (income minus rental expenses), but you could carry this amount forward to shelter rental income from the condo in future years. You also deducted the remaining $13,195 mortgage-interest and property tax as an itemized deduction on Schedule A.

3. Treat Your Home as Rental Property

This is a slightly less difficult case from above. If you use your vacation home for the lesser of 14 days *or* 10% of the time you rent it, you can treat the house as rental property. This lets you write off *all* rental expenses against rental income. You may also be able to write off rental losses against other income. Here's how it works:

♦ Report your rental income on Schedule E.

♦ Deduct your rental expenses, including mortgage-interest and property tax, plus depreciation against rental income on Schedule E.

♦ There's no deduction for mortgage-interest or property taxes on Schedule A.

♦ If rental expenses exceed rental income, you can write off the loss against any passive income you might have. If your adjusted gross income is under $150,000 and the average rental is longer than seven days, you may also be able to write off the loss against ordinary income. For more information, see Chapter 9, Real Estate.

To figure the rental portion of your expenses, divide the number of days of fair rental by the number of days of total use (including fair rental and personal use). This applies for mortgage-interest and property taxes as well as for maintenance and utilities. There's no separate formula for "empty days" with mortgage-interest and property taxes as there is when you treat the home as residential property. You can also deduct rental expenses such as advertising, commissions, and travel.

If your personal use varies, so that your home qualifies as rental property some years but not all, choose which method gives you the best advantage.

▶ **Example:**   In 1998, you used the condo just two days and rented it out for 48 days at $100 per day. You spent the same $14,000 on mortgage-interest and property taxes, the same $6,000 on maintenance and utilities, and the same $200 to advertise the rental. You reported $4,800 as rental income. You deducted $13,440 in mortgage-interest and property taxes (48 days of rental use divided by 50 days of total use, times $14,000 in mortgage interest and taxes), $5,760 in maintenance and utilities (48 days of rental use divided by 50 days of total use, times $6,000 of maintenance and utilities), plus $200 of rental expense, for a total of $19,400. Your deductions sheltered the entire $4,800 rental income. You deducted the remaining $14,600 in expenses, plus depreciation, against your remaining income as you were eligible.

FOUR

YOUR JOB
AND YOUR BUSINESS

YOUR JOB AND YOUR BUSINESS—the source of most of your income—are your first line of defense against the IRS. If you don't have to report income, you don't need sophisticated strategies to ease the tax bite. This chapter helps you make the most of your employer's pay package. You also learn how you can use a hobby or sideline business to shelter income. Finally, you learn how to make the most of home-office and car-expense deductions.

TAX-FREE FRINGE BENEFITS

❖ ❖ ❖

Your employer gives you a tax problem. It's called your salary, and you owe tax on it. But your employer can give you tax breaks too, from tax-free fringe benefits to tax-advantaged deferred compensation.

Most employees have no idea how much they cost their employer. But most employers, particularly governments and larger companies, give their employees a boat-load of tax-free benefits. Health insurance is usually the biggest, along with employer-retirement-plan contributions. Stock options aren't taxed until you exercise the option, and sometimes even later. Nonqualified deferred-compensation plans let the employer set aside money to pay you down the road—perhaps an extra income for retirement. Flexible-spending arrangements and dependent-care arrangements let you set aside pre-tax dollars for all sorts of day-to-day expenses. Tax-free fringe benefits also include:

- ◆ Group life-insurance coverage up to $50,000 (if your coverage tops $50,000, you'll owe tax on the value of the coverage over $50,000).
- ◆ No-cost company services (free flights for airline employees, free rooms for hotel employees, and so forth) are tax-free.
- ◆ Discounts on company services (so long as the discount doesn't top the company's gross profit margin) are tax-free.
- ◆ Athletic facilities owned or leased by the employer for the primary use of employees and dependents are tax-free.
- ◆ Dependent-care assistance is tax-free up to $5,000. This amount is reduced to the amount of your spouse's income if your spouse earns less, and reduced to $2,500 if you're married filing separately. Dependent-care assistance also reduces the expenses eligible for the dependent-care credit.
- ◆ Educational reimbursements for job-related courses and payment for undergraduate courses are tax-free up to $5,250 per year.

58

- Employees, retired employees, their spouses, and dependents may also receive $5,250 in tuition reductions for undergraduate courses.

- *"De minimis"* working condition benefits include any expense you could deduct if you paid it yourself. These also include company cars (for business use), transit passes and cash reimbursements up to $65 per month, free parking, and subsidized cafeterias. Meals are tax-free if served on the employer's business premises for the employer's convenience. Lodging on the employer's premises is tax-free if you have to accept it as a condition of employment for the employer's convenience.

- Reimbursed employee business expenses may or may not be taxable income. This depends on whether or not your employer reimburses expenses under an "accountable" plan requiring you to report expenses and return any unused reimbursements. For more information, see "Employee Business Expenses" in the Dictionary of Tax Deductions.

FLEXIBLE-SPENDING ARRANGEMENTS

◆ ◆ ◆

A flexible-spending arrangement, or "cafeteria plan," lets you set aside pretax dollars for a choice of nontaxable fringe benefits that can include health and disability insurance, dependent-care or adoption assistance, and even medical-expense reimbursement. You'll owe Social Security and local payroll tax on money you put in the plan, but no federal income tax. This saves you tax at your top on whatever you put in the plan. Your employer deducts your contributions from your paycheck and deposits it into your account until you need it. Here are the rules:

- When you enroll, you'll have to choose exactly how much to withhold each pay period. You can't change in the middle of the plan year unless there's a change in your family status.

- You can use contributions for expenses incurred during that plan year only.

- If you don't spend enough on qualifying expenses by the end of the plan year, you forfeit your remaining account balance. Wait until December before you buy those prescription sunglasses to soak up anything left.

A dependent-care account is a flexible-spending arrangement for day-care costs. The goal is the same: to let you pay day-care costs with pretax dollars. You can avoid tax on contributions up to $5,000 per year or the lower-paid spouse's earnings, whichever is less.

Contributions to a dependent-care account cut your expenses eligible for the dependent-care credit. So if your employer offers this benefit, you'll have to decide whether you're better off taking the deduction for FSA contributions, or the credit. For more information, see "Tax Breaks for Your Kids," in Chapter 2.

STOCK OPTIONS

◆ ◆ ◆

More than half of the nation's publicly traded companies offer stock options. Options are particularly popular with fast-growing technology companies. They let companies hire talent now without paying cash. And they let employees hitch their pay to their company's rising star. Of course, options can play *too* large a role in some employees' plans. It isn't healthy to tie too much of your pay and net worth to a single company. And disproportionately large options stakes affect marriage, divorce, and estate planning, to name just a few areas.

An option is an agreement to sell a specific number of shares, at a specific price, by a specific date (usually 10 years from the grant). The option value fluctuates with the price of the underlying stock. Generally, you have to stay with your employer for a specified period time. To "exercise" the option, you pay the "option price," which is the stock's market value on the date of the grant. You then take delivery of the specified number of shares. Your profit is the difference between the option price and actual value at exercise.

There are several types of stock incentives. Incentive stock options (ISOs) meet particular tax tests to let you defer tax until you actually sell the shares. Nonqualified stock options (NQSOs) face no such limits. A third type of stock incentive, stock-appreciation rights (SARs), is a cash bonus tied to the company's stock performance. Some companies let employees buy company stock at a discount. Finally, some companies offer restricted stock to key executives. The main differences are in how they're taxed.

◆ With ISOs, you pay no tax when the company grants you the option or when you exercise the option. You pay tax only when you sell the shares acquired with the ISOs. You'll pay capital-gains rates if you hold the shares two years from the grant date or one year from the exercise date, whichever is later. You'll pay ordinary rates if you sell before then. Also, the difference between the stock's option price and fair-market value is an adjustment for the AMT. For more information, see "Avoid the Alternative Minimum Tax" in Chapter 14.

◆ With NQSOs, you pay no tax when the company grants the option. When you exercise your option you pay tax at ordinary rates on the difference between the option price and the market value. NQSOs are actually more tax-efficient because the employer gets a deduction for the option price. The employer's deduction offsets the employee's income, resulting in a lower check for the IRS. Naturally, these are more common arrangements.

◆ With SARs, you're taxed when you exercise the rights or when you become entitled to the maximum bonus under the plan. Don't forget to exercise your SARs. If you forget, you'll still be taxed as if you had exercised them immediately before expiration.

◆ With employee stock purchases, any discount is ordinary income. Gain above the fair-market value on the purchase date is taxed as short- or long-term gain depending on when you sell the stock.

◆ Restricted stock isn't taxed when you receive the award. Instead, it's taxed in the year in which it's substantially vested—the year in which you can actually sell it or there's no longer substantial risk of forfeiture. You'll owe tax at that time on the difference between what it's worth and what you pay to buy it (if anything). If you're really confident your company's stock will rise, you can elect to pay tax now on the value as of the date you receive the award. There's no tax the year it's vested. When you finally sell the stock, the gain above its value at the time of the award is taxed as short-, mid-, or long-term capital gain. This strategy has the effect of converting gain from the date of the award to the date of vesting from ordinary income to capital gain. To make this election, you'll need to notify the IRS within 30 days of the award.

Deciding when to exercise an option (or sell stock you acquire with ISOs) is mostly an investment decision. The longer you wait, the more chance you have of winning (or losing) big. Stocks go up, but stocks can go down, and you can lose your entire gain if the stock price takes a tumble. This is especially true with the high-tech companies that fund so much of their payroll with stock options. These companies have a nasty habit of missing earnings forecasts and watching their stock prices tumble overnight, sending hoped-for options gains up in smoke. You might choose to exercise a predetermined number of options each quarter you're eligible, adjusting the amount as the underlying stock price rises and falls.

From a tax-planning standpoint you just need to know what the income you realize will do to your overall picture. Will a spike in income phase out your itemized deductions? Will it push you into a higher bracket? Consider the year-end planning strategies outlined in Chapter 14 when you exercise your options. Also, make sure to consider the effect of the alternative minimum tax before exercising ISOs.

Start Your Own Business

◆ ◆ ◆

Business owners, as a group, are the richest people around. *The Millionaire Next Door,* by Professors Thomas J. Stanley and William D. Danko, reports that while self-employed people make up less than 20% of the workers in America, they make up more than two-thirds of the nation's millionaires. The annual *Forbes* 400 list of America's wealthiest people lists more self-made millionaires—and billionaires—than Rockefellers and oil heirs.

For most business owners, their most valuable asset is their business. Business owners can choose whether to take income out, or retain profits to make the business grow. The value of the business grows tax-deferred. And if they do sell the business, they have plenty of ways to cut the tax bill. These include ESOP sales, installment sales, charitable remainder trusts, and exotic business and estate-planning techniques such as private annuities and self-canceling installment notes.

Tax rules for your own business could fill an entire tax planner. This discussion will outline the tax advantages of starting your own business. If you have a hobby or marketable skill, you'll learn how to use it to earn tax-advantaged income. Even if you don't make money, you can qualify for tax breaks. You don't have to start a computer company in your garage to take advantage of business tax breaks. A hobby or sideline business qualifies for the same breaks as those for General Motors.

The IRS treats hobbies as a one-way street. Income? That's taxable, thank you very much. Losses? We're sorry, hobbies aren't deductible. But if you operate with intent to make a profit—not even *expectation,* just *intent*—you can qualify your activity as a business. If you make money in three out of five consecutive years (two out of seven for businesses involving horses), you'll be presumed to be operating for profit. But even without profits, you can still qualify by spending time at the activity, keeping businesslike records, relying on appropriate advice, and showing that losses are common in your business.

Write Off Business Expenses

Once you've qualified your business, you can deduct just about all of your expenses. These include the cost of goods sold, if any, plus advertising, equipment, office expenses, rent or lease payments, repairs and maintenance, supplies, travel, and any other expenses. However, the costs of setting up a business—investigating potential markets, travel and expenses related to buying or establishing the business, and professional fees for attorneys and accountants—aren't deductible up front. Instead, file Form 4562 with your first return and amortize the cost over 60 months from the time you begin business.

Capital purchases—cars, computers, and business equipment—aren't actually deductible. Instead, you have to depreciate them over their expected life. However, you can use "first-year expensing" to write off tangible personal property you acquire from unrelated individuals. Here's how it works:

◆ You can expense up to $20,000 of property in 2000. This should cover most small business's capital equipment. (See "Business Use of Your Car," page 71, for special limits on cars.)

FIRST-YEAR EXPENSING

Year	1998	1999	2000	2001–2002	2003
Amount	$18,500	$19,000	$20,000	$24,000	$25,000

◆ You can expense the entire cost of property you buy as late as the last day of the year.

◆ If you use property for business and personal use—for example, you use a computer to keep your business records and "chat" online with your sister Margie in Cleveland—you'll need to use it more than 50% for business to claim first-year expensing.

◆ Your total first-year-expensing deduction can't exceed your total income from the activity.

- If you later sell the property, your basis for figuring gain or loss on the property is your actual cost, minus first-year expensing and depreciation. Any gain on the sale is taxed as ordinary income. Also, if you stop using the property more than 50% for business, you'll owe tax on the difference between the amount you expense and the amount you would have been able to depreciate under straight-line rules. This is more than you need to know in evaluating whether to start a sideline business. Just be aware that amounts you expense may be subject to later "recapture."

Use Form 4562 to claim first-year expensing and Form 4797 to report any later sales of depreciated property.

Filing Your Return

When it comes time to file an actual return, here's what you'll use:

- Sole proprietors file Schedule C or Schedule C-EZ. (You can file Schedule C-EZ if you have just one business expense of $2,500 or less, no inventories, employees, home-office expenses, prior-year suspended passive activity losses, or depreciation to report on Form 4562.) Schedule C should cover the bulk of sideline businesses.
- Partnerships file Form 1065, then give each partner a Schedule K-1 for reporting each partner's share of income and other items.
- "C" corporations file Form 1120. If the corporation pays you a salary, the corporation reports it on Form W-2; if it pays you a dividend, it reports it on Form 1099-DIV. Most small "C" corporations "zero out" their income with bonuses to avoid paying corporate tax on earnings.
- "S" corporations file Form 1120-S, then give each shareholder a Schedule K-1 for reporting each shareholder's share of income and other items. "S" corporations let you pay yourself a small salary—say, $12,000—to avoid self-employment tax on earnings and take the bulk of your income in dividends. However, if you choose to pay yourself a nominal salary, be aware that this will reduce your eventual Social Security as well as your earnings base for contributing to a retirement plan.
- Limited-liability companies generally file as partnerships unless they elect to be taxed as corporations.

Self-Employment Tax

If you report a net income from your sole proprietorship, you'll owe self-employment tax on that profit. The self-employment tax replaces Social Security withholding for self-employed workers. Since you're paying both the "employer" and "employee" portions of the Social Security, the tax is steep: 15.3% of your first $72,600 of net self-employment income (for 1999), plus 2.9% Medicare tax on anything above that amount. "Net" self-employment income equals 92.35% of gross self-employment income (to reflect the 7.65% Social Security that an employer would have withheld if your income had been from wages). This $72,600 figure, the "Social Security wage base," is indexed for inflation and rises every year. If you and your spouse both have self-employment income, you both must figure and pay the tax. Partners pay self-employment tax on their share of net partnership income. However, if you have income from wages as well as self-employment, you can subtract your wage income from your self-employment income to figure your self-employment tax.

> ▶ **Example:** In 1999, you reported $56,000 in wage income and $20,000 from part-time consulting. Your spouse reported $74,000 in wage income and $4,800 from teaching aerobics. You owed 15.3% self-employment tax on $16,600 (the $72,600 wage base minus your $52,000 in wages) and 2.9% Medicare tax on the remaining $3,400 of consulting income. Your spouse owed 2.9% Medicare tax on the $4,800 from teaching aerobics.

Self-Employed Audit Alert

One important caution is in order before discussing specific business-planning strategies. The IRS pays very close attention to business income and expenses. Small-business owners are the most frequent targets of audits. That's because business owners have more opportunity to hide income and more chances to turn personal expenses into deductible business expenses, than other taxpayers. So make sure you conduct your business to protect yourself from the tax man. Report all your income. Substantiate all your deductions. Don't mix business and personal writeoffs.

One partial solution to this problem is to operate your business as a partnership, corporation, or limited-liability company (LLC). You can incorporate your business, without a lawyer, through several nationwide firms that will take care of the paperwork for a small fee, usually a few hundred dollars. Incorporating your business gives you two advantages. First, you no longer report your income on the more closely scrutinized Schedule C. Also, you remove several other red flags from your return. For example, if you claim a home-office deduction for your sole proprietorship, you usually must file Form 8829. This has traditionally been a red flag. But you can claim the same home-office deduction for a partnership (Form 1065) or corporation (Form 1120) and avoid sending out the audit flags.

There are two main classes of corporations: regular, or "C" corporations, which pay taxes themselves, and "Subchapter S" corporations that pay no tax, instead "passing through" income directly to the owners. "S" corporations are available for corporations with a single class of shares and no more than 75 shareholders, all of whom have to be individuals, estates, and certain trusts. Most small businesses will choose "S" status because there will be no corporate-level income tax on corporate earnings. Instead, profits and losses will "flow through" to the shareholders directly.

You'll also have to choose between the cash and accrual methods of accounting. With the cash method, you report income and expenses as you receive them. With the accrual method, you report income as it is earned—regardless of whether it's paid—and expenses as you incur liability for payment. If you have inventories, you have to use the accrual method. The cash method lets you defer reporting income by deferring receiving income. This is useful for year-end planning strategies discussed in the Dictionary of Tax Deductions.

Buying into a Business

If you're successful enough to profit from this book's help, someday someone will ask you to join him or her in starting a business. It may be a local restaurant or perhaps an Internet startup. The person may just ask for a loan, or he or she may invite you into a partnership or corporation. There are two tax "safety nets" for you here. First, most businesses lose at first before they start to make money. You can use these losses to offset your other income if you structure the business right. Look for an "S" corporation that passes losses directly through to you, the shareholder, or a partnership, so that you can take advantage of start-up losses. Second, if the business goes belly-up, you can write off your loss in the year the investment becomes worthless. For more information, see "Worthless Securities" in the Dictionary of Tax Deductions.

SET UP YOUR OWN RETIREMENT PLAN

◆ ◆ ◆

Retirement plans can shelter up to 100% of your business income. This discussion will tell you which plan lets you shelter the most income for the least cost. Small business owners have a wide choice of retirement plans. These include IRAs, SIMPLE IRAs, Simplified Employee Pensions (SEPs), and Keogh Plans. If you're really ambitious, you can even set up your own traditional defined benefit pension plan. Before you choose a plan to shelter your income, you'll need to answer two main questions: First, how much do you want to put away for yourself? And second, how much are you willing to put away for any employees? Your answers will help decide which plan is best for you. Tax-favored retirement plans operate under strict rules designed in part to keep owners from discriminating against their employees. (Slightly different rules apply for qualified plans adopted by corporations.)

1. IRAs

IRAs, including regular deductible IRAs and nondeductible Roth IRAs, are available to anyone with earned income. IRAs are best for sideline businesses with little income, or for business owners who can't afford to contribute for employees. For complete information, see Chapter 12, Investing for Retirement.

2. SIMPLE IRAs

A SIMPLE IRA, which stands for Savings Incentive Match Program for Employees, is a "super-IRA" that lets you squirrel away more than the usual $2,000 limit. Here are the rules:

♦ You can contribute 100% of your earned income up to $6,000.

♦ Your business has to contribute 2% of each employee's earnings, whether the employee participates or not *or* match 100% of each participating employee's contributions up to 3% of his or her earnings. If you choose the match, you can reduce it as low as 1% for two out of every five years. Your match is due by the date for filing your business tax return, including extensions.

- You have to include any employees earning at least $5,000 in any two preceding years and who are reasonably expected to earn $5,000 this year.
- You have to open the plan by October 1 of the year you wish to start contributions.
- You have to establish IRAs for yourself and any eligible employees. The plan itself consists of SIMPLE IRA accounts for each employee.
- SIMPLE IRAs are good for "S" corporation owners paying themselves a small or nominal salary to avoid self-employment tax. That's because there's no limit on the percentage of income you can contribute, as there is with SEPs and Keoghs, following.
- If you participate in an employer's 401(k) or 403(b) plan, your total "deferrals" from the employer plan and your own SIMPLE plan can't exceed the overall deferral limit ($10,000 for 1998).

3. Simplified Employee Pension

A Simplified Employee Pension, or SEP, is another "super-IRA" that lets you squirrel away more than the usual $2,000 limit. In this case, it's 15% of net self-employment income up to $24,000 (indexed for inflation). Here are the rules:

- You can contribute up to 15% of net income, reduced by one-half of your self-employment tax and your SEP contribution. (Essentially, you can contribute up to 13.0435% of pay.)
- You have to include any employees age 21 and older who have worked three of the last five years and who earn $400 or more.
- You generally have to contribute the same percentage of compensation for your employees as you do for yourself. However, you can choose an "integrated" plan that lets you contribute more on behalf of higher-paid employees—presumably, yourself. The "integrated" plan lets you contribute up to 5.7% more of your net income from self-employment exceeding the Social Security wage base—$72,600 for 1999.
- You can establish the plan and make your contribution as late as the due date for filing the business's tax return, including extensions.

4. Keogh Plan

A Keogh Plan is a qualified plan for a self-employed person or partner. Here are the rules:

- A "money-purchase" plan requires you to make a fixed annual contribution of up to 25% of your net income, reduced by one-half of self-employment tax and the Keogh contribution itself. Essentially, this lets you contribute up to 20% for yourself and 25% for your employees. A money-purchase plan is best for mature businesses with the predictable cash flow necessary to make the required annual contribution.
- A "profit-sharing" plan lets you make a discretionary contribution of up to 15% of your net income, reduced by one-half of self-employment tax and the Keogh con-

tribution itself. Essentially, this lets you contribute 13.0435% for yourself and 15% for employees. A profit-sharing plan is appropriate for emerging businesses with less predictable cash flow.

- ◆ You can adopt both plans for flexibility to contribute between 10% and 25% per year.
- ◆ You have to include all employees who have reached age 21 and completed a year of service.
- ◆ You have to set up the plan by the end of the year you want to start contributions. Actual contributions are due by the filing deadline of the business, including extensions.
- ◆ If your Keogh account balance in a plan you maintain for yourself reaches $100,000, you'll need to file a Form 5500-EZ with the IRS each plan year.
- ◆ You can keep contributing to the plan past age 70½ so long as you keep earning income from the business. You don't have to begin making minimum required distributions until April 1 of the year after you finally retire.

5. Defined-Benefit Plan

A defined-benefit plan is a traditional pension plan, the kind that pays a specific income, usually based on salary and years of service. You may be surprised to learn that you can set one up for yourself. Defined-benefit plans are harder than other plans to set up and run. But they give you the mother of all tax deductions: enough to fund an annual income of 100% of pay, up to $120,000. If your business earns a steady income, this is a great way to avoid tax on the entire amount.

You can project whatever interest rate and retirement age you choose, within certain guidelines. This lets you shelter even more of your income. If you project a low interest rate, you'll have to stuff more into the plan to reach the required principal at retirement. Similarly, if you project a low retirement age, you'll need to stuff more into the plan to amass the required principal at retirement.

This chart sums up the key features of each self-employed retirement plan:

SELF-EMPLOYED RETIREMENT PLANS

Plan Type	Contribution Limit	Employee Coverage
IRA/Roth IRA	100% of earned income up to $2,000	None
SIMPLE-IRA	100% of self-employment income up to $6,000, plus 3% match up to $6,000	Minimal
SEP	15% of net self-employment income (13.04% of gross income) up to $24,000	Substantial
Keogh	25% of self-employment income up to $30,000	Substantial
Defined-Benefit	100% of self-employment income up to $120,000	Substantial

For sideline businesses with no employees, choose the plan that lets you make the biggest contribution. You can always choose not to fund it to the limit. But you'll appreciate the flexibility and control the plan allows.

SPECIAL BREAKS FOR BUSINESS OWNERS

❖ ❖ ❖

Here are five special tax breaks for business owners:

1. Medical Savings Accounts

Medical Savings Accounts, or MSAs, let you pay medical costs with pretax dollars. MSAs are available for self-employed workers and businesses with 50 or fewer employees. MSAs come in two parts. The first part is a "high-deductible" health-insurance policy to cover catastrophic costs. (Deductibles have to be between $1,500 and $2,250 for single coverage and between $3,000 and $4,500 for family coverage. Out-of-pocket limits can't be more than $3,000 for singles and $5,500 for families.) The second part is a tax-deductible savings account for routine medical costs. You can contribute up to 65% of your deductible if you are single, or 75% of your deductible for family coverage. A single person with a $2,250 deductible, for example, can contribute up to $1,462.50. A family with a $4,500 deductible can contribute up to $3,375. Withdrawals for medical expenses are tax-free. Withdrawals for any other reason are taxed as ordinary income, plus a 15% penalty. The goal is to give you incentives to keep down medical costs.

Let's say you're an attorney in the 28% bracket. You and your family buy a health-insurance policy with a $4,500 deductible. You put the maximum $3,375 into your MSA. During the year you spend $2,000 on medical care. Your contribution saves you $945 in taxes. And at the end of the year you'll still have $1,375 to compound for future bills.

MSAs haven't taken off like sponsors hoped they would. High deductibles can leave employees with bills that top an entire year's worth of contributions. And as the self-employed health-insurance deduction rises, MSAs become less attractive in comparison. Why spend money for routine costs when you can simply deduct your health insurance? But if you're healthy, wealthy (and wise) enough to pay your routine costs from *other* funds, MSAs can let you squirrel away some serious cash. Congress didn't envision it, but MSAs can even help you save for retirement. Let's say you contribute the maximum $3,375 for 20 years. If you earn 10.5% per year, your $67,500 in contributions will grow to $158,615. You can use that money to pay for medical costs in retirement, even including the cost of long-term care. Even if you take it out to pay for a cruise or leave it to your heirs, you'll get decades of tax-deferred compounding on your funds.

Use Form 8853 to figure your MSA deduction (then carry the balance to Form 1040 as an adjustment to income) and any taxable distribution (carry that amount to Form 1040 as "Other Income").

2. Medical-Expense-Reimbursement Plans

Medical expenses can be a self-employed person's biggest nightmare, particularly since most self-employed people don't have the same comprehensive health plans as company employees do. Medical-expense-reimbursement plans let you pay your medical expenses with pretax dollars. The catch is, you have to establish the plan for your employees. The solution is to hire your spouse and pay the benefits through him or her. You can also use this strategy to deduct a full 100% of your self-employed health insurance, which would otherwise be limited as a percentage of your income.

3. Voluntary Employees' Beneficiary Associations

If you have employees, you can consider funding a Voluntary Employees' Beneficiary Association, or VEBA. This is a welfare-benefit trust that lets you deduct an unlimited amount of contributions for "life, sick, accident, or other benefits" for employees, dependents, and designated beneficiaries:

- ◆ "Life benefits" include life insurance or other death benefits.
- ◆ "Sick and accident" benefits include health insurance, sick pay, medical reimbursement, and long-term-care insurance.
- ◆ "Other benefits" include vacation pay, child-care facilities, severance pay, and educational benefits.

A VEBA's biggest break may be to let you buy your life insurance with pretax dollars. As long as you include your employees and figure the amount you buy on an equal basis, you can buy a huge amount of coverage for yourself. The taxes you save on your own coverage can easily pay for your staff.

4. Nonqualified Deferred Compensation

A nonqualified deferred compensation plan is a promise by the business to pay a future income or benefit. This could be a lump sum, a benefit for a period of years, or even a lifetime annuity. There's no requirement that the business actually funds the promise. However, most deferred-comp plans, as they are called, involve some sort of tax-advantaged funding to pay the promised benefit. Usually this involves putting money into trust and buying insurance on the life of the owner. That way, earnings grow tax-advantaged, and the entire death benefit is available for the corporation and the owner. Money you put in the trust isn't deductible by the business or taxable to you until the benefit "substantially vests," or you actually become entitled to the money. This risk of forfeiture is what preserves the tax break. There are two main types of trust for funding deferred-compensation plans. A "rabbi trust" (so-named because the first one the IRS approved was set up for a rabbi) provides that money you put in the trust remain subject to the claims of the employers' creditors. A "secular trust" is not subject to creditors' claims; however, the IRS argues that contributions to a secular trust are immediately taxable to the employee.

Deferred-compensation plans are useful when you reach the limits of a qualified-retirement plan. The plan can be as creative as you need. For more information, see an attorney who specializes in business planning or a financial planner who works in this area.

5. Split-Dollar Life Insurance

A "split-dollar" life-insurance plan is not a kind of policy. Instead, it's a method of sharing the costs and benefits of a policy between two parties. For example, a corporation might pay for a policy on the life of its president. The president pays tax each year on the value of the death protection he or she receives. (IRS tables show you this value according to your age and the amount of coverage. If the corporation wants, it can pay the president a bonus to take care of the tax bill.) The corporation pays the premium, lets the president designate the beneficiary, and reserves the right to collect its cumulative contributions to the policy. If the president dies, the corporation gets back its contributions, and the president's beneficiary gets the rest. If the president retires, the corporation might "roll out" the cash value to give the president extra retirement income.

Split-dollar insurance, like nonqualified deferred-compensation plans, is a creative benefit that you can design around whatever resources are available. Again, for more information, see an attorney who specializes in business planning or a financial planner who works in this area.

THE HOME-OFFICE DEDUCTION

❖ ❖ ❖

Working at home—commuting 20 feet in your pajamas instead of 20 miles in rush-hour traffic—is a reality for more and more of us. Whether you run a sideline business out of a spare bedroom or telecommute for your employer, you can use a home office to qualify for tax breaks. But this deduction might be one of the most misunderstood and overrated tax breaks out there. And the IRS takes a careful look at home-office expenses. So be sure you qualify before you claim the break.

You can claim a home-office deduction for any space you use "regularly and exclusively" as your "principal place of business." Starting in 1999, you can also claim the deduction for any space you use "regularly and exclusively" to conduct administrative and managerial activities where you have no other fixed location to do so. The space doesn't have to be an office. You can claim the deduction for a workshop, studio, or space you use to store samples and products. It doesn't even have to be an entire room. If you use it for more than one business, both have to qualify to take the deduction. If you and your spouse both use the office, both of you have to qualify to take the deduction.

"Regularly and exclusively" mean just that. Don't use your home office to manage your personal business. Don't use your office computer to download games from the net. The principal-place-of-business test is easy for home-based businesses where you perform the actual work in the office. It's tougher if you're a contractor or consultant and you do your actual work outside your home. Starting in 1999, the administrative-

and-managerial-activities rule will give you a break. The test is hardest if you're a regular employee. You can take the deduction only if the employer requires you to maintain your home office for the employer's convenience.

Once you determine you qualify, here's how to claim the deduction. First, figure what percent of your home you use as the office. You can divide the total space by the number of rooms, if they're roughly equal. Or you can figure the actual percentage of the home's square feet you use. You can then deduct that percentage of rent, mortgage interest, property taxes, utilities, repairs, insurance, plus incidental home expenses such as garbage pickup, lawn maintenance, and security.

You can also depreciate the percentage of your home's purchase price covering the office space. But you'll probably be disappointed by the amount. Let's say you bought your house for $100,000; $20,000 is for the land, $80,000 is for the house. (Land isn't depreciable. Check your property-tax valuation for the amount of the purchase price to allocate to the land.) In June, you start a mail-order business that occupies 10% of your house. This gives you a "depreciable basis" of $8,000, or 10% of your $80,000 purchase price. Looking at the following table, you see that you can deduct 1.391% of your $8,000 depreciable basis, or $111.28. The next year, you can deduct the "full" $205.12. In the 28% tax bracket, that "full" deduction saves you less than $60. By all means, take it. Just don't spend it all in one place.

NONRESIDENTIAL PROPERTY

Year	Jan	Feb	Mar	Apr	May	Jun	Jul	Aug	Sep	Oct	Nov	Dec
1	2.461	2.247	2.033	1.819	1.605	1.391	1.177	0.963	0.749	0.535	0.321	0.107
2–39	2.564	2.564	2.564	2.564	2.564	2.564	2.564	2.564	2.564	2.564	2.564	2.564

Here's a final tip on home offices: Don't claim depreciation in any year you sell your home. The $250,000 tax-free exclusion for home sales doesn't apply to business use of your home. So the tax-free exclusion won't apply to the portion of your home that you claim as your home office. When you sell your home, you'll owe a 25% "recapture" tax on amounts you've depreciated. The easy solution is simply not to claim the deduction the year you sell the house.

Sole proprietors claim the deduction on Form 8829, then carry the total to Schedule C. You can use the deduction to shelter profits, but not to take a loss against other income. If your home-office expenses exceed your income, carry forward the loss to next year. Partnerships and corporations claim these expenses directly on Form 1065 or 1120.

BUSINESS USE OF YOUR CAR

◆ ◆ ◆

If you use your car or light truck for business, you can deduct your car expenses. There are two ways to calculate your deduction for business use of your car: the actual-expenses method and the mileage allowance.

- To use the actual-expense method, you'll need to keep track of all your car expenses. These include lease or purchase payments, garage fees, gas, insurance, licensing and tags, oil, maintenance, parking, tires, tolls, and even washing. Deduct whatever percentage of your total expenses equals your business use of the car. If you choose this method the first year you use the car for business, you'll have to use it for all future years for that car.

- To use the mileage allowance, keep track of your deductible mileage and deduct the appropriate amount per mile—currently 31 cents per mile for most purposes. You have to choose this method the first year you use the car for business if you want to use it for future years. You can switch from the mileage allowance to the actual-expense method, but you can't switch back.

If you choose to claim actual expenses, you can also claim depreciation on the car. You can deduct up to $3,160 in the first year, $5,000 in the second, $3,050 in the third, $1,775 in the fourth and fifth, and $1,152 in the sixth. Personal use cuts your depreciation by whatever percentage you use the car personally. For example, if you use the car 75% for business, your maximum first-year depreciation is 75% of $3,160, or $2,370. To claim depreciation as an employee, you have to show that you use the car for your employer's convenience. If you use a car more than 50% for business, you can choose first-year expensing or "modified accelerated-cost-recovery system" (MACRS). If you use it less than 50% for business, use straight-line depreciation.

DEPRECIATING YOUR CAR

MACRS Depreciation						
Year	1	2	3	4	5	6
Half-Year	20.00%	32.00%	19.20%	11.52%	11.52%	5.76%
Q1	35.00%	26.00%	15.60%	11.01%	11.01%	1.38%
Q2	25.00%	30.00%	18.00%	11.37%	11.37%	4.26%
Q3	15.00%	34.00%	20.40%	12.24%	11.30%	7.06%
Q4	5.00%	38.00%	22.80%	13.68%	10.94%	9.58%

Straight-Line Depreciation						
Year	1	2	3	4	5	6
Half-Year	10.00%	20.00%	20.00%	20.00%	20.00%	10.00%
Q1	17.50%	20.00%	20.00%	20.00%	20.00%	2.50%
Q2	12.50%	20.00%	20.00%	20.00%	20.00%	7.50%
Q3	7.50%	20.00%	20.00%	20.00%	20.00%	12.50%
Q4	2.50%	20.00%	20.00%	20.00%	20.00%	17.50%

- If you choose first-year expensing, you can deduct whatever percentage of the $3,160 limit applies to your business use of the car. In future years, you'll reduce your depreciable basis by the full $3,160, even if personal use cuts your actual deduction. For example, if you claim first-year expensing for a car that you use 80% for business, reduce your basis by the full $3,160 even though you claim only $2,528 of first-year expensing (80% of the $3,160 limit).

◆ If you choose MACRS, your deduction depends on when you buy the car. If the car is the only capital equipment you buy in a year, use the "midyear" convention, following, if you buy it in January through September, or the "fourth-quarter" convention if you buy it in October, November, or December. If you buy other capital equipment, you'll need to add the cost of the car to any other equipment you buy. If the cost of the car is more than 40% of the total cost of equipment you buy, then use the appropriate quarter convention for when you buy the car. (If the midquarter convention limits your deduction to less than the $3,160 annual limit, consider using first-year expensing, instead.) Otherwise, use the midyear convention. In future years, you'll reduce your depreciable basis by the full amount of depreciation allowable, whether or not you claim the full deduction.

◆ If you choose MACRS and your business use of the car falls below 50%, you'll have to "recapture" the difference between what you actually claimed (including first-year expensing) and what you could have claimed using straight-line depreciation. Report this "excess depreciation" as ordinary income the year business use falls below 50%.

◆ If you use the car 100% for business and you can't deduct 100% of the depreciable basis in the aforementioned six-year periods, you can continue deducting the remaining balance over future years at the sixth-year rate until you finish writing it off.

◆ If you're subject to the AMT, you may have to use a slightly different schedule instead of MACRS. This "150% rate" for half-year convention lets you deduct up to 15% in year one, 25.50% in year two, 17.85% in year three, 16.66% in years four and five, and 8.33% in year six. The difference between MACRS "200% rate," shown, and the "150% rate" is an AMT adjustment.

◆ Sport-utility vehicles with a gross vehicle weight, loaded, of 6,000 pounds or more don't count as "cars," so they aren't limited to the annual depreciation ceilings. You can deduct the full amount of depreciation under any of these three methods. Your dealer can tell you if your vehicle qualifies.

◆ If you lease your car, you can deduct whatever part of your lease payment equals your business use of the car. For example, if you lease a car for $300 per month and use it 75% for business, you can deduct $225 per month. If the fair-market value of the car at the beginning of the lease is $15,800 or more, you may have to report income to reflect the value of the car. The purpose of this rule is to limit your deduction to what you could take if you had bought the car outright.

◆ When it's time to replace a car you've depreciated, sell it before you buy a new one. Don't trade it in. If you sell your old car, you can claim a capital loss if your loss on the sale is more than the depreciation you've claimed over time. If you merely trade in the old car, you'll have to "carry over" the basis of the old car in a complicated formula involving the depreciated basis of the old car plus any cash you pay at the trade in, reduced by the excess of any depreciation that would have been allowed on the old car had it been used entirely for business over the actual depreciation allowed.

Let's put it all together. We'll assume that you buy a car for $18,000 in October 1998. You use it 60% for business that year. Since you use it more than 50% for business, you can use first-year expensing to deduct $1,896 (60% of the $3,160 first-year expensing limit). You could also use MACRS to deduct $540 (60% of the $900 fourth-quarter depreciation limit).

Now let's say that in 1999, your business use of the car falls to 30%. Your allowable deduction for 1998 under straight-line depreciation would have been $270. Your straight-line deduction for 1999 will equal the car's depreciable basis (the $18,000 purchase price minus the $3,160 first-year expensing deduction, or $14,840) multiplied by the fourth-quarter depreciation limit (20%), multiplied by your business use of the car (30%), or $890.40. You'll also "recapture" and report as income the "excess depreciation" of what you claimed in 1998 ($1,896) minus the amount you could have claimed under the straight-line method ($270), or $1,626.

Here's something you'll like after all that bookkeeping. You can even deduct payments you make to settle an accident you have while driving on business. You can also deduct 100% of any property tax you pay on a car, regardless of business use, as an itemized deduction on Schedule A.

If you travel for business, keep a log of your business travel and receipts. If you use the "per-mile" method, it's not necessary to record every mile. You can record a month's worth of travel each quarter so long as you choose a "typical" month.

FIVE

MAKE THE MOST
OF CHARITABLE GIFTS

IF YOU VOLUNTEER or make charitable gifts, the tax law lets you do well for yourself while you do good for others. You can deduct volunteer expenses and charitable gifts from your taxable income. You can give away appreciated property without paying tax on the gain and still deduct the entire value of the gift. You can also use a wide variety of charitable trusts to avoid tax on capital gains.

Volunteer work and charitable gifts let you control your contributions to our nation's social capital. Your tax dollars go where Uncle Sam wants them to, mainly Social Security and Medicare, interest on the debt, and defense. Only a tiny fraction goes toward education, arts, and social welfare. Your volunteer work and charitable gift dollars go where you direct them. You alone decide which causes to champion, which organizations to trust, and which programs to support.

The Congressional Joint Committee on Taxation reports that in 1996 the charitable-gift deduction was worth $18.1 billion in tax savings. The average taxpayer gave just over 3% of income. That figure actually slides as income rises. For 1995, taxpayers reporting incomes between $15,000 and $30,000 claimed an average of $1,338 in charitable contributions, while taxpayers reporting incomes between $100,000 and $200,000 claimed just $3,433. Be sure you claim credit for all your gifts.

In the "bad old days," when marginal tax rates ranged up to 91%, you could give away a dollar for just nine cents. With today's lower rates, these strategies aren't quite as valuable. And charitable gift strategies are, first and foremost, *gift* strategies, not *tax* strategies. You'll have to make a gift to get the breaks. So if you aren't philanthropically inclined—if your Christmas ties sport images of Ebeneezer Scrooge and the Grinch—skip this chapter. But if you're philanthropically inclined, read on. You'll learn how to get a tax break for nearly every gift you make, whether it be cash, property, or even gifts in trust. They might even throw a snazzy dinner in your honor.

WRITE OFF VOLUNTEER EXPENSES

◆ ◆ ◆

Volunteer work should be rewarding all by itself. But the tax code gives you an extra lift and lets you deduct any expenses involved in your volunteer work. These expenses include:

◆ Meals and lodging on a trip away from home on behalf of a charity
◆ Commuting expenses to and from volunteer and charitable activities (actual expenses or 14 cents per mile, plus tolls and parking)
◆ Phone calls and office supplies
◆ Convention expenses

- A portion of your organizational dues (the organization should be able to tell you how much is deductible)
- Clothing expenses, including laundry and dry-cleaning, for clothing not usable as ordinary street clothing (Girl Scout uniforms, and the like)

Deduct these expenses as charitable gifts on Schedule A. Keep records such as canceled checks and credit-card receipts to substantiate the deduction. If you claim any unreimbursed expense over $250, you'll need a statement from the organization acknowledging your services.

GENERAL RULES FOR CHARITABLE GIFTS

Charitable gifts are heavily abused, so the IRS insists that you document your gifts. This chart sets out the basic rules. See discussions of specific property for more specific rules.

DOCUMENTING CHARITABLE GIFTS

Under $250
Check

$250–$500
Check plus receipt
Receipt must show value received

$500–$5,000
Check plus receipt
Receipt must show value received
Gifts of property over $500 require Form 8283

$5,000 and up
Check plus receipt
Receipt must show value received
Gifts of property greater than $5,000 require a written appraisal, (except publicly traded securities and nonpublic stock under $10,000)
Gifts of art worth more than $20,000, attach appraisal to Form 8283

Most gifts are made in plain old American cash. Here are the basic rules:

- You can deduct up to 50% of your adjusted gross income for gifts to public charities.
- You can deduct up to 30% of your adjusted gross income for gifts to private foundations.
- If gifts to public charities exceed 50% of your adjusted gross income, you can carry forward the unused deduction to future years. If your gifts to private foundations

exceed 30% of your gross income, you can carry over any unused deduction for up to five years.

- Gifts you make by check are deductible the year you present the check, even if it isn't cashed until the next year.

- If your donation exceeds $75 and the organization gives you anything in return, such as dinner or entertainment at a banquet, the organization must disclose the value of the benefits you receive. You don't, however, need to reduce your deduction for token items such as calendars and tote bags or "intangible religious benefits." It's good to know that everlasting karma isn't taxable income.

- Gifts of cash over $250 require a written receipt as well as a canceled check. The receipt has to be dated no later than the filing date of your return.

- If your donation to a college entitles you to buy sporting tickets, you can deduct 80% of your donation. The right to buy tickets is valued at 20% of the gift, regardless of the amount. Presumably, Ohio State, Notre Dame, and similar schools expect bigger gifts than the Akron Zips of the world.

- Lots of employers match their employees' gifts to favorite charities. Before you make a gift, check to see if your employer will match all or part of your gift.

- Don't forget to deduct gifts you make through payroll deductions at work.

There are nearly as many ways to make charitable gifts as there are property. Here's how to handle some of the more common gifts:

- Raffle tickets are deductible as gambling losses, up to your total gambling winnings.

- Donations of used clothing and household items are deductible at fair-market value, such as the price they would bring at a resale shop. (Are Bill Clinton's used undershorts really worth what he claimed on that infamous tax return?)

- You can give a life-insurance policy to charity by irrevocably naming the charity as beneficiary of the policy. This lets you direct a large sum of money for a relatively small ongoing premium. Your deductible gift equals the policy's cash value, plus any ongoing premiums you give to support the policy. If you contribute annual premiums, make sure to give them to the charity first, rather than to the company.

- You can give a remainder interest in your home or other property and still keep the right to use it for the rest of your life. Simply retitle the property in the name of the charity with a restriction letting you use the property for the rest of your life. You'll get a charitable deduction now for the value of the house at the time of your death figured in much the same way as a gift to a charitable remainder trust (see following).

- If you donate the use of your vacation home, there's no deduction for the fair-market value of the use. Plus, the days of charitable use will count as personal use for purposes of qualifying your vacation home as rental property.

- Similarly, there's no deduction for free use of property. You can't write off a gift of office space, for example, or an interest-free loan.

- Many charities offer pooled income funds, gift annuities, and similar arrangements that provide you an income in exchange for a gift. For more information, see the discussion of charitable trusts, following.

GIFTS OF APPRECIATED PROPERTY

⬦ ⬦ ⬦

There comes a point as gifts get larger when what to give is as important as how much to give. Gifts of appreciated property—specifically, gifts of securities, mutual funds, real estate, and artwork held for more than a year—are an ideal choice for charitable gifts. They can give you two tax breaks at once. First, you get to deduct the value of the gift. Second, you'll avoid tax on capital gains that you'd pay if you sold it.

> ▶ **Example:** In 1995 you bought 100 shares of Microsplat for $4,000. The stock is now worth $10,000. You're in the 28% bracket, and you'd like to give the stock to your alma mater. Your tax breaks include a $2,800 deduction for the gift, plus $1,200 in capital gains, for a total tax saving of $4,000—a full 100% of your purchase price!

Here's how to claim these two tax breaks at once:

- First you'll need to figure the value of property you donate. With securities, fair-market value is the average of the high and low sale prices on the date of the donation. With real estate and works of art, you'll need an appraisal. The IRS Art Advisory Board helps the IRS decide whether to accept or contest these valuations. Appraisal fees are a miscellaneous itemized deduction subject to the 2% floor.
- You have to hold the property for at least a year to deduct the fair-market value. If you hold the property yourself for less than a year, you can deduct only your purchase price.
- Make sure the charity sells the property, not you. If you sell it in your own name, you'll wind up owing tax on the capital gain.
- You can deduct up to 30% of your adjusted gross income for gifts of appreciated property to public charities and qualifying private foundations. You can carry over any unused deduction for up to five years.
- If you donate property that's worth less now than when you bought it, you get no deduction for the loss.

Bargain Sales of Appreciated Property

If you sell appreciated property to a charity for less than its fair-market value, you can deduct the difference between the proceeds and the fair-market value. But the transfer will be treated partly as a sale, and you may owe tax on the "sale" portion. Here's how it works:

- First, divide the sale price by the fair-market value to figure what percentage of the transaction will be treated as sale proceeds. If the property is mortgaged, include the value of any mortgage discharged in the price.

♦ Next, take your aforementioned "sale" percentage and multiply it by your adjusted basis in the property. That amount will become your basis allocated to the sale.

♦ Finally, subtract the basis allocated to the sale from the sale price to figure the gain from the sale.

> ▶ **Example:** In 1990, you buy an office for $50,000. The office is now worth $100,000, with a $30,000 mortgage balance, and you'd like to sell it for $50,000 to a charity. Your $50,000 sale price and $30,000 mortgage, divided into the $100,000 sale price, equals 80%. Eighty percent of your adjusted basis, or $40,000, will be allocated to the "sale" portion of the transaction. Your taxable "sale" portion equals your $50,000 sale price minus your $40,000 adjusted basis, or $10,000.

Gifts of Mortgaged Property

If you donate mortgaged property, you can deduct the fair-market value, minus the amount of the mortgage. However, the transferred mortgage counts as cash received in a part-sale transaction such as the aforementioned one, and you may owe tax if the transferred mortgage exceeds the basis allocated to the sale.

> ▶ **Example:** In 1990, you buy property for $50,000. The property is now worth $100,000, minus a $40,000 mortgage, and you'd like to give it to charity. The mortgage equals 40% of the property's fair-market value. Forty percent of your adjusted basis, or $20,000, will be allocated to the "sale" portion of the transaction. Your taxable "sale" portion equals the $40,000 mortgage transferred minus your $20,000 adjusted-cost basis, or $20,000.

GIFTS OF ART AND PERSONAL PROPERTY

❖ ❖ ❖

If you donate art or other tangible personal property—books, furniture, and the like— you can deduct just your actual cost if you've owned it for up to one year. If you've owned it for more than a year, your deduction depends on how the charity plans to use the property. If the charity plans to use it for "exempt" purposes, such as a college planning to display art for students to study, you can deduct the fair-market value. If the charity plans to sell it to raise cash, you can deduct only your cost.

> ▶ **Example:** You own a painting that you bought ten years ago for $1,000, now worth $10,000, and an antique desk that you bought two years ago for $1,000, now worth $2,000. You'd like to give them to good old alma mater. If the college displays the painting and uses the desk in an office, you can

deduct the full market value for each. If the college sells the desk, you can deduct only the $1,000 cost.

If your gift is worth more than $500, you'll need to file Form 8283. If it's worth more than $5,000, you'll need an appraisal. And if you're a really heavy hitter, giving art worth more than $20,000, you'll need to attach a copy of the appraisal. Gifts this large might attract attention from the IRS Art Advisory board. In order to avoid any penalty or interest in case of dispute, you can request an advance Statement of Value. The fee is $2,500 for up to three appraisals, plus $250 for each additional appraisal.

CONSIDER CHARITABLE TRUSTS

❖ ❖ ❖

Charitable trusts aren't just for "the rich" anymore. Charitable trusts, along with pooled income funds, donor-advised funds, and even private foundations, let you sell property without paying tax, increase your income from the property, take a charitable-gift deduction, and cut your eventual estate tax, all at the same time. Jacqueline Kennedy Onassis is only the most famous charitable trust donor; she used these techniques to avoid almost all tax on her estate. The Taxpayer Relief Act of 1997 made charitable trusts less attractive by lowering capital-gains rates, doubling the tax exclusion for sales of primary residences and closing a loophole for particularly abusive trust arrangements. But they remain an attractive strategy if you have highly appreciated property, such as stocks or investment real estate that currently yields little or no income, and capital-gains tax you'd pay on a sale would "spike" your income into a higher tax bracket or cost you deductions and personal exemptions.

The subject of charitable trusts has filled entire books. There's a wide variety of charitable trusts, with different rules and different advantages to each. And this isn't something to try yourself at home. If you decide to establish one of these trusts, you'll need a competent attorney. This discussion should give you enough information to decide if it's worth further study, then help you do some of the groundwork to speed the process and keep the fees as low as possible.

A trust, in general, is when one party holds property for the benefit of another. The person giving the property is a "grantor." The person holding the property is the "trustee." And the people getting the benefit of the property are "beneficiaries." With charitable trusts, you as grantor donate property to yourself or someone else as trustee, for benefit of yourself, your heirs, and one or more charitable organizations. Simple, right? Yes, it takes a lawyer to set one up. But the IRS has published sample charitable trust forms that should help bring down the cost.

There are two main flavors of charitable trusts: "lead trusts," where the charity gets a stream of income and you or your heirs get the eventual principal; and "remainder trusts," where you and your family get the income and the charity gets the eventual principal, or remainder. Each type of trust is further divided into two types according to how that income is paid out: "annuitrusts," which pay a specific dollar amount, or annuity;

and "unitrusts," which pay a fixed percentage of the trust's value. Typically, the income lasts until the grantor's death. So, a charitable lead annuitrust results when you first grant income to the charity, then leave the remainder to your heirs. A charitable remainder unitrust results when you grant yourself an income, then leave the remainder to the charity. This table should help you keep track of these types:

CHARITABLE TRUST ARRANGEMENTS

	Annuitrust	*Unitrust*
Lead Trust	Trust pays fixed dollar income to charity; remainder to heirs	Trust pays percentage income to charity; remainder to heirs
Remainder Trust	Trust pays fixed dollar income to donor or family; remainder to charity	Trust pays percentage income to donor or family; remainder to charity

If the trust doesn't earn enough to pay the target income in a given year, you can direct the trustee to "make up" the shortfall from future surpluses. Surprisingly, this is called a "makeup" provision.

Now that you know what kinds of trusts are available, what are the advantages?

- You avoid capital-gains tax on property you donate to the trust.
- The trust can trade investments, to pay more income or diversify holdings, without paying tax on sales.
- You get an immediate charitable deduction for the gift you make to the trust.
- You remove the value of the donated property from the value of your estate.

▶ **Example:** You and your spouse are both 60 years old. Years ago you bought $50,000 worth of stock. The stock is now worth $100,000 and pays a 2% dividend. You'd like to boost your current income and use the stock to benefit your college. You donate the stock to a charitable remainder unitrust. The trust sells the stock and avoids capital-gains tax on the sale. The trust invests in a balanced portfolio yielding 5% per year and growing at another 5%. You keep the 5% income and, at your death, the charity keeps the portfolio. This increases your income from $2,000 to $5,000 per year. It avoids capital-gains tax on the sale of the stock. And it gives you a charitable deduction equal to the remainder interest you donate to the college.

Figuring the value of the gift is the hard part. You don't know when you'll die, and you don't know how much the trust will be worth when you die. How do you calculate what to deduct from your income today when you make the gift? Fasten your seat belt—this road is rough. The gift equals the fair market value of the property you donate, minus the percent value of the income you retain. Generally, you figure the present value using standard valuation tables that reflect your life expectancy and the "applicable federal rate" that the IRS publishes monthly to make sure you use a reasonable interest-rate assumption. Your attorney or CPA can calculate the actual value of your gift.

Your maximum deduction for gifts to charitable trusts is limited to 30% of your adjusted gross income. If the value of your gift tops 30% of your adjusted gross income, you can carry the excess deduction forward five years. So it's important to plan correctly and project your future income to make the most of particularly large gifts exceeding 150% of a single year's adjusted gross income.

Charitable-Trust Alternatives

If you like the tax advantages of a charitable trust, but you don't want to jump through the legal hoops to establish one yourself, here are several alternatives:

- ◆ Charitable-gift annuities let you donate property to a charity in exchange for an annuity income from the charity itself. You get a charitable deduction today, figured the same as if you had given the money to a charitable trust. You can take an annuity income now, or defer it until a later date—retirement, perhaps, or when you're in a lower tax bracket. A charitable-gift annuity avoids the legal hassle of setting up a trust. The main difference is that you no longer direct the investment of assets you give. Also, you have to count on the charity, rather than an insurance company or investment adviser, to make the ongoing annuity payments.

- ◆ Pooled income funds are charitable trusts set up to accept donations from several donors. You transfer cash or property to the trust and get an up-front deduction based on the value of the gift and your life expectancy. The trust pays you an income, now or later, in proportion to your share of the trust's total contributions. At your death, the assets pass to the charity.

- ◆ Donor-advised funds are another charitable trust alternative. You make a gift of cash or securities to the fund—generally, $5,000 or more—and get a tax deduction now. The fund manages the assets and perhaps allows you to choose among a group of "mutual-fund" options. You can direct the fund to make a gift at any time.

Finally, if you're a truly heavy hitter, with $500,000 or more to give, you can establish a private foundation. A private foundation is a perpetual, irrevocable trust that has to distribute at least 5% of its assets per year to whatever charities the trustees choose. None of the income comes back to you, as it would with the aforementioned vehicles. This arrangement lets you control the foundation, its board of directors, and the causes you choose to support. You can also use a private foundation to shift income to your family, by naming them as officers and trustees and paying them for their services. At your death, the trustees continue to manage foundation assets according to the terms of the foundation.

SIX

TAX-ADVANTAGED INVESTMENTS TO MEET YOUR NEEDS

YOU HAVE MORE CONTROL over taxes with your investments than with any financial choice you make. Whether you're just starting out with a $100 monthly IRA contribution, or you're retired and living off a million-dollar portfolio, your investment choices give you more control over your taxes than any part of your finances. That's because you can arrange your investments to avoid paying a single dime of tax. What's more, you can control exactly when you pay the taxes you do.

You'd better believe just how much that control is worth. Over time, taxes, like inflation, positively *crush* your investment returns. Wharton School finance professor Jeremy Siegel, author of *Stocks for the Long Run,* has calculated just how much damage taxes had on investment returns over time. His study looked at returns from 1801 to 1997. A dollar invested in bonds grew to $727 before taxes—but just $73 after taxes, barely 10% of the pretax total. (By contrast, municipal bonds grew to $413.) The damage is even worse with stocks. A dollar invested in stocks grew to $514,605 before taxes—but just $23,684 after taxes, a puny 4.6% of the pretax total. Inflation is devastating too. But you don't have control over inflation.

The fact is, tax efficiency can mean even more than security selection. Most financial advisers agree that asset allocation—the choice you make regarding what percentage of your portfolio you distribute among stocks, bonds, cash, and other broad-asset classes—accounts for the largest part of your investment return. One influential study argues that asset allocation controls over 90% of your investment return. The same study argues that choosing specific securities within these asset classes accounts for 4% of returns over time, while market timing accounts for 2% more. But choosing tax-efficient investments can have a profound effect on your real, after-tax returns. And choosing tax-efficient investments is easier. It's hard to beat the market—that's why so few investment managers do it. But it's easy to find investments that jealously protect themselves from the tax man.

Before talking about specific investment choices, it's important to emphasize one fundamental rule: Investment choices are, first and foremost, *investment* choices, not tax choices. Don't put the tax cart before the investment horse. Choose your investments because they fit your investment plan. (What! You don't have an investment plan?) Make sure that you're properly diversified, your investments match your risk tolerance, and you've chosen the proper mix of stocks, bonds, cash, and other investments. Take time to find good managers and put an appropriate portion of your assets abroad. The 1980s tax shelter disaster is a glaring warning against letting tax considerations overwhelm investment choices. Thousands of investors sank billions of dollars into real-estate and energy-limited partnerships, cattle-breeding and feeding arrangements, master recordings, and other schemes, not because they were such appropriate investments, but because the tax code let them write off more than their actual investment. When Congress pulled the plug in 1986, the tax-shelter industry slid down the drain, sucking thousands of hapless victims along with it.

Having said all that, it's what you *keep* that counts. Your quick killing on a hot Internet stock looks a lot less impressive after the IRS confiscates 40% of your gain. If you don't plan carefully, you'll find that the IRS is your not-so-silent partner in every investment you make. And here's one more reason to integrate taxes into every investment decision you make. You can invest your money today in any number of different investments. Only time will tell if you choose right. That's because investment choices are a matter of opinion. But taxes aren't a matter of opinion. Taxes are a matter of fact. Why gamble on that hot Internet stock when you can count on the tax code to give you a break? The point is, while you don't enjoy control over investment results, you do enjoy control over tax results. Use this control whenever you can.

In the end, your goal should be to earn the highest after-tax return consistent with your ability to handle risk. This is an area where your own investment temperament is more important than objective tax-planning advice. The most tax-efficient way to invest is to find the next Microsoft—a hot growth stock with no dividend—and simply hang on for the ride. It worked for Microsoft founder Bill Gates, and he's the richest man in America. But Gates has seen his stock's value plunge by as much as $3 billion in a single *day*. Do you have the stomach for that kind of volatility? If not, ignore the tax advice and find investments you can live with. Let's say you're a young attorney, married to a computer programmer. You've got no kids, and you're 30 years from retirement. Conventional wisdom says you should be aggressive and put most, if not all, of your money in stocks. But if you've examined the reasons, and you're not convinced—in your *gut,* which is what keeps you up nights worried about your investments—then by all means reject the conventional wisdom. (Hey, if everyone's right, how come everyone isn't rich?) Choose the best investments for your needs, buy and sell them as efficiently as you can, and be done with it.

There are two main strategies for cutting tax on investments:

1. Choose Tax-Efficient Investments

First, choose tax-efficient investments. This includes investments that favor capital gains over income. It also includes investments that pay partially or fully tax-free income.

- Municipal bonds are free from federal and most state taxes.
- Treasury securities are free from state taxes.
- Certain U.S. Savings Bonds may be free from federal and most state taxes if you use the income to pay for college costs.
- Withdrawals from College IRAs are tax-free if you use them to pay for qualified college costs.

2. Buy and Sell Investments Efficiently

Second, buy and sell your investments efficiently. This means taking advantage of capital gains when you finally sell, as well as strategies for reaching your cash without paying tax on sales. It means considering investments that permit tax-free exchanges instead of taxable sales: life insurance, annuities, and real estate. Finally, it means holding appropriate investments in tax-deferred accounts. Tax deferral delays tax until you take your money out of the account. But tax deferral is a double-edged sword, because all income from tax-deferred accounts is eventually taxed as ordinary income, regardless of how the underlying investment itself would be taxed.

Keep these in mind as you read the next few chapters. Where can you find chances to shelter your money with tax deferral? Where can you find chances to buy investments that pay you later?

Many of the general strategies in this chapter overlap with specific strategies in other chapters. If you're saving for retirement, be sure to make the most of qualified plans and IRAs. If you buy mutual funds, be sure you do so as tax-efficiently as possible. And if you're saving for your kids' college educations, take advantage of opportunities to shift income to them. So make sure you follow up the general advice here with specific recommendations for specific goals and investments.

> Here's the secret to winning the investment game. Choose the most tax-efficient investments you can to meet your goals. Hold them for the long run. Draw as little income as you can. Try as hard as you can to avoid selling. Sleep well.

Choosing Tax-Efficient Investments
❖ ❖ ❖

Investments pay you two different ways: now (income) and later (capital gain). Income takes a number of different forms: interest on cash and bonds, dividends from stock and mutual funds, and rents from real estate. Capital gain is profit or loss on the sale of the asset. Together, income and gain produce total return, the measure of an investment's profit or loss.

Tax-wise, income is less efficient than gain. Why? Because income is taxed now, at your marginal rate, when you receive it. Gain is taxed in the future, at lower rates, when you sell the asset. This is the key to comparing tax efficiency. What do investments pay today compared to what they pay tomorrow? This actually involves two questions. First, what do they pay before taxes? And second, what do they really give you, after taxes?

Different Returns for Different Investments

Cash investments—bank deposits, bank CDs, and money-market funds—are the least efficient securities because they pay all their return in current interest. Bonds are inefficient because most of their return comes from current interest. Stocks are the most efficient because they pay the largest portion in long-term gains. But even stocks vary in tax efficiency. Dividend-paying stocks—utilities and real-estate investment trusts, for example—are less efficient than small-growth stocks that pay no dividend and pay all of their return in capital gains. Real estate is the most tax-favored investment because depreciation deductions can shelter current income. Finally, retirement accounts, life insurance, and annuities shelter any investment by wrapping it in a warm, snuggly blanket of tax deferral.

Morningstar Mutual Funds is a prominent mutual-fund rating service. *Morningstar's* tax-efficiency ratings tell you how much of a fund's return it keeps after taxes. These ratings are a useful proxy for the funds' underlying investments and reveal which investments pay the most efficient returns:

SECURITIES' TAX EFFICIENCY

o	**Small-Cap Growth Stock**
High o	**Large-Cap Growth Stock**
o	**Small-Cap Value Stock**
o	**Large-Cap Value Stock**
o	**Foreign Stock**
o	**Junk Bond**
o	**Long-Term Bond**
o	**Intermediate-Term Bond**
Low o	**Short-Term Bond**
o	**Money Market**

TAX BREAKS FOR CAPITAL GAINS

❖ ❖ ❖

Capital gains are the first place to look for lower tax on your investments. This is a good place to review the definition gains we discussed in the first chapter. Capital gains enjoy three significant advantages over ordinary income.

- ◆ Long-term capital gains are taxed at lower rates than ordinary income—no more than 20%, even for taxpayers in the top tax brackets.

- ◆ You don't pay tax until you "realize" your gain (actually sell your property), so you can choose when to pay the tax.

- ◆ If you hold on to appreciated property until your death, you avoid income tax entirely. Your heirs inherit the property with a basis equal to its value on your date of death. This "stepped-up basis" is an important tax- and estate-planning tool. Probably half of all capital gains escape taxes this way.

Property you hold for more than 12 months is taxed at 10% for taxpayers in the 15% tax bracket and capped at 20% for taxpayers in higher brackets. Property you buy after December 31, 2000, and hold for more than five years will be taxed at 8% for taxpayers in the 15% bracket and capped at 18% for taxpayers in higher brackets. (The 8% rate for 15% bracket taxpayers kicks in for post-2000 gain on assets held for five years regardless of when you buy the property. The 18% rate or higher-bracket taxpayers won't kick in until property is sold after 2006.)

Special rates apply for collectibles and for "recapture" of depreciated real property. Also, you can choose to treat property you buy before January 1, 2001, as if you had bought it on that date to take advantage of the lower rate for "five-year" capital gains. To do so, you'll have to "mark to market" and pay the tax due on the appreciation to that point. The property's value at that time will be your new cost basis, and your future appreciation will be taxed at the "five-year" rate.

CAPITAL-GAINS TAX RATES

Ordinary Income Rate	15%	28%	31%	36%	39.6%
Short-Term Capital Gains (property held less than 12 months)	15%	28%	31%	36%	39.6%
Long-Term Capital Gains (property held more than 12 months)	10%	20%	20%	20%	20%
"Five-Year" Capital Gains (property held more than five years and sold after 12/31/2000)	8%				
"Five-Year" Capital Gains (property bought after 12/31/2000 and held more than five years)		18%	18%	18%	18%
Collectibles	15%	28%	28%	28%	28%
Real-Estate Depreciation Recapture (capital gains attributable to amounts previously depreciated)	15%	25%	25%	25%	25%

If you have both gains and losses on separate sales in a single year, use your losses to cut your tax on your gains. Here's how:

- ◆ First, "net out" your gains and losses from short-term and long-term gains and losses. You'll finish with a single gain or loss for each category.

◆ Then, net out gains and losses between categories. You can use long-term losses to net out short-term gains and vice versa. Let's say you have a $2,000 short-term gain and a $4,000 long-term loss. The $4,000 long-term loss shelters the $2,000 short-term gain, leaving you with a $2,000 long-term loss.

You can use your losses to shelter 100% of your gains. If you finish the year with a net loss, you can use the loss to offset up to $3,000 of ordinary income. If your net loss tops $3,000, you can carry it forward to offset future gains and future ordinary income.

Married couples filing jointly can combine carryover losses from separate returns. But separate filers can carry over only their own separate losses. If you die with more than $3,000 in carryover losses, your losses die with you. You can't use them to cut your estate tax, and you can't leave them to your spouse.

The fact is, even with lower rates it pays to avoid selling. Turnover kills your returns, plain and simple, regardless of what you buy. Let's look at the case of two investors with $100,000 for retirement. Investor one takes his $100,000 and holds it in an index fund earning 10.5% per year. We'll call investor one the tortoise. Investor two takes her $100,000 and switches funds every year, beating the index and earning 12%. We'll call investor two . . .never mind, you've already guessed who wins. After 20 years, the tortoise finishes with $736,623. The hare finishes with just $524,560. The tortoise owes $114,592 in tax on his gain—but still beats the hare even after her phenomenal pretax achievement. (This example assumes for simplicity's sake that both investors are in the 28% bracket.)

BUY AND HOLD VS. FUND SWITCHING

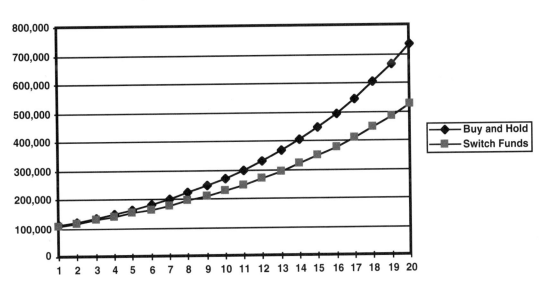

Here's a tip to cut your tax *and* simplify your life. Ignore the magazine covers telling you which hot funds to buy *NOW!*—except for *new* investments. Your money almost always takes you further without turnover.

The following chapters show you how to pick investments that reward you with capital gains. You learn where to find them and how to buy and sell them. You also learn which investments benefit most from tax deferral and which you should hold in taxable accounts for capital gains.

TEN WAYS TO AVOID TAX ON CAPITAL GAINS

❖ ❖ ❖

Special capital-gains rates are powerful tax-cutting tools. But why pay even that if you can avoid it? Here are ten strategies you can use to defer or eliminate tax on appreciated assets:

1. Borrow Against Your Assets

This is the easiest way to avoid tax on gains: just say no to sales. Borrowing lets you tap your equity without triggering tax. You can use your home, your real estate, and even your securities as collateral for a loan or line of credit. You can also borrow against a permanent life-insurance policy. Borrowing against an asset also lets you continue to enjoy the asset's growth.

2. Defer Sales

If you have to sell an asset, can you defer the tax by deferring the sale? This won't avoid tax completely, but it might push back the tax a year. They say that justice delayed is justice denied. Taxes deferred aren't always taxes denied, but at least they're taxes reduced. For stock sales, consider "selling short against the box." For more information, see "Stock-Investing Strategies" on page 114.

This strategy also works in reverse if your tax rate this year is lower than it will be in future years. Let's say you're between jobs, and this year you're likely to be in the 15% bracket. Next year, when you find a job, you'll be in the 28% bracket. You have 1,000 shares of Microsplat you bought two years ago for $10 per share. It's worth $20 now, and you're hoping to sell it next year at $25. Consider selling the stock now, in the low-bracket year, and immediately buying it back. Your capital-gain rate on the increase from $10 to $20 this year will be 10%, half as much as next year's rate of 20%. By selling this year, you pay $1,000—10% of the $10,000 gain. If you wait and sell it at the same price next year, your tax would be $2,000—20% of the same $10,000 gain. Even if you resell it next year for more than $20 per share, you'll have cut your tax on the gain from

$10 to $20. But before you use this strategy, figure out how much gain you can realize before you move up tax brackets.

3. Installment Sales

Installment sales let you defer your tax until you actually receive your payments. Tax is divided among the actual installments and due as you receive them. No payment is necessary the year of the actual sale; you must receive at least one payment in a year after the year of the sale. Installment sales are especially good for "big-ticket" sales such as businesses and real estate. The basic concept is simple. First, figure your profit on the sale. Next, figure what percent of the sale price consists of gain. Finally, multiply each installment by your profit percentage to figure taxable gain from that installment. For example, if you buy a building for $600,000 and sell it for $1 million, 40% of your sale price is gain, so 40% of each installment is taxed as capital gain. Here are some rules for some extra wrinkles:

- You have to charge interest on future installments or a portion of each installment will be treated as interest, taxed at ordinary rates, rather than capital gain. The minimum rate you have to charge is the "applicable federal rate" (published monthly by the Treasury), or 9%, compounded semiannually, whichever is less. Interest you earn on unpaid installments is taxed as ordinary income.

- If you sell a property on which you've claimed depreciation, the entire depreciation is "recaptured" the year of the sale. Recapture is taxed as ordinary income, except for real property, which is taxed at no more than 25%.

- You can't make an installment sale of depreciable property to a business you control or to a trust with you or your spouse as a beneficiary.

- If you sell property with no fixed price—as with an "earnout" sale of a business or rental property for a fixed percentage of sales or rent—divide the property's basis into the term of the installments, then pay tax on any gain above that amount.

- If the total of installment payments owed to you in any year tops $5 million, you'll owe interest at the federal underpayment rate on the balance exceeding $5 million. This rule keeps sellers from abusing the installment sales rules to defer tax on huge sales.

- If the buyer assumes a mortgage, subtract the mortgage amount from the gross sale price before figuring gain on the sale.

- If you elect installment treatment on a sale to a relative (spouse, child, grandchild, parent, grandparent, sibling) and the relative resells the property within two years of the original sale date, you'll owe tax on the entire balance the year the relative sells the property.

Let's say in 1990 you buy a rental duplex for $50,000. Over the years you depreciate $7,180. In 1998 you sell it for $100,000, payable in five installments of $20,000 plus 9% interest on the unpaid balance. Your gain is $50,000, or 50% of the sale price. Each $20,000 installment includes $10,000 of taxable gain. You'll also owe "recapture" on the $7,180 in 1998, plus ordinary income tax on the interest as you earn it.

Report installment-sale income on Form 6252, then carry the amount forward to Schedule D.

4. Match Gains and Losses

This strategy involves pairing your gains and losses to shelter income when you can't avoid a sale. Even if you have to sell and report income now, you can eliminate tax by matching gains with offsetting losses. It may make sense to hold your "losers" until you can use them to wipe out a gain.

This strategy is even more effective if you have old limited partnerships or other passive investments with "suspended" passive losses. Remember, passive losses are available only to offset passive gains. Most investors don't earn passive income, so they don't have any use for passive losses. There they sit, year after year, locked up as tight as the IRS's vault. But when you sell the investment, your suspended losses are "unlocked" and finally available to offset other income. There isn't much liquidity for used limited partnerships. But several organizations match buyers and sellers. For more information, see "Buying and Owning Rental Real Estate," in Chapter 9.

5. Consider Tax Swaps

A tax swap is when you sell an asset at a loss and replace it with a similar, but not identical, investment. The tax swap leaves your portfolio looking the same, but lets you book the loss on your original asset. You can use tax swaps with individual securities, mutual funds, and even real estate. For example, you can swap one computer company for another, one growth fund for another, or one apartment for another. If you buy back your original investment within 31 days before or after the original sale, your loss (but not any gain) will be disallowed as a "wash sale." Buying back shares in the same security counts as buying your original asset.

If you want to keep your same investment and still realize a loss, consider "doubling up," buying an identical lot more than 31 days before selling your old lot. You can also use your IRA to avoid the wash-sale rule. Sell an investment from a taxable account, and buy it back in your IRA. The taxable account lets you take the loss, but buying it back in an IRA is not the same as buying it back yourself. Of course, if the asset's value continues to fall, you can't take additional loss from the IRA.

6. Make Charitable Gifts

Charitable gifts of appreciated property let you do good for others while you do well for yourself. Giving a gift of appreciated property lets you deduct the full-market value—just as if you had given the same in cash—without paying tax on the gain in the property. You can also profit from bargain sales of appreciated property. For general limits on charitable gifts, see Chapter 5, Make the Most of Charitable Gifts.

> ▶ **Example:** In 1995, you buy 100 shares of Microsplat for $4,000. The stock is now worth $10,000. Give the stock to your alma mater and deduct $10,000 as a charitable gift.

7. Give Assets to Lower-Bracket Taxpayers

If you have appreciated property you'd like to sell to benefit a lower-bracket taxpayer—a child, a parent, or anyone else—consider giving the property to the other person to sell. If you sell it, you'll owe tax at your own rate. If the other person sells it, he or she will owe tax at their lower rate. This is especially useful for helping your kids with college or first-time home-buying costs.

> ▶ **Example:** In 1995, you bought 100 shares of Microsplat for $4,000. The stock is now worth $10,000 and you'd like to use it to help your daughter buy a house. Your capital gain rate is 18%; hers is 8%. If you sell the stock and give her the money you'll owe $1,080. If you give her the stock and she sells it herself, she'll owe just $480.

Unfortunately, there's a built-in limit to this strategy—$10,000 per year, per recipient. (If you and your spouse give jointly, you can give $20,000). If you give more, you may wind up owing gift tax.

8. Sell Your Business to an ESOP

An employee stock-ownership plan, or ESOP, is an employer-retirement plan that owns shares in the corporation itself. ESOPs give employees a bigger stake in the company's success and give departing owners a huge tax break. You can sell shares in your business to an ESOP without paying any tax on the sale. Here's how to qualify:

- ◆ You have to have owned the business for at least three years. (This is a fairly new requirement, passed after buyout artists abused the ESOP sale for short-term speculation. In one case, former Treasury Secretary William Simon and a group of partners used an ESOP to escape tax on $700 million of gain from selling Avis to employees less than two years after buying it. Apparently, the IRS had to try harder to get its tax.)
- ◆ You have to sell at least 30% of the company to the plan.
- ◆ You have to reinvest your proceeds in domestic corporate securities.
- ◆ You can't sell those securities during your lifetime.

The 1990s have seen an explosion of entrepreneurs with multimillion-dollar businesses to sell. The ESOP sale is a fabulous way to avoid income taxes in these sales. Investment banks have enthusiastically created special units to manage these sales and have even created new "domestic corporate securities" called ESOP notes that qualify to hold the proceeds.

9. Tax-Engineered Products

Tax-engineered products are a class of sophisticated strategies for heavy hitters. These are usually offered by Wall Street firms with the resources to hire and support the creative tax-and-accounting "rocket scientists" who dream them up. Most of these are limited to investors with at least $1 million—in a single stock! That's not as much as it used to be. Some of these strategies turn on separating ownership of a stock from any risk. Other strategies involve creating "derivative" securities based on underlying qualities.

"Equity swaps" are one strategy that lets owners lock in profits without selling. Let's say you have $5 million worth of stock in your former company. The stock yields 2% and pays just $100,000 a year. You'd rather buy some Treasury bonds and make three times that amount. You'd sell the stock to buy the bonds, but there's the small matter of $1 million you'd have to pay in tax. No problem! Your broker takes the risks and rewards of owning the actual stock and, in exchange, pays you the income you would earn from the Treasuries. You keep legal title to the stock. Since there's no sale, there's no tax. Sure, you'll pay your broker a fee for the service. But it's far less than you'd pay in tax on the stock.

"Swap funds" are a similar device for diversifying low-basis stock or other assets without selling. Transferring property into a partnership is generally not a taxable event. That is, there's no capital-gains tax on appreciated property you transfer into a partnership. So, you contribute your low-basis stock or other assets into a partnership made up of other wealthy investors. You end up owning shares in a more diversified portfolio consisting of all the investors' various assets. Alternatively, the fund itself sells the assets and invests in a diversified portfolio. The IRS has clamped down on these funds by barring tax-free transfers into partnerships with too much of their assets invested in "readily marketable" securities and that raise the holding period before the fund can distribute diversified assets back to the partners. Still, they remain useful tools for investors with $1 million or more.

"Zero-cost collars" are one more way to reach your cash and diversify without selling. First, you set up a hedge to protect your position. Sell a "call"—an option requiring you to sell the stock at a certain price. Then, buy a "put"—an option protecting you from a fall in the price. The money you make from selling the call pays for the cost of the put, hence the name zero-cost collar. Your biggest danger is the chance that the price of the stock will soar and the call buyer will exercise the option, forcing you to sell and realize the gain. Then, simply borrow against the stock, safely knowing the put protects your position. Without the collar, most lenders will give you only 50% of the stock's value. The collar gives your lender confidence to lend you up to 90%.

Tax-engineered products are a creative and changing field. By the time you read these words there may be new strategies that didn't exist when they were written. If you have at least $1 million invested in a single stock, find the firms that do these deals. You can save yourself tens of thousands in tax. What's more, you'll be the envy of your spiked-shoe friends at the club.

10. Offshore Opportunities

Offshore opportunities include bank accounts, investment accounts, and partnerships and corporations in foreign countries. The term "offshore" may conjure up images of Caribbean drug pirates and money launderers. The fact is, the vast majority of offshore investments are legitimate. The primary goal is protecting assets from U.S. creditors. Can they help protect your income from the tax man?

Congress has closed most of the loopholes that once let U.S. citizens send money offshore and avoid taxes. Now you have to report the mere existence of offshore accounts and trusts. You'll also owe tax on income from any offshore trust that you establish with U.S. beneficiaries. However, there are still a few limited offshore opportunities.

◆ You can use minority ownership in an offshore corporation to shelter offshore income. The singer Nat King Cole used a Bahamas corporation to shelter income from foreign tours and royalties. The catch is, under U.S. law you can't own a legal controlling interest. You can use an offshore trust to own the corporation. But if you're a beneficiary of the trust, the IRS will still tax you as if you owned the corporation yourself.

◆ You can use offshore annuities, taxed the same as U.S. annuities, to manage your own investments. A "self-directed" annuity lets you manage the underlying investments yourself, rather than choosing from a commercial annuity's existing portfolios. You can also transfer appreciated assets to the annuity without gain. (You can set up similar "private-placement" annuities and variable universal life-insurance contracts with some U.S. insurers. The problem is, you'll need to invest *at least* $1 million to do it. Some insurers who serve this market look for as much as $20 million to justify the special effort required.)

Both of these are expensive options for most U.S. investors. Who has offshore income they need to shelter? Offshore annuities seem attractive because they let you manage your funds yourself. But if asset allocation theory is true, and the majority of your returns are explained by asset class rather than by security selection, the marginal gains you squeeze out yourself might not justify the additional costs. The real attraction to these funds is asset protection.

THE MAGIC OF TAX-DEFERRED COMPOUNDING
◆ ◆ ◆

Albert Einstein is said to have called tax-deferred compounding the eighth wonder of the world. You probably already know about compound interest: you earn interest on your original principal, plus interest on the interest. In a taxable account, you pay tax on the interest each year and lose a little piece of your earnings. But in a tax-deferred account, you don't pay tax until you take out your money. With tax-deferred compounding, you earn interest on your principal, interest on the interest, and interest on the tax savings.

Let's consider the income you earn on a $2,000 IRA contribution. The amount per year may not sound like much, but it adds up over time. If you invest $2,000 per year for 20 years at 10.5% (the long-term historical return for U.S. blue-chip stocks), you'll finish with $134,000, more than three times your original investment.

What happens if you invest outside the IRA and pay taxes? If you invest the same $2,000 annually in a blue-chip stock fund, earn the same 10.5% per year, but pay 28%

TAXABLE ACCUMULATION VS. TAX-DEFERRED ACCUMULATION

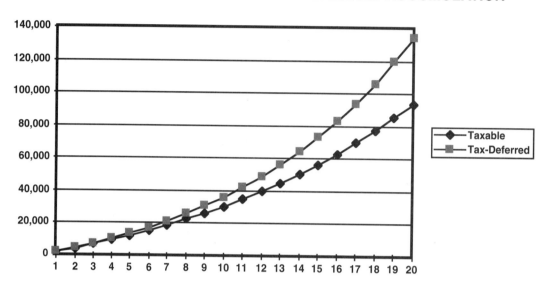

tax on the earnings, you'll have just $94,000. Income taxes will cost you more than your entire original investment.

If you invest the same $2,000 per year at the same 10.5% for 40 years, the difference is even more dramatic. In an IRA, your contributions grow to over $1,121,000. But if you pay taxes on this hypothetical mutual fund, your contributions grow to just $819,000. The difference, $302,000, is *more than three times* your total investment.

For a particularly dramatic example of tax-deferred compounding, consider this: Peter Minuit and the Dutch bought Manhattan island from the Indians for $24 in 1624. America's first land swindle, right? Yes, but the swindlers weren't who you think. If the Indians had invested that $24 in an IRA paying just 5%, they'd have over $252 *billion* dollars today—enough to buy Manhattan *and* all the buildings. But if they'd paid taxes at 28%, they'd have just $442 *million* today—less than 2% of the tax-deferred total. Taxes eat up *over 98%* of the growth. That difference over time is huge.

Tax deferral makes your savings grow faster and your income last longer. But tax-deferred accounts, including employer-retirement plans, IRAs, and tax-deferred annuities, have one significant disadvantage: plan withdrawals are taxed as ordinary income. There's no chance to take advantage of lower rates on capital gains, and there's no stepped-up basis for assets held until death. In some cases, the advantages of capital gains outweighs the advantage of tax-deferred compounding. This is even more true after the Taxpayer Relief Act of 1997 cut capital-gains rates. So, if your portfolio is large enough to include investments outside your tax-deferred accounts, you need to plan which investments to hold in tax-deferred accounts (to take advantage of tax-deferred compounding) and which to hold in taxable accounts (to take advantage of capital gains).

▶ **Example:** You have $100,000 invested in a bond fund compounding at 8% and $100,000 in a stock paying no dividend but appreciating at 8% per year. Which should go in the IRA? If you hold the bond fund in the IRA, you'll save tax on the 8% growth each year. But if you hold the stock in the IRA, you'll save—nothing. That's because the stock doesn't generate taxable income in the first place. At the end of the 20 years, the bond and accumulated interest will be worth $466,000 in the IRA and $306,000 outside it. The stock will be worth $466,000 whether it's inside the IRA or not. Clearly, the bond fund belongs in the IRA.

Since capital-gains rates are lower than ordinary income rates, it makes more sense to hold growth stocks and stock funds *outside* the IRA, to avoid converting capital gains into ordinary income. You also keep the chance to let your losers offset winners. Let your capital gains accrue in taxable accounts where you can take advantage of lower capital-gains rates. If you hold those investments until death, your heirs will receive them with a stepped-up basis equal to their value at the time of your death and escape capital-gains tax entirely. Use your IRA to shelter bond interest and other current income.

It's easy to look at an existing portfolio and choose which investments to protect from taxes. It's harder to tell whether you should rely on tax deferral going forward. The more time you have to let your investments grow, the more tax deferral is worth.

Different stock-investing strategies produce different tax results, so even if you buy just stocks, you can take advantage of these strategies. Large-company stocks and value stocks tend to pay higher dividends, which are taxed immediately as ordinary income. Small-company stocks and growth stocks tend to pay little or no dividends and return more in the form of capital appreciation, taxed only when you sell your shares. So tax-deferred accounts make more sense for large-cap and value investing. Leave your small-cap and growth investments in a taxable account.

This same principle applies to all types of tax-sheltered investments, including qualified plans, permanent life insurance, and annuities. Variable annuities have become tremendously popular in recent years as a way to invest in stocks without paying current tax. But variable annuities can actually *increase* your tax bill by converting capital gains into ordinary income. Also, variable annuities charge higher fees than do comparable mutual funds. These fees eat away at returns. Be sure you make the most of tax deferral by choosing the right investments for your tax-deferred accounts.

This principle is especially important if you find yourself in a higher tax bracket at retirement. This is possible even if your income drops. Your deductions will almost certainly be limited. If your house is paid off and your kids have graduated from college, you can find yourself paying more tax just because you lose your deductions.

There are some investment strategies that work best in tax-deferred accounts regardless of how the underlying investments are taxed. If you trade frequently, try to do as much as you can in your tax-deferred accounts. Also, if you try to time the market—switching your entire portfolio among cash, stocks, and bonds—do it in your tax-deferred accounts. You'll avoid whacking your profits each time you make a switch. It's tough enough to beat the market to start with. It's even tougher to do it with the IRS on your back.

Finally, tax-deferred investments, like any other investments, should fit within your overall portfolio. That means you should have the right mix of stocks, bonds, and other asset classes; your investments should match your risk tolerance; and you should have the right exposure to international investments.

TAX-ADVANTAGED INVESTMENTS TO MEET YOUR NEEDS

❖ ❖ ❖

Now that you know how to hold down your tax on investments, it's time to look at specific investment choices. Fortunately, there are tax-advantaged investments for every investor, from conservative retirees to go-go speculators. Income investors can choose among U.S. Treasuries, municipal bonds, and a wide range of fixed and variable annuities. Growth investors enjoy built-in tax breaks with stocks and stock mutual funds, plus their own set of annuity options. There are tax-advantaged alternatives to almost every taxable investment: bank savings accounts, CDs, and money-market funds; government, corporate, and even foreign bonds; even stocks and stock mutual funds. Tax-advantaged investments are valuable because they don't add to your final tax bill. They also keep down your adjusted gross income, preserving the value of your personal exemptions and itemized deductions.

You have your own unique goals and appetite for risk. These are actually more important than choosing specific tax strategies. That's because there are tax-advantaged investments to suit every combination goals and appetite for risk. So, rather than set out a laundry list of tax-advantaged investments, without putting them in the context of your own portfolio, see which tax-advantaged investments meet your current needs. Plan your investments to meet your needs, not just to cut your taxes.

Once you've figured which investments meet your needs, the following table can help you explore tax-advantaged alternatives.

TAX-ADVANTAGED INVESTMENTS TO MEET YOUR NEEDS

If you currently own:	Consider:
◆ Bank savings accounts ◆ Bank CDs ◆ Money-market mutual funds	◆ U.S. Savings Bonds ◆ U.S. Treasuries ◆ Municipal money-market funds ◆ Municipal bonds ◆ Immediate annuities ◆ Fixed annuities ◆ Whole life insurance
◆ U.S. Treasury/Agency securities (including mutual funds)	◆ Immediate annuities ◆ Fixed annuities ◆ Variable annuities—bond funds ◆ Whole life insurance ◆ Universal life insurance ◆ Variable life insurance—bond funds ◆ Real estate
◆ Corporate/high-yield/Foreign bonds (including mutual funds)	◆ Immediate annuities ◆ Variable annuities—bond funds ◆ Variable life insurance—bond funds
◆ Income stocks (including mutual funds)	◆ Immediate annuities ◆ Real estate
◆ Growth stocks (including mutual funds)	◆ Tax-managed mutual funds ◆ Index funds ◆ Variable annuities—equity funds ◆ Variable life insurance—equity funds

SEVEN

INVESTMENT SECURITIES

THE WORLD OF INVESTMENTS includes a bewildering range of competing choices, most with different tax rules, and most with different appeal for different investors. The next three chapters concentrate on finding the most tax-efficient investments for you. You learn the basic tax rules for any investment you might consider. You learn which investments pay the most efficient returns. You learn how to choose from various items on the investment "menu." And you learn how to buy and sell these investments to your best advantage.

"CASH" PAYS TAXABLE INTEREST

◆ ◆ ◆

"Cash" includes actual cash under the mattress, as well as bank deposits and money-market funds. Cash is an essential part of most investors' asset allocations and a safe harbor when markets are rough. But cash has historically paid the lowest return over time, and cash is the least efficient investment for taxes.

Bank savings accounts are the first place most people venture when they pull their cash from the mattress. Banks pay lousy interest rates. The interest is taxable immediately. And there's not even much reward for shopping rates. The extra 0.25% you might earn on a $10,000 balance (a fat $25 per year) doesn't justify the time it takes to shop around and move your account.

Bank CDs are the next step up the "investment" ladder. The bank pays you a guaranteed rate for a fixed length of time. These are especially sneaky "investments." They promise absolute safety. But do they deliver? After taxes and inflation, they leave you with little or no real return. And if you're trying to live off the income, good luck! Rates jump with every twitch of the economy. You can buy a five-year CD to lock in a steady income now—then renew, five years later, at less than half of your previous rate. It's no surprise that many investment advisers dismiss CDs as "going broke—safely." And it's no surprise that so many banks are adding securities brokerages—to keep their grip on investors finally wising up to lousy CD returns. (If you cash in a CD early and pay a penalty for early withdrawal, report the total interest credited. Then deduct the penalty as an adjustment to income on Form 1040.)

Most investors use money markets to hold the cash portion of their portfolios. Money markets pay the highest cash yields over time and offer instant liquidity to move your money to better-paying investments.

There are plenty of tax-advantaged places to stash your cash. There's no law that says you have to hold that part of your portfolio in a bank. If you're spending your income now, consider tax-free money markets and immediate annuities. If you're saving the interest, consider a variable annuity money market or fixed account. The annuity offers the extra advantage of tax-free transfers between accounts—a benefit you'll appreciate if you choose to sell stocks and retreat to cash.

BOND-INVESTING STRATEGIES

◆ ◆ ◆

In Shakespeare's *Julius Caesar,* Polonius warns us "neither a borrower nor a lender be." If Shakespeare manages your money, then you won't be buying bonds. A bond is simply a loan security promising a specified rate of interest and return of principal. The issuer pays a stated rate of interest. At the end of the term, the issuer pays a predetermined "face value." There are literally thousands of bond issues available. Government issues range from the U.S. Treasury to local agencies. Corporate bonds range from blue-chip giants to Internet start-ups. And foreign issues range from super-safe British "gilts" to speculative paper issued by former Third World colonies.

Bonds are generally known as safe investments. But bonds are full of hidden risks despite their steady interest income.

- ◆ "Credit risk" is the risk that the borrower won't repay. U.S. Treasuries have the lowest credit risk in the world. If the U.S. government ever defaults, the only investments worth holding will be canned goods and shotguns.

- ◆ "Interest-rate risk" is the risk that the price of your bond will rise and fall with interest rates. Long-term bonds generally fluctuate more than short-term bonds. You can buy adjustable-rate bonds whose yields move up and down with interest rates to eliminate this risk.

- ◆ "Reinvestment risk" is the risk that you won't be able to reinvest your proceeds at similar rates.

- ◆ "Currency risk" is the risk that interest and principal from foreign bonds will be worth less.

Bonds pay you now, with interest income, and possibly later, with capital gain on a sale. Most bonds aren't tax-efficient because most of their total return comes as current interest, taxed immediately when you receive it. (Some bonds get special breaks that shelter some or all of their interest income. Municipal bonds pay interest that's free from federal income tax. Treasury bonds pay interest that's free from state and local tax. And U.S. Savings Bonds let you wait to pay tax when the bond matures.)

Current interest isn't the only tax consideration with a bond. That's because interest rates rise and fall over time. Bond prices themselves rise and fall as interest rates rise and fall. This lets you profit when you sell or your bond matures. Bond prices rise and fall in the opposite direction of interest rates. If you buy a bond paying 8% and interest rates rise, the value of your bond will fall. Investors won't pay full price when they can earn more interest somewhere else. If you buy a bond paying 8% and interest rates fall, the value of your bond rises. Savvy investors are willing to pay a higher price for a bond paying higher interest. The farther away the bond matures, the more its price swings with interest rates. These price swings also open the door to tax swaps.

If you buy a bond at a premium—a price above its face value—you'll lose money when the bond matures. That's because the issuer won't return your full purchase price. So the IRS gives you a break for the loss you take on the premium. You can choose to write it off as a loss when the bond matures. Or you can choose to "amortize" it over the life of the bond. If you choose to amortize, you can deduct that amount from your annual income. To amortize a premium, simply divide it by the time remaining to maturity. Report your amortization on Schedule B where you report the income from the bond.

> ◆ **Example:**   You pay $1,040 for a four-year Treasury paying $80 per year. Your premium is $40, which, divided by four years, gives you $10 of amortization per year. You can choose to take a $40 loss when the bond matures. Or you can choose to amortize $10 and report just $70 of income per year. If you choose to amortize the premium, then sell the bond after two years, your basis for figuring gain or loss will be $1,020. So, if you sell the bond for $1,030, you'll report a $10 gain and not a $10 loss.

Your best choice in bonds depends on your own tax rate as much as it does on the bonds' interest income. Let's look at three different bond buyers to see how personal tax rates affect the choice. Our buyers each have four available choices (returns are from *The Wall Street Journal,* November 28, 1997).

- ◆ High-yield corporate bonds pay the best return at 8.46 percent. But these are subject to federal and state taxes.
- ◆ Long-term investment-grade corporate bonds pay the next best return at 6.78%. But these are also subject to federal and state taxes.
- ◆ Long-term Treasury bonds pay 6.04%. These are subject to federal taxes only.
- ◆ Finally, long-term municipal bonds pay the lowest return at 5.31%. But these are free from both federal and state taxes.

> ◆ **Example 1:**   You live in California. Your 31% federal rate and 10% state rate give you a combined rate of 37.9%.

BOND-YIELD COMPARISON
37.9% COMBINED RATE

Category	Pretax Yields	After-Tax Yield
High-yield Corporates	8.46	5.25
Long-term Corporates	6.78	4.21
Long-term Treasuries	6.04	4.17
Long-term Municipals	5.31	5.31

▶ **Example 2:** You live in Ohio. Your 28% federal rate and 6% state rate give you a combined rate of 32.32%.

BOND-YIELD COMPARISON
32.32% COMBINED RATE

Category	Pretax Yields	After-Tax Yield
High-yield Corporates	8.46	5.73
Long-term Corporates	6.78	4.59
Long-term Treasuries	6.04	4.35
Long-term Municipals	5.31	5.31

▶ **Example 3:** You live in Florida. Your federal rate is 15% and there's no state tax.

BOND-YIELD COMPARISON
15% FEDERAL RATE

Category	Pretax Yields	After-Tax Yield
High-yield Corporates	8.46	7.19
Long-term Corporates	6.78	5.76
Long-term Treasuries	6.04	5.13
Long-term Municipals	5.31	5.31

In Example 1 you're better off with the seemingly lowly municipal bond. In Example 2 the high-yield corporates come away the winner. And finally, in Example 3, the municipals lose their luster. (Realistically, a state with no income tax would pay an even lower rate on its municipal bonds.) You need to look at your own tax results before you buy your bonds.

In the end, bond investing is more than simply finding the highest yield. It's all about you, your comfort level, and your need for interest income. If you buy in a tax-deferred account, look for the highest total return consistent with your taste for risk. If you buy in a taxable account, look for the highest after-tax return consistent with your taste for risk. Consider tax swaps to capture breaks for paper losses. If you're investing for current income, consider municipal bonds, U.S. Treasuries, and immediate annuities for tax-advantaged income. And if you're reinvesting your interest, consider universal life insurance, variable life insurance, and variable annuities to protect your earnings from taxes.

BEWARE OF TAX ON ZERO-COUPON BONDS

❖ ❖ ❖

Zero-coupon bonds don't pay actual interest. Instead, you buy the bond at a deep discount to face value. The value of the bond increases steadily as it moves toward maturity, finally maturing at face value. In some cases, the issuer sells a zero-coupon bond directly. In other cases, a broker "strips" the coupon from a regular bond and sells the principal and coupons separately. You pay tax each year on the "original issue discount," or OID—the interest accrued—even though you don't get any cash. How's that for a deal!

Generally, your broker or the bond issuer will report the amount of OID to include on your return with Form 1099-OID. However, if you bought the bond at a premium (more than the total of the issue price plus all accumulated OID), or your zero-coupon is a "stripped" bond or coupon, you'll have to adjust the amount reported using complicated rules set forth in IRS Publication 1212.

Each year, as you report original issue discount, you add that amount to your basis for figuring gain or loss on a sale. If you sell a zero-coupon bond before maturity, you'll owe separate taxes on the portions representing income and capital gains.

Zero-coupon bond prices move dramatically with interest-rate swings, so bold investors use them to bet on rates. But the immediate tax bill on "phantom" income, along with complicated rules for figuring how much income to report each year, make them best suited for tax-deferred accounts.

TREASURY BONDS PAY TAX-ADVANTAGED INCOME

❖ ❖ ❖

It shouldn't surprise you to learn that the U.S. government is the world's largest debtor. The national debt stands at $4 trillion and counting. Every few years, the American public is treated to the embarrassing spectacle of Congress, holding its nose, raising the federal debt ceiling. This debt includes a tremendous variety of different instruments, with maturities ranging up to 40 years.

U.S. Treasury Bonds

U.S. Treasuries are bonds issued by the U.S. Treasury and backed by the full faith and credit of the United States government. Treasuries include T-bills (with maturities up to one year), notes (with maturities between one and ten years), and bonds (with maturities up to 30 years). Treasury interest is free from state and local income taxes. Your "taxable equivalent yield" equals the Treasury rate divided by 100 minus your state rate. For someone in a 10% state tax bracket, a Treasury paying 7% is equal to a fully taxable bond paying 7.78%. Obviously, there's no tax advantage to buying Treasuries in a state with no income tax.

Treasuries are available from any bank or brokerage house. You can also buy them directly through the Treasury Direct program (202-874-4000). If you can't afford to buy Treasuries directly, you can buy Treasury mutual funds. In fact, *Forbes* magazine recommends that investors with less than $50,000 to buy Treasuries do so through funds for diversification. Most Treasury funds differ little from each other. If you buy funds, pay careful attention to average maturities, which determine price volatility, and expense ratios, which can add up over time and make a tremendous difference in your long-term rate of return.

Treasury bills, with maturities up to one year, don't pay periodic interest. Instead, they're issued at a discount to their face value at maturity. The difference between the discounted price you pay and the $1,000 you receive at maturity is the income you receive. You don't pay tax until the year the T-bill matures. So if you bought a one-year T-bill on February 1, 1997, you could earn 11 months of interest and pay no tax until you file your 1998 return in 1999.

If you buy a Treasury at a premium—a price above its face value—you can amortize the premium over the life of the bond, or deduct it as a capital loss when the bond matures. If you amortize the premium, you can deduct the amortization from the interest you report. Remember, if you amortize the premium, you'll have to subtract the amortization from your basis for figuring gain or loss on a sale.

Treasury Inflation Protection Securities

Treasury Inflation Protection Securities, or TIPS, are Treasury securities "indexed" to inflation. Each year, your interest and your face value rise with the consumer price index. The rising interest, naturally, is taxable as you receive it. The principal "resets" each year to reflect the rise in the consumer price index. Here's the rub: Your rising principal is taxed as well. If inflation spikes like it did in the 1970s, you could wind up paying enormous taxes on inflationary, paper gains.

> ▶ **Example:** In 2000, you pay $1,000 for a ten-year TIP. The bond pays a stated interest rate of 3%. The 2000 inflation rate is 4%. At the end of 2000, your bond's value will rise to $1,040, and your annual interest will increase to $31.20, or 3% of $1,040.

TIPs pay a lower stated interest because you get the inflation protection. But since both the interest and principal gain are taxed each year as paid, they're best suited for tax-advantaged accounts.

U.S. Agencies

Agency securities are issued by U.S. governmental agencies. They usually consist of federally funded or guaranteed loans that are packaged and sold to investors. Agencies issuing securities include the Federal National Mortgage Agency, "Fannie Mae" (mortgages), and the Student Loan Marketing Agency, "Sallie Mae" (student loans). Agency securities generally aren't backed by the full faith and credit of the U.S. Treasury and aren't free from state and local taxes. They pay slightly more interest to make up for these disadvantages.

Mortgage-backed securities have a tax twist of their own. Usually a portion of every payment is a tax-free return of your own principal. The concept is easy to grasp if you think of the bond as a mortgage. Every mortgage payment you make includes both interest and principal. So if you act as lender—which you do when you buy these bonds—every monthly payment you get includes both interest and principal. The principal boosts your monthly payment. This makes your yield look awfully high in comparison to regular Treasury bonds. But remember, like a mortgage, there's nothing left at the end. If you spend 100% of your monthly payments, you'll wind up with nothing at the end. What's more, your payments will rise and fall with interest-rate changes. With Ginnie Maes, for example, if rates drop, you'll get large chunks of your principal back as homeowners refinance to take advantage of lower rates.

U.S. Savings Bonds Pay Tax-Deferred Interest

❖   ❖   ❖

U.S. Savings Bonds aren't as dull as they used to be. Savings bonds have traditionally paid a miserly interest rate. The main appeal was patriotism, not returns. But that has changed, and they now pay a market rate tied to Treasury yields. And savings bonds have attractive tax advantages. You can report your interest income every year *or* when you redeem the bond. And savings bond interest used to pay for college costs may be tax-free depending on your income.

New savings bonds are issued at half their face value. The bond's redemption value grows monthly or semiannually according to tables published annually. Bonds issued between May 1, 1995, and April 30, 1997, pay 85% of the average six-month T-bill rate for the first five years and 85% of the five-year Treasury rate for the next 12 years. New bonds issued after April 30, 1997, earn 90% of the average market yield on five-year Treasuries for the preceding six months. If the bonds haven't reached their face value in 17 years, the Treasury will "reset" the redemption value at that time.

Here's how U.S. Savings Bonds help you with your taxes:

♦ You can include the annual gain on your tax return if you choose. Or, you can include your accumulated gain the year you redeem the bond.

♦ You can change from annual reporting to deferral, and vice versa. To change from annual reporting to deferral, file Form 3115 the year you stop reporting annual gain. You have to continue deferring at least five years following the year of the change. To change from deferral to annual reporting, simply report the accumulated gain that year and annual gain as you receive it in future years.

♦ Savings-bond interest is free from state and local taxes.

♦ Savings bonds redeemed to pay your children's college tuition may be partially or fully tax-free if your income is below $65,850 ($106,250 for joint filers). For more information, see Chapter 11, Investing for College.

- If you buy a bond in a child's name and report the interest annually, the gain in the bond's value may be subject to the "kiddie tax." If your kids are reporting interest annually and the income grows to the point where they face the tax, consider changing to deferral reporting until they reach age 14 and the kiddie tax no longer applies.

- Savings bonds eventually stop paying interest at maturity. If you have old savings bonds, be sure to redeem them in time to avoid losing interest. You don't want to cut your taxes by losing interest.

CONVERTIBLE BONDS OFFER TAX-FREE CONVERSIONS

◆ ◆ ◆

Convertibles bonds pay regular interest, but can be converted into stock if the stock reaches a certain price. Convertible buyers like the profit potential coupled with the safety of regular interest payments and a fixed price at the bond's maturity. If you convert your bond into stock, there's no tax until you sell the stock. Your basis in the stock will be the same as in the original bond, and your holding period will start with the date you bought the bond. Convertibles are good for cautious investors who want a chance to profit from stock moves but keep an interest-paying safety cushion.

MUNICIPAL BONDS PAY TAX-FREE INCOME

◆ ◆ ◆

Municipal bonds, or munis, are issued by cities, counties, and their agencies, including universities, water and sewer districts, and even municipally backed private activities such as stadiums and aquariums. Munis are called "tax-free" bonds because their interest is free from federal income tax. But there are several wrinkles you'll need to know before you buy.

- Municipal bond interest is free from federal income tax.
- Most municipal bonds are free from state tax in the state of issue.
- Puerto Rico bonds and funds are free from state tax in any state. These are a good alternative for investors in states that tax their own bonds.
- Municipal bonds are still subject to federal estate tax.
- "Private activity" municipal bonds issued to finance stadiums and similar projects are subject to the Alternative Minimum Tax.
- Never buy a municipal bond or fund in a tax-deferred account. Not only do you earn a lower rate, you convert tax-free interest into ordinary income. This might seem like an obvious mistake. But IRA custodians report hundreds of tax-deferred accounts holding municipal bonds.

Individual munis generally carry no commission, but your purchase price includes a markup to pay the broker. It pays to shop around; markups can range as high as 3% for some long-term bonds. If you buy from your regular broker, ask her to discount the markup. The lower price you receive will boost your yield.

Taxable-Equivalent Yields

Since municipal bond buyers don't pay tax on their interest, issuers can pay lower rates. The key rate is taxable-equivalent yield—the rate you'd have to get with a taxable bond to equal the muni's tax-free yield. Your taxable-equivalent yield equals the muni bond rate divided by (100 minus your tax rate). For someone in the 28% tax bracket, a muni paying 5% equals a taxable bond paying 6.94% (5 divided by .72). For someone in the 39.6% bracket, the same muni equals a taxable bond paying 8.28% (5 divided by .604).

TAXABLE-EQUIVALENT YIELDS

Tax Rate	4%	5%	6%	7%	8%	9%	10%	11%	12%
15%	4.71	5.88	7.06	8.24	9.41	10.59	11.76	12.94	14.12
28%	5.56	6.94	8.33	9.72	11.11	12.50	13.89	15.28	16.67
31%	5.80	7.25	8.70	10.14	11.59	13.04	14.49	15.94	17.39
36%	6.25	7.81	9.38	10.94	12.50	14.06	15.63	17.19	18.75
39.6%	6.62	8.28	9.93	11.59	13.25	14.90	16.56	18.21	19.87

Remember, state and local taxes affect your true taxable-equivalent yield.

♦ If you're comparing a municipal bond's yield against a Treasury bond, include state tax only if your state taxes the muni-bond interest.

♦ If you're comparing a municipal bond's yield against a fully taxable corporate or foreign bond, include all state and local taxes, plus deduction and credit phaseouts.

♦ If you're collecting Social Security, don't forget to include the effect of tax on Social Security benefits. In some cases, a muni bond may make more sense than a taxable bond, even if the taxable equivalent yield is lower, because the taxable bond subjects more of your Social Security to tax. For more information, see "Make the Most of Social Security," in Chapter 12.

Municipal bonds are even more valuable if your adjusted gross income is high enough to phase out exemptions, deductions, and credits. Muni-bond interest doesn't increase your adjusted gross income, so your true tax break can be even higher.

Capital Gains on Municipal-Bond Sales

You may still owe tax on a municipal bond or bond fund if you sell it at a gain. Although the interest is tax-free, any gain or loss on a sale is taxable.

If you buy a municipal bond at a premium—a price above its face value—you'll have to amortize the premium over the remaining term of the bond. With muni bonds, amortization doesn't reduce the interest you receive. That's because you pay no tax on the interest to begin with. Amortization just reduces your "basis" for figuring gain or loss on the sale.

> ▶ **Example:** In 2000, you pay $1,040 for a muni maturing in four years at $1,000. Each year you have to reduce your basis by $10. If you sell the bond after two years, your basis will be $1,020. So if you sell the bond for $1,030, you'll report a $10 gain, rather than a $10 loss.

Since gains and losses on sales are taxable, muni bonds are still terrific candidates for tax swaps. If your bond's value falls, you can exchange it for another to realize a capital loss. You can increase your income, improve your credit quality, and lengthen or shorten your bond's maturity, all at the same time.

Zero-Coupon Municipal Bonds

Zero-coupon municipal bonds pay no current interest. Instead, you buy the bond at a deep discount to face value. The value of the bond increases steadily as it moves toward maturity, finally maturing at face value.

Since muni-bond interest is not taxed, you pay no tax on the gain if you hold to maturity. All of your gain will be considered interest. But if you sell the bond before maturity, it's necessary to calculate how much of your gain consists of nontaxable interest and how much consists of taxable capital gain. The process works the same as with any other zero-coupon bond. For more information, see the aforementioned "Beware of Tax on Zero-Coupon Bonds."

Municipal-Bond Funds

Municipal-bond funds and unit investment trusts (closed-end, unmanaged portfolios packaged and sold by brokers) come in all shapes and sizes. Tax-free money-market funds invest in short-term municipal bonds to maintain a stable net-asset value and pay tax-free income. Short-term, intermediate-term, and long-term bond funds invest in appropriate bonds for buyers seeking different maturities. Insured bond funds buy insured bonds for ultimate safety, while high-yield funds buy lower-rated and unrated municipal "junk" for highest possible returns. Finally, national funds buy bonds from all across America, while single-state funds invest in a single state to avoid state income tax in that state. Income dividends are tax-free; capital gains distributions and sales of fund shares are taxable.

Forbes magazine recommends that if you have less than $500,000 to buy munis, you buy funds. A fund will give you instant diversification among issuers and maturities. This can cut both your credit risk and interest-rate risk as well. A fund will also reinvest your interest at the same rate as the rest of your money if you aren't spending the interest. (If you buy individual bonds, the small size of the interest checks will make them hard to reinvest.) Finally, a fund lets you cash out any time at published net-asset value.

Single-state funds are popular in states that don't tax their own bonds. The obvious advantage is "double tax-free" treatment: interest is free from both federal and state income taxes. (New York City residents can buy funds of local bonds for "triple tax-free" income.) The less obvious disadvantage is lost diversification: All your muni-bond "eggs" are in a single state's basket. Single-state funds also carry higher expenses than do their national counterparts: Costs are spread over fewer shareholders, and demand for the state's bonds may push up prices. Higher expenses can eat up state tax savings, particularly with money-market funds. However, if you live in a high-tax state such as California or New York, it may pay to find a single-state fund with low expenses.

Here's a curious muni-bond perversion: single-state funds for states with no income tax. Why on earth would you buy a single-state fund, with less diversification and higher fees, except to avoid state taxes? So why on earth would you buy such a fund for a state with no tax to avoid? This surely represents the triumph of marketing over reality, especially with higher expenses on single-state funds.

STOCK-INVESTING STRATEGIES
◆ ◆ ◆

Stocks represent ownership of a company. When you buy stock, you're actually buying a piece of the business, one that entitles you to elect a board of directors, vote on various issues, and receive dividends if the board of directors chooses to pay them out of corporate profits. As the company's earnings grow, your piece of the business grows more valuable. The share price goes up and lets you sell at a profit. At least that's how it's supposed to happen. . . .

Stocks, like other investments, pay you now (with income dividends) and later (with capital gains). Since most stocks return more in capital gains than they do in income, stocks are considered a tax-advantaged investment. This is far more valuable now, with dividend yields averaging less than 3%, than in previous years with higher dividend yields and less difference in capital-gains rates. Here are the basic rules:

◆ Cash dividends are taxed as ordinary income the year the company pays the dividend.

◆ Profit or loss when you sell your shares is capital gain when you sell.

◆ Commissions you pay when you buy and sell are added to your cost or deducted from your proceeds to figure adjusted-cost basis and adjusted-sale proceeds.

◆ If you hold stocks in a fee-based account, where you pay a single fee for an unlimited number of trades, there's no specific commission for each transaction. Instead, deduct the annual fee as an investment expense, up to net-investment earnings, subject to the 2% floor on miscellaneous itemized deductions.

You probably already know that different stock-investment strategies give you different results. Small, growth stocks can rocket up and down with the day's headlines, while stodgy utility stocks give smoother, more predictable returns. But did you know that your investment style makes a big difference on your tax bill?

The main reason for this is dividends. Dividends are income, taxed now, rather than gain, taxed later at lower rates. And different investment styles are usually characterized by differing reliance on dividends.

- Value investors look for stocks with relatively low price-earnings ratios and stocks that have been beaten down in the market. Their goal is to buy low and to profit when prices rebound. Value stocks are usually mature companies paying higher dividends. These dividends help cushion share prices from further declines and smooth out market swings. Academic studies show that value stocks generally outperform growth stocks over time. However, dividends make them less tax-efficient.

- Growth investors look for fast-growing companies with rising earnings to push share prices higher. They don't mind buying high if they think they can later sell even higher. Growth stocks generally pay little or no dividend, choosing instead to plow profits back into the company. Growth stocks are more volatile than value stocks, with prices swinging wildly on sudden good or bad news. However, low dividends make growth stocks more tax-efficient than value stocks.

- Equity-income investors look for stocks with fat dividends for steadier returns and a safety cushion during market downturns. Naturally, the dividends make this a relatively inefficient investing style.

- Utility stocks generally pay the highest taxable dividends of any common stock.

- Preferred stock pays a "guaranteed" dividend that has to be paid before common shareholders get any dividend. If the company issuing the stock goes bankrupt, preferred shares stand in line before common. The higher level of guarantee makes the stock itself trade more like a bond. "Convertible preferred" is convertible into shares of common at a specified price. These shares generally pay a lower dividend in exchange for the conversion privilege. Preferred stock doesn't just *trade* like a bond. It's *taxed* like a bond. Paying today's tax on today's dividend takes away much of the tax advantage of buying stock to begin with.

Remember, the proper goal is to earn the highest after-tax return, consistent with your own willingness to take risk. That's important—in fact, it might be more important than actual return. If you're the type who lies awake nights in fear of a market crash, you won't do yourself any favors buying Internet start-up stocks to avoid tax on dividends.

Minimize Turnover

What would you do if you heard that the market had fallen by 10%? Would you call your broker, or your fund company's "800" number to dump your shares? The fact is, the market crashes every time you sell a winner. Why? Because the taxes you pay on your profits take a bite out of every gain. If you trade stocks frequently, you'll whack your gain even harder than if you buy and hold. Not only do you whack your gain more often, but every dollar of tax you pay costs you the chance to make that dollar grow.

The one exception to the turnover rule is this: Don't be afraid to walk away from a loser. The new science of behavioral finance tell us that most of us feel more pain from losses than joy from gains. Faced with the choice between selling a winner and selling a loser, most of us sell the winner. That way, we don't have to admit we were wrong when we picked the loser. But dumping the winner costs you tax and cuts your profits short. Selling the loser cuts your tax and lets you reinvest your cash in a winner.

Convert Dividends to Capital Gains

Cash dividends are taxed immediately as ordinary income. There's no tax break on dividends as there is for capital gains.

However, you can time your stock sales to capture your final dividend as a capital gain, taxable at lower rates. Stocks that pay dividends do so to investors who own them as of a certain date, called the "record date." After the record date, the stock trades "ex-dividend," meaning without the dividend. Naturally, the stock's price drops on that date by an amount roughly equal to the missing dividend. If you sell your stock just before it goes ex-dividend, when it's fat with the dividend amount, you get the full value of the stock *and* the dividend. But you pay lower capital-gains rates on the dividend since you receive it as part of the sale price rather than as a dividend payment.

This same strategy works for mutual funds as well.

Identify Specific Shares to Sell

If you're like most investors, you've bought different lots of the same stock at different times and prices. This is especially true if you've bought shares through a dividend-reinvestment program. You can control the tax you pay just by identifying shares to sell. If you hold certificates yourself, choose the highest-priced lot to pay the lowest tax. Or, if you have losers to match, choose the lowest-priced lot to realize the biggest gain without paying tax. If you hold shares in "street name" with a broker, instruct your broker which shares to sell. If you don't, the IRS will treat you as having sold your oldest shares first.

Short Sales

"Selling short" is when you sell borrowed shares and hope the price goes down, so that you can buy it back for less to "cover" the borrowed shares. When it works, it's buying low and selling high—in reverse. Your "closing" date for figuring gain or loss is the date you deliver the replacement shares. While you hold a short position, you'll have to pay your broker the dividends paid on the stock. You can add your dividend to your basis, or, if you hold the "short" position 46 days or more, you can deduct it as investment interest.

"Selling short against the box" is a strategy for deferring tax on stock sales until the next taxable year. When you short "against the box," you borrow shares in a stock you already own. This lets you profit from your existing position (by selling an equal amount of shares) without paying tax as you would on a sale. At the same time, you "hedge" the value of your shares. If the price falls, the profit you make on the short position offsets the loss on your own shares.

Before the Taxpayer Relief Act of 1997, you could hold a short period forever without paying tax on the "sale." Now you can use this strategy to delay taxes only if you close your short position by January 30 of the following year *and* hold the underlying stock for 60 days more. You'll have to accept the risk that your stock's value can fall during that 60-day period. Shorting against the box is less useful than before. But it's still worth considering to delay this year's tax bill until next year.

Dividends Paid in Stock

Common-stock dividends paid in additional stock generally aren't taxed when you receive them. Instead, they're taxed as capital gains when you sell the dividend shares. Your basis for figuring gain or loss is your original cost in the stock, divided by your total number of shares. Your holding period for determining short- or long-term gain is the date you bought the original stock.

Let's say on January 1, 1998, you bought 100 shares of Microsplat for $1,100. On December 31, the company pays a dividend of 10 additional shares. On August 1, 1999, you sell the dividend shares for $20 each. Your basis in the new shares is $10 each, which equals your $1,100 purchase price divided by 110 total shares. Your gain on the shares is $10 each, taxed as long-term capital gain.

However, these stock dividends are taxed when they're paid.

- If you choose to reinvest cash dividends in a dividend-reinvestment program, the dividend is taxable when paid. If the plan lets you buy shares at a discount, your taxable dividend and basis for figuring gain or loss when you sell the new shares is the fair-market value of the dividend date. There's no immediate tax on the discount; instead, it's taxed as capital gain when you sell.
- Preferred-stock dividends are taxable when paid.
- Dividends paid in the stock of another company—say, shares in a subsidiary or sibling company in a controlled group—are taxable when paid.
- If you have a choice between taking cash or taking stock, the dividend is taxable when paid. Your holding period in the new shares begins the day after the distribution; your basis for figuring gain or loss is the value of the distribution.

The "Dogs of the Dow" Pack a Nasty Tax Bite

The "Dogs of the Dow" is a popular proven strategy for beating the Dow Jones Industrial Average. The theory is simple: Stocks with high dividends outperform the average as a whole. Yields are high, the theory says, because prices have fallen too low. These low prices set the stage for a comeback. The dividend further boosts your returns. The actual mechanics are simple: At any particular day of the year, survey the 30 stocks of the Dow Jones Industrial Index to find the 10 with the highest dividend yields. Buy them, and hold them for a year. At the end of the year, rerank the stocks according to dividend yield and replace those that have fallen out of the high-yield group. If you don't have the money to buy individual stocks, several firms offer unit investment trusts (unmanaged portfolios resembling mutual funds) that buy the Dow 10 stocks.

Results have been impressive. One study shows that from 1973 to 1994, the strategy returned 17.23% per year, far more than the S&P 500's 11.19% for the same period. Put another way, if you had invested $10,000 at the start of the period into the S&P 500, you would have $103,145 before taxes. That's great! But if you'd put the same $10,000 in the Dow 10 group, you'd have $330,258 before taxes—fully three times more than in the S&P 500! The "Dow 5" group does even better for more aggressive investors willing to concentrate their funds on just five stocks. Yet this is at heart a very conservative value strategy. The Dow stocks are the safest, most recognizable blue chips available.

Impressive as they are, can you see how these dogs practically sit up and beg the IRS to grab your gains? The high dividend yields are taxed immediately. And the constant annual turnover clips your profits every time you sell. These dogs pack a nasty tax bite. If you're going to use this strategy, do it in your tax-deferred accounts.

OPTIONS, FUTURES, AND COMMODITIES
❖ ❖ ❖

Options, futures, and commodities are the crack cocaine of the investment world. Why? Because most of these investments use tremendous leverage to magnify gains and losses. As with crack cocaine, the highs are higher (and the lows, lower) than with any other investment. Trading exchanges are littered with the bankrupt accounts of traders who crash and burn. When trading closes, the nearby bars fill with traders craving one more fix. If riverboat gambling hasn't found its way to a state near you, options, futures, and commodities might fill that void in your life.

These investments aren't for amateurs. Studies consistently show that over 80% who play end up losing money. If you need more proof, just look around for someone who made a killing. (While you're at it, look for someone who's actually retired on Beanie Babies.) And they're not for investors who want to keep down their tax bill. Options, futures, and commodities use short-term trading to generate quick profits. In some cases, investors hold their position for less than a day. This can rack up quick profits, but racks up tax bills, too. What's more, some contracts don't even let you delay taxes by holding on through the end of the year. The "mark-to-market" rules require you pay tax each year as if you had sold at the end of the year. And 60% of your gain is taxed as long-term capital gain; the remaining 40% is taxed as ordinary income.

Options have one specific use for investors looking to save taxes. Options can "hedge," or protect, a position you don't want to sell. Let's say you have $1 million worth of Microsplat. Your cost is just $200,000. If you sell, you'll pay over $300,000 in taxes. You can buy a "put" option that pays off if the price of Microsplat drops. Hold the stock as long as you like, secure in knowing the option "ensures" your stock against a fall. You can sell the stock in pieces, or you can borrow against its value. Of course, the insurance has a cost. But the "premium" you pay for the option will be far less than you'd pay in taxes if you sold.

Certain options also help investors manage risk. Conservative covered call writing—selling an option to buy a stock you already own, in order to pick up extra income from selling the option—can help increase your income (at the cost of losing control over timing sales). The premium you get from selling the option is taxable income the year the transaction closes. And commodities have a place in diversifying your holdings. They don't rise and fall in synch with financial markets. Properly used, they can boost returns and cut your overall risk. But if those are your goals there are specialized money managers to help. Managed accounts and commodity-linked mutual funds are just two ways to harness the power of these markets. Individual contracts are best for aggressive investors willing to learn the markets cold.

TAX SHELTERS

❖ ❖ ❖

Old-fashioned tax shelters died a terrible death with the Tax Reform Act of 1986. Oil and gas, equipment leasing, cattle feeding, master recordings, and the like let investors write off more in a year than they paid for the entire investment. Then Congress cooked up the passive-loss and at-risk rules, and the cops shut down the party. For more information, see Chapter 9, Real Estate. Tax shelters still survive, but today they emphasize tax-advantaged income over losses.

Oil and gas investments include exploratory programs that search for new resources, development programs that drill in areas with proven deposits, income programs that generally purchase existing reserves, and combination programs. These deals carry three main tax advantages:

◆ You can write off "intangible drilling-and-development" costs, such as labor, fuel, and supplies involved in drilling a well.

◆ You depreciate the cost of capital equipment you use to extract the resources.

◆ Finally, you can write off up to 15% of your gross income as a depletion allowance, a sort of "depreciation" for natural resources. This depletion allowance reflects the reality that someday the well will run dry.

Timber deals get similar depletion breaks: Someday the trees will all be cut.

Equipment-leasing deals use depreciation to defer income. The Modified Accelerated Cost Recovery System introduced in 1986 lets equipment buyers "front-load" their depreciation deduction for fatter writeoffs their first few years of ownership. Equipment-leasing partnerships buy equipment to lease to users, then pass the writeoffs through to the partners along with the income. The depreciation delays or shelters out all or part of the income. Some of these deals are structured so that eventual profits depend on reselling the equipment. Even if the deal itself shows a loss, investors can gain from the use of their money during the period when depreciation shelters income.

Most of these deals are organized as limited partnerships, subject to the passive-loss and at-risk rules. The general partner will report income and writeoffs on Schedule K-1 for you to report on Schedule E and other parts of your Form 1040. If you've made the most of your traditional tax-planning opportunities, it may be worth your while to consult a CPA or tax attorney about some of these tax shelters. They can diversify your portfolio as well as give you tax-advantaged income. But it's important to evaluate these deals as investments. And be aware that they generally won't cut your tax from salaries, wages, and other investments. That old gray mare, she just ain't what she used to be.

EIGHT

MUTUAL FUNDS

MUTUAL FUNDS HAVE fast become America's favorite investment. Fund managers have become celebrities, writing best-sellers and brandishing performance statistics like batting averages. The Investment Company Institute, a Washington, D.C.-based trade group, reports that as of April 1998, nearly 40 million American households owned over $5 trillion worth of mutual funds. Over $1 trillion of that was invested in retirement accounts. Twenty-three percent of households own stock funds; 16% own bond-and-income funds; and 16% own money-market funds. The typical shareholder is a 44-year-old college graduate, makes $60,000 per year, and has financial assets of $50,000.

A mutual fund is an investment company that pools money from shareholders and invests in a diversified portfolio. The fund hires a professional manager to choose individual securities, who then chooses investments according to guidelines set forth in a prospectus. Each fund share is worth its proportional piece of the fund's underlying investments. With "open-end" funds, the bulk of today's offerings, shares are priced daily, and new investors buy their shares at the price set on the day of purchase. The fund provides semiannual reports to shareholders listing all of the fund's holdings and audited-performance figures. Shareholders who wish to exit the fund sell their shares directly back to the fund. (Another type of fund issues a fixed number of shares that later trade on an established exchange. For more information, see "Closed-End Fund Strategies," following.

Mutual funds are generally offered in families of up to 100 funds. You can switch money from one fund into another, usually just with a phone call. If you buy your fund from a broker and pay a sales commission, you can switch funds within the family without paying additional commission on your original investment. Mutual funds are also regularly audited to protect investors. The Securities and Exchange Commission (SEC) regulates and oversees mutual funds to ensure they invest under the terms of their prospectuses. The National Association of Securities Dealers (NASD) regulates fund advertising and communication, as well as the brokers who sell funds and advise clients.

Mutual funds (including open-end funds, closed-end funds, and unit-investment trusts) may be the smartest way for most investors to buy securities.

* Funds offer professional management at a reasonable fee. This is an important plus for new investors without the experience to assemble portfolios on their own. It's also valuable for experienced investors venturing into new areas, such as junk bonds or international stocks.

* Funds provide instant diversification for a minimal investment. Investors get a complete portfolio with a single purchase. Experienced investors venturing into new areas can acquire a complete portfolio that they couldn't confidently or economically assemble themselves with individual securities.

* Funds offer instant liquidity and, in most cases, 24-hour trading access. You can buy funds at the day's closing net-asset value without worrying about execution.

* Funds are ideal for IRAs, custodial accounts, and systematic investment plans because you can buy them in bite-sized chunks. A $250 or even $1,000 stock invest-

ment can't buy enough individual shares to justify the steep commissions for that size purchase.

◆ Funds are the most convenient way to dollar-cost average. This is a strategy for buying a set dollar amount of shares at constant intervals regardless of underlying share price, which yields higher average gains per share in rising markets.

◆ Since so many fund families offer funds with similar investment objectives, funds are ideal for tax swaps.

At the same time, funds have these disadvantages that make it harder to manage your taxes:

◆ Your fund manager exercises most control over taxes, choosing which gains to realize and when to do so. Most funds don't manage their investments with an eye toward shareholders' eventual taxes. The only control you exercise is when you sell the fund.

◆ You can't separate out your fund's winners from losers, or realize a single underlying holding's gain. For example, you can't "carve out" a big winner and give those shares to charity. (Of course, you can carve out a portion of your shares in the overall fund and give *that* to charity.)

◆ Management fees are an ongoing expense that you wouldn't bear if you bought and held individual securities yourself.

Today there are nearly 10,000 mutual funds: open- and closed-end funds; "load" funds and no-load funds; stock, bond, money-market, and combination funds; domestic funds and foreign funds. There are "socially responsible" funds that avoid companies involved in alcohol, tobacco, gambling, weapons, and other ostensibly irresponsible corporate citizens. There's even a socially *irresponsible* fund that buys the stocks the responsible funds don't buy.

The same general rule applies to mutual funds as to any other investment: Investment choices are, first and foremost, investment choices, not tax choices. Choose your mutual funds to fit your investment plan, not your tax plan. Make sure you're properly diversified, your funds match your risk tolerance, and you've chosen the proper mix of stocks, bonds cash, and other investments. The name of the game is picking tax-efficient investments that meet your particular needs.

KEYS TO MUTUAL-FUND TAX EFFICIENCY

◆ ◆ ◆

Mutual funds are "pass through" entities that pay no tax themselves. Instead, they pass through earnings directly to you. Funds are generally taxed like their underlying investments. Bond funds are taxed like the underlying bonds, stock funds are taxed like the underlying stocks. But mutual funds have a few unique wrinkles arising out of their structure. They complicate the picture by returning capital gains on sales within the underlying portfolio now, as ordinary income, rather than when you sell. But the general principal of tax efficiency is the same. The greater the part of total return that comes from future gains, the more efficient the fund is. The key to your tax efficiency is the proportion of total return coming from current income versus the proportion coming from capital gain.

Funds pay a wide variety of distributions taxed in different ways. These distributions play a big part in establishing how much tax you pay.

- Income dividends consist of income earned by the fund's portfolio investments, such as interest earned by bonds and dividends paid on stock. Income dividends may be distributed monthly, quarterly, or annually, depending on how much income the fund's investments generate. Income dividends are taxed as ordinary income whether you take the dividend in cash or reinvest it in additional shares. Some income dividends, such as from Treasury bond and municipal-bond funds, pay interest that's partially or fully free from state taxes. If so, the fund will send a statement telling you the percentage of the dividend that's free from state tax. You can then exclude the appropriate amount on your state tax return.

- Capital-gains dividends, not surprisingly, consist of profits from sales of securities within the fund's portfolio. Capital-gains distributions are generally taxed as long-term capital gains, regardless of how long you own the shares. And, like income dividends, capital-gains distributions are taxed when distributed whether you take the distribution in cash or reinvest in additional shares.

- Return-of-capital distributions are a return of your original investment. These distributions generally aren't included in taxable income. Instead, they reduce your basis in your shares when you finally sell. If your basis is already down to zero, then report these distributions as capital gains.

- Some funds may retain long-term capital gains and pay tax themselves, rather than distributing those gains to shareholders. You still owe tax on the gain, but you can claim a credit for the tax the fund pays. The fund will report your share of the tax on Form 2439. To claim the credit, enter the amount on Form 1040, line 59, check the box for Form 2439, and attach a copy of the form.

- Some funds also pay foreign tax on foreign income. You can claim a deduction or a credit for your share of the fund's foreign taxes. To claim the deduction, report it on Schedule A, along with state and local income and property taxes. The credit will usually cut your tax more. For tax years beginning after January 1, 1998, if your foreign tax is $300 or less ($600 for joint filers) and your only foreign income is qualified passive income (including mutual-fund income), you can claim the credit directly on Form 1040. If your share of the fund's foreign tax is higher than those amounts, figure the credit on Form 1116. This involves figuring some complicated ratios for different kinds of foreign income. But it beats paying the same tax twice.

The same general rules apply in cutting tax on your funds. First, choose tax-efficient funds. Strategies for choosing tax-efficient funds include paying attention to turnover ratios, using *Morningstar Mutual Funds* tax-analysis ratings, and considering index funds and tax-managed funds. Second, buy and sell your funds efficiently. Strategies for buying and selling shares include writing off sales loads, avoiding purchases and favoring sales near dividend distributions, recording reinvested dividends, and using tax swaps.

Fund investors looking for tax deferral should also consider variable annuities. A variable annuity is a contract with an insurance company offering a group of "subaccounts" that resemble a mutual-fund family in a tax-deferred wrapper. Your income grows tax-deferred, and you can make tax-free transfers among subaccounts. In fact, many variable-annuity subaccounts are virtual "clones" of popular mutual funds. They are particularly useful for sheltering interest income from the fixed-income portion of your portfolio. However, by offering tax deferral, variable annuities wipe out the chance to profit from lower capital-gains rates. For more information, see Chapter 10, Life Insurance and Annuities.

Four Ways to Pick Tax-Efficient Funds

❖ ❖ ❖

Here are four ways to choose tax-efficient funds. These strategies, along with the buying-and-selling strategies discussed later, will help cut your fund taxes to the lowest amount appropriate for your individual goals.

1. Pay Attention to Turnover Ratios

Mutual-fund managers generate taxable gains and losses every time they trade. It follows that managers who trade less, cost less. The "turnover ratio" tells you what percentage of a fund portfolio trades every year. A fund with a turnover ratio of 100, for example, turns over the equivalent of 100% of its portfolio per year. Since the fund has to distribute all capital gains from this trading, higher turnover ratios mean higher capital gains at tax time. Funds with high turnover also have higher expense ratios to pay for research, trading, and operations costs.

You can find a fund's turnover ratio in the prospectus, the annual report, and sometimes in the semiannual report. You can also find turnover ratios in *Morningstar, CDA/Wiesenberger,* and other third-party mutual-fund evaluators.

Turnover isn't a perfect measure of tax efficiency. The same 10% of a fund turned ten times a year won't generate the same amount of tax as if the entire fund had turned just once. And a fund with a 40% turnover ratio won't necessarily generate twice the tax of a fund with a 20% ratio. Some studies suggest that turnover's effect is greatest as it commences and diminishes as it increases past 30% or so. Holding period may be a better measure of tax efficiency, although average holding periods aren't widely reported as turnover is. Still, turnover is a useful indicator once you've narrowed your fund choices to a few final candidates.

Some funds that troll for new business by touting their latest performance figures wind up boosting their own turnover. They buy stocks with the new investors' money, then wind up selling those stocks as the "hot money" leaves for the next new fund to come along.

It's also worth checking to see if a fund has just hired a new manager. This is obviously an investment consideration. A new manager might not have the proven track record of an experienced hand. But it's a tax consideration, too. When new managers take over funds, they usually "clean house" by selling stocks that they would not otherwise have bought and replacing them with their own favorites. This artificially gooses turnover, which boosts your eventual tax bill as a shareholder.

2. Consult *Morningstar Mutual Funds* Tax-Analysis Ratings

Morningstar is a popular mutual-fund rating service. A *Morningstar* rating is a single page jam-packed with information, including the fund's performance history, top holdings, a brief editorial description, and a much-misunderstood "star rating," which ranks the fund's risk-adjusted return against its peers. *Morningstar*'s tax-analysis ratings are particularly valuable for investors looking to make the best after-tax return.

Morningstar's "tax-adjusted return percentage" tells you each fund's after-tax total return. To calculate this figure, *Morningstar* "taxes" all income and capital-gains distributions at the highest applicable rate and "reinvests" the remaining amount into new shares, but does not include any taxes that would result from selling the fund. The final figure doesn't represent your after-tax return. Obviously, that will depend on your own tax bracket. But it's useful whatever your tax rate to see which funds pay a greater portion of their total return in immediately taxable dividends and distributions.

Morningstar's "% Pretax Return" figure tells you what percentage of a fund's return consists of taxable distributions. This direct measure of tax efficiency equals the fund's after-tax return divided by its pretax return. A fund with a score of 100% would have no taxable distributions whatsoever.

Finally, *Morningstar*'s "Potential Capital Gains Exposure" figure tells you what percentage of a fund's total assets represents undistributed capital appreciation. If the fund were liquidated today, this amount would be taxed as capital gains. As a fund's assets grow, this percentage is diluted over a larger total pool of assets. Just for laughs, here's the formula *Morningstar* uses to calculate this figure:

$$\frac{\begin{array}{c}[\text{Unrealized Appreciation or Depreciation} + \text{Realized Gains or Losses} + \\ (\text{Ending NAV} + \text{Sum of Capital Gains Paid} - \text{Beginning NAV (Avg \# of shares)})] - \\ (\text{Capital Gains Paid})(\text{\# of Shares at Time of Distribution})\end{array}}{\text{Current Assets}}$$

Kids, don't try this at home.

Together, these ratings tell you which funds protect you the best from taxes. They certainly aren't the place to start your search. But they can be useful once you've narrowed the field. The following table summarizes the percentages of pretax return for various fund categories. Use it as a guide as you evaluate fund purchases.

3. Consider Index Funds

Most funds are "actively managed"; they hire managers who try to "beat the market" in whatever securities they manage. Active managers then score themselves against an

PERCENTAGE OF PRETAX RETURN BY FUND CATEGORY

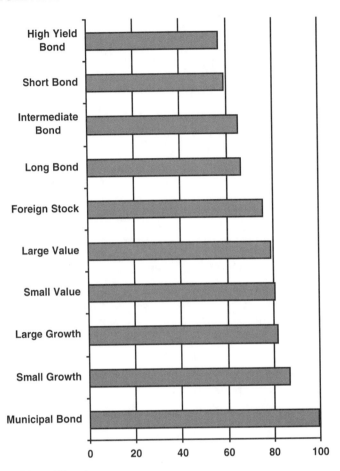

Source: Morningstar Mutual Funds

index that tracks the market in the appropriate securities. Large-cap managers, for example, generally aim to beat the S&P 500, an index of the 500 largest companies by market valuation (share price multiplied by outstanding shares). Index funds don't try to beat the market. Instead, they aim to match a particular index. The largest funds do it by buying every security tracked in the index. Smaller funds do it by buying a representative sample, or by buying options on the index. Index funds have exploded in recent years. There are large-cap, mid-cap, and small-cap index funds, foreign index funds, and fixed-income funds. U.S. large-cap fans can even choose value- and growth-stock indexes. There's even a fund that purports to track an "index" of "tombstone" stocks: funeral homes, cemeteries, and casket makers.

"True" index funds that buy the entire index, and hold it, enjoy a huge tax advantage over traditional actively managed funds. Low turnover means scant realized capital gains, therefore, scant taxable gains. Each time an active fund manager sells a stock at a profit, it generates a capital gain to be distributed and taxed to shareholders. Index funds sell only when necessary to redeem exiting shares or when the index itself changes. Index funds can also hold less cash than active funds since index investors redeem their shares less often. In fact, many index funds limit transfers just to hold down this sort of expensive turnover.

Indexing is controversial among investment advisers. Fans argue that low expenses outweigh chances to beat the market. Because index funds don't actively try to beat the market, they don't incur the costs of trying to do so: manager's fees, research, and trading costs. Index funds generally have the lowest expense ratios in the business. The average stock fund, for example, costs 1.47% per year. The average index fund costs just 0.62%, with some funds ranging as low as 0.20%. That means the average actively managed fund must beat the average index fund by 0.85% just to break even. Critics respond that fees, and even raw performance, aren't everything. Actively managed funds can still add value by cutting investors' losses in market slides. A fund that gains 90% as much as the market, with just 80% of the risk, actually "beats" the market on a risk-adjusted basis. Lots of funds accomplish this. Index funds, in contrast, expose you to all the risk of the market.

Here are some general rules for examining index funds:

◆ Indexing works best with efficient markets. Large-cap American stocks are one example of a relatively efficient market: Research analysts cover most of the companies, information about stocks is readily available, and there are fewer earnings surprises. Consequently, the S&P 500 itself outperforms more than 80% of actively managed large-cap stock funds. But small stocks, and foreign stocks, are less efficient markets. There's more opportunity to beat the market with careful research and stock selection. For proof, just look at the results: 74% of actively-managed small-stock funds beat the benchmark Russell 2000, and 70% of actively managed international funds beat the Morgan Stanley Capital International Europe, Australasia, and Far East index.

◆ Indexing is also more tax-efficient for stable indexes without a lot of substitution. The S&P 500, for example, includes the 500 largest U.S. stocks, by market capitalization. This index changes very little. The Russell 2000, in contrast, consists of the 1001st through 3000th largest U.S. stocks. This is a more volatile index, with many substitutions each year. These substitutions boost turnover, which in turn boost taxes.

◆ Some index funds don't actually *buy* their underlying index. Instead, they buy a representative sample to *track* the index. "Enhanced" index funds may use options or futures to track the index or even beat it. These options and futures generate short-term gains—and lots of them. They don't give you the tax advantages of true index funds. So be careful when you index. Hold "true" index funds in taxable accounts. Buy "proxy" index funds and "enhanced" index funds in your IRA or retirement accounts.

If you want long-term growth from U.S. stocks, you can't do much better than an S&P 500 index fund. Use it as your "core" holding and build the rest of your portfolio around it. You'll get the long-term growth that domestic stocks provide. You'll get to ignore those annoying articles touting the latest hot funds. And the IRS will be an occasional visitor—not "the guest who wouldn't leave."

INDEX FUNDS VS. ACTIVELY MANAGED FUNDS

Index Funds	Actively Managed Funds
Low fees and passive management guarantee market-matching performance.	Active management can beat market on absolute or risk-adjusted basis.
Low turnover guarantees tax-efficiency.	Active management may generate expensive turnover.
"Efficient markets" are difficult to beat and lend themselves to indexing.	"Inefficient markets" are easier to beat and lend themselves to active management.

4. Consider Tax-Managed Funds

Most funds focus on raw returns, not buyers' bottom lines. Tax-managed funds are a new breed designed for high after-tax return. Their goal is to marry the tax benefits of passive index funds with possible better returns of active management. They do this by avoiding turnover, matching gains with losses, selling specific shares within holdings to minimize taxable gain, and avoiding stocks that pay large dividends. Some tax-managed funds also hit sellers with an early-redemption penalty to discourage withdrawals that might force the manager to sell shares and realize gains. These funds are best suited for college savings and retirement planning outside tax-deferred accounts. They're also good for avoiding "kiddie tax" on funds in your children's names.

Today there are more than two dozen tax-managed funds you can buy. New ones come to the market all the time. Their biggest problem is the lack of adequate track records. Most advisers will tell you to wait for managers to prove themselves before trusting them with your money. If you buy a tax-managed fund, make sure the manager has the seasoning to deserve your business. Remember, mutual-fund choices are foremost investment choices, not tax choices. But tax-managed funds bear watching.

SIX TIPS FOR BUYING AND SELLING FUNDS

◈ ◈ ◈

Once you've chosen the right funds, it's time to build a portfolio. Here are six ways to buy and sell funds efficiently. Many of these strategies are the same as for individual securities. Others take advantage of mutual funds' unique tax structure.

1. Limit Turnover

Limiting turnover must be starting to sound like a broken record. Still, here it is again. Frequent fund switching whacks your profits, just as it does with individual stocks. What's more, frequent trading subjects more of your gains to punitive short- and mid-term rates, rather than long-term capital-gain rates.

There are two exceptions to this rule. First, as with individual stocks, don't be afraid to walk away from a loser. And second, tax swaps may be an appropriate strategy to convert paper losses into tax savings. For more information, see the following.

2. Write Off Sales Loads

If you buy a fund through a broker, you'll pay some sort of commission, or "load," for the broker's service. There are three main flavors of load. "Front-end loads" are traditional sales commissions paid up front to acquire shares. "Back-end loads" are contingent deferred sales charges, similar to the penalty on early withdrawals for bank CDs, for shares redeemed within the first few years of ownership. And "level-load" shares charge an ongoing "trail" commission of up to 1% per year, similar to the management fee you'd pay to a bank trust department or a private money manager.

Here's strategy to write off front-end loads. Remember, once you've paid your load, you're free to move funds within the family at no additional charge. If you buy into a family and then immediately switch into another fund, you'll show a capital "loss" equal to the load. You can use the loss to offset capital gains, or up to $3,000 of ordinary income. For example, if your broker recommends the Gambino Emerging Markets Fund, have him first buy shares in the Gambino Equity Fund (or any fund with the same sales load), then immediately transfer your funds into the emerging-markets fund. (This strategy works in taxable accounts only, not IRAs.)

When you finally sell your shares, your basis for figuring gain or loss will be lower than if you hadn't used this strategy. Still, the extra "gain" you create at the end will be taxed at lower long-term gain rates (assuming you keep the shares long enough), while your up-front "loss" will offset ordinary income and short-term gains. Your savings up front are greater than the extra tax at the end. In fact, this strategy effectively converts an amount equal to your "load" from ordinary income into capital gains.

3. Don't Buy Funds Near Capital-Gains Distributions

Want to buy your neighbor's tax bill? Buying funds near the end of the year does just that. Avoid buying funds near the end of the year when funds pay capital-gains dividends. You could find yourself paying tax on a portion of your original investment before you make a dime. Even worse, you could find yourself paying tax on a loss.

Funds generally accumulate capital gains throughout the year, then pay out some or all of the gain near the end of the year. Shareholders who own the fund on a designated date, called the ex-dividend date, pay tax on the accumulated gains whether they actually profited from the gain or not. If you buy the fund just before the ex-dividend date, you'll end up paying tax on gains you never actually earn. Let's say you buy 1,000 shares of the Gambino Growth & Income Fund for $10 apiece. The next week, the manager declares a capital-gains distribution of $2 per share. You'll now own 1,000 shares worth $8,000, plus a taxable check for $2,000. Congratulations! You've just turned your principal into taxable income—with nothing but a tax bill to show for it. The process works the same if you direct the fund to reinvest your dividends. Now, instead of owning 1,000 shares at $8 each, plus a $2,000 taxable check, you'll own 1,250 shares at $8 each, and you'll still owe tax on your 250 "new" shares.

Brokers who sell "load" funds are specifically prohibited from "selling the dividend" and have to inform investors if a distribution is due. No-load investors have to do a little more homework themselves. Either way, be sure to avoid this rookie mistake.

4. Convert Dividends into Capital Gains

This strategy also takes advantage of the ex-dividend date to convert ordinary income into capital gains. It's actually the reverse of avoiding purchases near year-end.

When a mutual fund distributes a dividend, the price of each share actually falls by the amount distributed as a dividend. That dividend is then taxed as ordinary income or capital gain. If you're ready to sell shares you've held for more than a year, and you sell when the shares are "fat" right before a dividend, you'll pay capital-gains tax on the portion of the value that would otherwise soon be distributed as a dividend. This strategy makes little difference with capital-gains dividends that are taxed as long-term capital gains already. But you can squeeze out some extra tax savings by selling these "ripe" shares as capital gains.

This strategy can also help with year-end tax-planning strategies discussed in the Dictionary of Tax Deductions. If you buy shares in a high-tax year, use this strategy to cut that year's income.

5. Keep Appropriate Records Before You Sell to Cut Your Tax

Reinvested dividends can be a nightmare when it comes to sales. The rules themselves are fairly simple. It's recordkeeping that becomes a chore. Many funds, especially income-oriented funds, pay dividends every month that are reinvested at different prices. A fund account held for five years might include shares with 60 different prices, including ordinary income, capital gains, and even fractional shares.

When you sell your shares, you pay tax on the gains on your shares. This is simple if you sell all your shares in a fund. Just add up the cost of all of your shares (including sales loads and reinvested dividends, if any), subtract that amount from the proceeds you get from the sale (minus contingent deferred sales charges, if any), and pay your tax on the difference. It gets tricky, though, if you sell just a part of your holdings. There are three ways to account for fund-share costs. The method you choose can make a huge difference in your tax bill.

- The "average-cost" method is the simplest way to calculate gains. You don't need to keep track of purchase prices or designate specific shares to sell. Just divide the number of shares into your total basis (including reinvested dividends) to figure your basis for each share sold. You can also divide your shares into three groups: those held less than a year (to be taxed as short-term gains), those held more than one year but less than 18 months (to be taxed as mid-term gains), and those held more than a year (to be taxed as long-term gains). You can figure a separate basis for each group before figuring your gain.
- The "first-in, first-out" (FIFO) method requires you to keep track of your purchase price for each share. When you sell, you're considered to sell your oldest shares

first. In rising markets, your oldest shares will generally be your least expensive shares, generating your highest taxable gains.

♦ The "specific shares" method requires you to keep track of your purchase price for each share and designate which specific shares to sell. If you've bought shares over a period of months or years at different prices, this method lets you report the lowest gain. By selling the highest-priced shares, you pay the lowest tax, since your gain will be less on the higher-priced shares.

CALCULATING TAX ON MUTUAL-FUND SALES

Jan. 1, 1997: You buy 500 shares at $20 each for a total investment of $10,000.

Dec. 1, 1997: You receive a $200 income dividend and a $300 capital-gain dividend. You reinvest your $500 into 20 shares at $25 each.

Dec. 1, 1998: You receive a $210 income dividend and a $315 capital-gain dividend. You reinvest your $525 into 17.5 shares at $30 each.

Dec. 1, 1999: You receive a $220.50 income dividend and a $330.75 capital-gain dividend. You reinvest your $551.25 into 15.75 shares at $35 each.

Jan. 1, 2000: You sell 100 shares at $40 each. What is your taxable gain?

Average-Cost Method: Your gain is $1,908 (553.25 shares at $11,576.75 equals $20.92 average cost).

FIFO Method: Your gain is $2,000 (100 original shares at $20 each).

Specific-Share Method: Your minimum gain is $1,488.75 (15.75 shares bought for $35 each on 12/1/99 are taxed as short-term capital gains; 17.5 shares bought for $30 each on 12/1/98, 20 shares bought for $25 each on 12/1/97, and 46.75 of your original 500 shares bought on 1/1/97 are taxed as long-term capital gains).

If you buy funds in a tax-deferred account, such as an IRA, none of this record keeping is necessary. Every dollar you withdraw from the fund is taxed as ordinary income, unless you've made nondeductible contributions.

Finally, keeping good records will keep you from paying twice on reinvested dividends. Once you've paid tax on a dividend distribution, the amount on which you pay tax increases your basis in the fund. It can be easy to forget that you've already paid tax on reinvested dividends and wind up paying tax again when you finally sell. Don't pay tax twice on your mutual-fund dividends.

6. Use Tax Swaps to Profit from "Paper" Losses

A tax swap is when you sell an investment at a loss and then replace it with a similar or identical investment. Mutual funds that invest in similar assets let you sell a poor performer and replace it with a different family's fund. Your portfolio looks the same, but you realize a loss to offset gains or even ordinary income. Mutual-fund tax swaps let you realize capital losses while keeping the same sort of fund.

Why not just buy back the same fund? The "wash-sale" rule says that if you sell an investment at a loss, then buy it back within 31 days before or after the original sale date, your loss is disallowed as a "wash sale." This rule limits your chance to net out capital gains with unrealized losses. But individual mutual funds are considered unique securities, even those that invest in similar assets. If you sell one family's growth fund to buy another family's fund, you'll beat the wash-sale rule even if both funds' portfolios are exactly the same.

The strategy, then, is to find another fund with the same investment objective and similar holdings as your current fund. After you sell your current fund at a loss, transfer your money into the new fund. You can use the loss to wipe out an equal amount of capital gains, or up to $3,000 of ordinary income.

> ▶ **Example:** You buy the Gambino Emerging Markets fund for $10,000. The Mexican peso collapses, and your fund is now worth $7,000. You'd like to realize the loss to shelter your $3,000 dividend income from the Gambino Bond Fund. But you'd also like to stay invested in emerging markets. What do you do? Consider selling the Gambino Emerging Markets Fund and buying the Lucchese Emerging Markets Fund. You realize a $3,000 capital loss to offset your capital gain and stay invested in your chosen market.

This strategy is even more useful for index funds and "commodity"-fund categories such as Treasury bond funds, where most fund families' portfolios are similar. It's also useful for funds held less than a year, since short-term capital gains are taxed at ordinary income rates. But be careful with this strategy. Don't pay unnecessary loads or higher expense ratios for the sake of short-term tax savings.

Closed-End-Fund Strategies

❖ ❖ ❖

Closed-end funds are different from their more popular open-ended cousins. Closed-end funds issue fixed numbers of shares to an original group of investors. Then, instead of redeeming shares directly from investors, the fund trades on an open market such as the New York Stock Exchange. Investors looking to sell their fund must find another investor who's willing to buy—and not necessarily for the net asset value of the fund's underlying portfolio. Out-of-favor funds can sell at considerable discounts to Net Asset Value (NAV), while popular funds in hot sectors can carry hefty premiums. In fact, one popular strategy for investing in these funds calls for buying at a discount, then waiting for the price to catch up to NAV. This way, investors can make money even if the value of the fund's underlying portfolio remains flat.

Closed-end funds are taxed like their open-ended cousins. Income dividends are taxed immediately as ordinary income, just as with open-ended funds. When you sell your shares you'll owe capital-gains tax on the profits from the sale. However, since there are no reinvested dividends, closed-end funds avoid the confusion "open-ended" funds cause with reinvested dividends.

America's most famous investor, the legendary Warren Buffet, runs a unique alternative to traditional closed-end funds. His company, Berkshire-Hathaway, is a former textile mill with stock holdings in some of America's greatest companies: Coca Cola, GEICO, and The Washington Post Company, among others. These holdings themselves are a viable alternative to closed-end funds. The shares have traded north of $80,000 each, and carried a "premium" of up to 50% above net-asset value. (Buffet himself has sported a net worth over $20 billion.) The company is wonderfully tax-efficient: it pays no dividend, so shareholders pay no tax until they sell their shares.

Finally, there is a small group of closed-end funds that have issued preferred shares paying a guaranteed income taxed partially as capital gains. They do this by distributing long-term gains to the preferred shareholders and reserving the bulk of ordinary income dividends for common shareholders. The capital-gain portion of the dividend is taxed at your capital-gains rate rather than your ordinary income rate. Of course, if fund income isn't enough to cover preferred yields, the funds' common shareholders lose. Preferred shares may be an attractive option for investors seeking high current income.

Tax Tips for Mutual-Fund Alternatives

❖ ❖ ❖

Mutual funds certainly aren't the only professional money-management "package" available. Wrap accounts, bank trust departments, private money managers, and hedge funds all provide professional investment management similar to mutual funds. These vehicles all require larger investments and usually charge higher fees. They also provide more service and hand-holding than their publicly available mutual-fund cousins. These services include greater control over realized capital gains, giving investors greater control over their final tax bills.

1. Wrap Accounts

Wrap accounts combine a bundle of services including professional management by a "name" money manager, trading commissions, and account maintenance fees for a single fee. These accounts let smaller investors hire "name" money managers they might not otherwise be able to afford. The all-inclusive fee reassures investors that trades aren't made to generate commissions. Fees are deductible as an investment expense (up to the amount of investment income) subject to the 2% floor on miscellaneous itemized deductions.

Wrap fees are generally higher than mutual-fund expenses. They start as high as 3% of your assets and decline as assets under management increase. Mutual-fund expense ratios, by contrast, average just 1.47% (equity funds). A wrap account charging 2.25% has to beat the average mutual fund by 0.78% per year just to break even. However, wrap-account fans note that many wrap accounts let investors time their buys and sells, which gives them greater control over their taxes. (Obviously, this makes no difference in retirement accounts). And some wrap managers aim specifically for tax efficiency. Does control over taxes justify the additional cost?

If a wrap-account manager's performance, after charging additional fees, compares to a mutual fund with the same objective, by all means consider the wrap account. You'll enjoy extra hand-holding you can't get from a fund. What's more, you'll score points on the golf course when you talk about the conference calls and local dinners with your manager, the one the rest of the foursome just read about. But make sure you actually use your tax-timing opportunities. And make sure the manager's performance justifies the fees, especially if he or she also manages a mutual fund. Wrap accounts are marketed as a couture product in order to justify higher fees. Don't pay higher fees for features you won't use.

2. Bank Trust Departments

Banks provide a similar service for a similarly all-inclusive fee. Trust departments are best known for managing actual trusts, but most of them manage private accounts and pension funds as well. Trust departments usually charge less than wrap accounts. Fees may start at just 1% per year, with all the hand-holding you'd get from a wrap account, including investment management, trading commissions, and account services such as trust tax-return preparation. The main difference is the choice of investment advisers. Wrap accounts let you choose from up to dozens of different managers, while bank trust departments use the bank's own money managers.

Trust-department fees are deductible as an investment expense, up to the amount of investment income, subject to the 2% floor on miscellaneous itemized deductions.

3. Private Money Managers

Private money managers provide portfolio-management services directly to investors without going through a brokerage firm. In fact, many private money managers also market their services through wrap accounts and mutual funds. Some private money managers build portfolios of individual securities. Others build portfolios of mutual funds. They generally charge less than wrap accounts, often starting at 1% of assets under management and declining as account size rises. You'll generally get more face-to-face contact with the actual manager than you would with a wrap account. They also offer tax-timing advantages. Investors usually maintain their own accounts at a brokerage firm, giving the manager discretionary authority over the assets and paying their own trading costs and account fees in addition to investment management fees.

Money-manager fees, like wrap-account and trust-department fees, are deductible as an investment expense, up to the amount of investment income, subject to the 2% floor on miscellaneous itemized deductions. You can also write off account costs, such as annual fees. Include commissions to buy and sell individual securities in your adjusted cost basis and sales prices for figuring gains and losses on sales.

4. Hedge Funds

Hedge funds, along with their cousins, venture capital funds and buyout funds, are private investment partnerships, the glamorous celebrities of the managed money world. Managers such as George Soros capture headlines and move markets. They also catch the blame when markets fall and currencies collapse. The funds themselves usually accept only "qualified investors," those with $1 million and up. Some funds operate offshore and require as much as $10 million to join. They use sophisticated and risky strategies such as options, futures, and short sales to try to whup the pants off the market. They're also very expensive: A typical fee is 1% of assets under management, *plus* 20% of profits. Hedge funds trade furiously; turnover is high. They generally pay no attention to taxes. The theory is that superior pretax returns will outweigh the drag of taxes. And, in fact, they're right. A hedge fund that doubles the market pays you more, even after fees and taxes, than the most efficient index fund. The trick, of course, is actually reaching that goal.

Hedge-fund-management fees, like wrap fees, trust fees, and money-manager fees, are deductible as an investment expense, up to investment income, subject to the 2% floor on miscellaneous itemized deductions. But most hedge-fund investors have adjusted gross income high enough to phase out these deductions. The deduction doesn't mean anything to them. So don't count on any help from the IRS. They want to see you succeed, of course, so they can collect more taxes. They just won't throw you a line if you fail.

Hedge-fund investors with an extra $5 million or so can profit from special strategies to convert short-term hedge-fund gains into lower-taxed long-term gains. Here's how it works: Instead of buying the actual fund yourself, you buy a "swap" or "option" from your broker. You give the broker money to buy the fund. The broker buys the fund and pays you the return. Instead of paying short-term gains on the actual fund itself, you pay long-term gains on the "swap" or "option" the two of you create.

Hedge-fund investors can usually qualify for the special tax breaks available from the clubby world of tax-engineered products. For more information, see "Tax-Engineered Products" (page 95) in Chapter 6.

NINE

REAL ESTATE

REAL ESTATE IS the foundation of more American fortunes than any other single investment. It's the classic inflation hedge because it provides a steadily rising income. And it's a unique asset class for diversifying securities holdings. Most investors already own it in the form of their own home.

This chapter covers rental real estate—everything from a handyman's-special two-family, to shares in giant national real-estate investment trusts, to low-income-housing tax credits. The purpose is to help you decide if real estate's tax advantages have a place among your holdings. For personal-residence tax strategies, including vacation-home rental rules, see Chapter 3, Buying, Owning, and Selling Your Home.

REAL-ESTATE TAX BASICS

❖ ❖ ❖

Real estate, like most other investments, pays you now (with rent) and later (with capital gain). But real estate gets special breaks that help you shelter current income. And real estate gets more breaks to cut your tax when you sell. Congress ended the glory days of real estate with the 1986 tax reform. The passive-loss and at-risk rules ended abusive tax shelters, and real estate spiraled into a recession from which it's still recovering. But real estate still offers tremendous opportunities for smart investors willing to do their homework. And real estate remains the nation's most tax-favored investment. These breaks include leverage, depreciation, tax-deferred growth, tax-free exchanges, and tax-deferred installment sales.

- ◆ You can buy real estate for a fraction of its purchase price by putting down a portion of the price, borrowing the rest, and deducting the interest you pay.
- ◆ You can depreciate, or write off, a portion of your purchase price each year. Depreciation cuts your tax without affecting your cash flow.
- ◆ Your equity grows tax-free until you choose to sell.
- ◆ You can exchange one investment property for another "like-kind" property, tax-free.
- ◆ You can defer tax you pay on a sale with an installment sale.
- ◆ You can write off up to $25,000 worth of losses against regular income if you meet certain participation and income requirements.

1. Leverage Fuels Your Equity Growth

Leverage is using borrowed money to buy your investment. Leverage lets you buy more property than you could afford on your own. This boosts your equity-growth and depreciation deductions. If you choose your property carefully, the additional rent you earn should cover the mortgage. Leverage can also bump up available credits from the low-income-housing tax credit.

2. Depreciation Shelters Current Income

Depreciation is writing off the cost of property over a specified life or recovery period. Depreciation shelters your income by giving you a paper tax loss without a corresponding cash-flow reduction. You can write off a portion of your investment every year until you've written off nearly every dime. (There's no depreciation for raw land and none for the land portion of any real-estate investment.) Residential real estate depreciates over 27.5 years. Nonresidential real estate placed in service after May 12, 1993, depreciates over 39 years.

> ▶ **Example:** You buy a four-family apartment building for $180,000, of which $110,000 of the price is for the building and $70,000 is for the land. The building nets $4,000 after mortgage interest, utilities, and maintenance. However, you can depreciate $4,000 per year ($110,000 ÷ 27.5). Your taxable income from the property is zero, and you pocket the $4,000 tax-free.

Depreciation reduces your basis in the property when you sell. There is a special 25% capital-gains rate for "recapture" of depreciated real property.

> ▶ **Example:** In the preceding situation, you depreciate the property for three years, then sell the building for $200,000. Your gain on the sale is $32,000, of which $12,000 is taxed as depreciation recapture at 25%. The rest is taxed as long-term capital gain at your regular long-term gain rate.

IRS tables tell you how much to depreciate the year you buy a property, depending on what month you place it in service.

REAL-ESTATE DEPRECIATION RATES

Residential Property

Year	Jan	Feb	Mar	Apr	May	Jun	Jul	Aug	Sep	Oct	Nov	Dec
1	3.485	3.182	2.879	2.576	2.273	1.970	1.667	1.364	1.061	0.785	0.455	0.152
2-9	3.636	3.636	3.636	3.636	3.636	3.636	3.636	3.636	3.636	3.636	3.636	3.636
10	3.637	3.637	3.637	3.637	3.637	3.637	3.637	3.637	3.637	3.637	3.637	3.637
11	3.636	3.636	3.636	3.636	3.636	3.636	3.636	3.636	3.636	3.636	3.636	3.636
12	3.637	3.637	3.637	3.637	3.637	3.637	3.637	3.637	3.637	3.637	3.637	3.637

Nonresidential Property

Year	Jan	Feb	Mar	Apr	May	Jun	Jul	Aug	Sep	Oct	Nov	Dec
1	2.461	2.247	2.033	1.819	1.605	1.391	1.177	0.963	0.749	0.535	0.321	0.107
2-39	2.564	2.564	2.564	2.564	2.564	2.564	2.564	2.564	2.564	2.564	2.564	2.564

▶ **Example:** In May 2000 you buy an apartment building with a depreciable basis of $200,000 and an office building with a depreciable basis of $300,000. For 2000, write off 2.273%, or $4,546, for the apartments and 1.605%, or $4,815, for the office building. For 2001 write off $7,272 for the apartments and $7,692 for the offices.

However, mortgage amortization—actual principal payments—isn't deductible, even though it cuts your cash flow. If your mortgage amortization is more than your depreciation, the difference may be taxable income even though you don't receive any cash. This "phantom income" counts as "passive income" for purposes of the passive-loss rule. So "passive losses" (see the following) can shelter your phantom income.

▶ **Example:** You buy an apartment building in January 2000 for $100,000. You put $20,000 down and take out a 15-year mortgage at 8%. Your monthly mortgage payment is $764.25, and in the first year you pay $2,878.26 toward principal. Just 60% of your purchase price is depreciable, for a first-year depreciation deduction of $2,091. At the end of the year, your net cash flow leaves you with a $100 gain. Your depreciation deduction leaves you with a net loss of $1,991. But wait! The $2,878.26 of your mortgage payment that goes toward principal isn't deductible. Your actual income on the property is $2,978.26—your $100 gain plus your $2,878.28 principal payment. After depreciation, you're left with $887.26 in taxable income, even though your cash flow nets you just $100.

3. Equity Grows Tax-Deferred

Like any capital asset, your real-estate equity grows tax-deferred. There's no tax until you sell. When you do sell, you pay a lower capital-gains rate depending on when you bought it, how long you held it, and your regular tax bracket. (There is a special tax rate to "recapture" amounts previously depreciated.) Finally, if you die owning the property, its value is "stepped-up" for your heirs.

4. Tax-Free Exchanges

You can exchange one investment property for another "like-kind" investment property, tax-free. Like-kind property is liberally defined according to how you use the property—investment property, property held for business use, or residential property—and not character. You can exchange raw land for developed acreage, a city apartment for a suburban strip center, and even fee-simple property (outright ownership) for a leasehold of 30 years or longer. (You can't trade American property for foreign property.) Postponing the tax gives you the same advantage as an interest-free loan in the amount of tax you save. Here are the rules:

- You have to hold both the old and new properties for investment. For example, you can't trade investment property for a primary residence.

- Both transfers have to happen within a 180-day period. If you don't specifically identify one of the properties to be traded, you must do so within 45 days of the first transfer.

- If you receive additional property in the exchange—cash or nonlike-kind property—called "boot," you'll owe tax on the value of the boot.

- If you trade mortgaged property, the value of the mortgage released is boot. If both parties transfer mortgaged property, the one giving up the larger mortgage reports the difference in mortgage amounts as taxable boot.

- Ordinarily you can't declare a loss on a like-kind exchange. However, if you give up boot in the trade, you can declare the amount you give up as a loss.

- You have to carry over your basis in the old property to the new property. This can limit your depreciable basis in the new property, plus increase your taxable gain if you eventually sell.

Report exchanges of like-kind property, along with boot, on Form 8824. If you report a loss on the trade, carry the loss to Schedule D as well.

You don't actually have to find the property to trade yourself. Creative brokers can arrange "three-corner exchanges," "four-corner exchanges," and "deferred exchanges" to help their clients close their deals. For more information, see a broker who specializes in investment property.

You can swap one primary residence for another. This is useful if your gain in your primary residence tops the $250,000 exclusion ($500,000 for joint filers), although finding the right home to swap is harder than finding investment property. But here's a way to use the rule to acquire a primary home. Simply exchange a rental property for a residence suitable to rent. Hold the new residence as investment property and rent it until you're ready to move. Then "convert" the investment into your primary residence. When you sell, the gain above your basis in your investment property will be sheltered by the $250,000 exclusion. For example, you own a rental condo in your home city of Chicago. You plan to retire to Scottsdale in five to ten years. Make the exchange now, and rent the Scottsdale condo to tenants until you're ready to move.

5. Installment Sales Defer Taxes

You can defer tax when you finally do sell by collecting the proceeds in installments. For more information on installment sales, see "Ten Ways to Avoid Tax on Capital Gains," in Chapter 6.

You can't use the installment method to sell real estate to a business you control or a trust of which you or your spouse are a beneficiary. If you use the installment method to report a sale to a relative (spouse, child, grandchild, parent, grandparent, sibling, controlled corporation), the buyer has to hold the property for at least two years from the date of the sale. If the buyer sells before the end of this period (except for death or involuntary conversion), you'll owe tax on the entire amount of the sale, minus any payments taxed in the previous year, minus any loss on the related party's sale.

6. The Rental Real-Estate Loss Allowance Shelters Other Income

Tax-sheltered income from real estate is pretty sweet all by itself. But if your adjusted gross income is $150,000 or less, you can deduct up to $25,000 in losses from property you help actively manage. (The loss allowance phases out by 50 cents for each dollar of adjusted gross income between $100,000 and $150,000. For purposes of this allowance, adjusted gross income does not include Social Security or Railroad Retirement benefits and is not reduced by IRA contributions or the exclusion for savings-bond interest used to pay higher education expenses.) Let's say your adjusted gross income from salary is $80,000. You also manage two apartments in a building you own. The apartments pay you $200 a month after you've paid all your expenses. Depreciation is $300 a month. You pocket the $200, plus take a $100 loss to offset your salary. Here's how to qualify for the allowance:

- You have to participate actively in managing the property.
- You have to net out losses first against other real estate in which you materially participate, then any other passive income, before using the allowance.
- The allowance isn't available to married couples filing separately.
- You can carry forward a loss disallowed by the allowance phaseout.
- The allowance isn't available for six specific uses treated as businesses rather than rental real estate: (1) "incidental" rentals of property, where the main reason for holding the property is to profit from the gain and the rental income is less than 2% of the property's value; (2) short-term rentals averaging seven days or less; (3) rentals averaging between 7 and 30 days where you provide significant personal service; (4) rentals involving extraordinary personal service (nursing-home facilities, and the like); (5) rentals to a partnership or S corporation not engaged in the business of renting property (such as renting an office building to your S corporation or medical partnership); or (6) property opened for use of customers during regular business hours (such as a golf course or swimming pool).

7. Passive-Loss and At-Risk Rules May Limit Your Loss

At the same time, the passive-loss and at-risk rules limit your ability to write off real estate losses against other income. Passive-loss rules were imposed to keep investors from using tax-shelter losses to offset nonpassive income. At-risk rules were imposed primarily to limit deductions from nonrecourse financing—loans for which the investor isn't personally on the hook.

- Passive income is income from any trade or business in which you don't materially participate. You're considered to materially participate if you're involved in operations on a "regular, continuous, and substantial" basis. This usually means performing substantially all the work of an activity or participating more than 500 hours per year. However, rental real estate is considered a passive activity, so rental income and losses are passive income and losses. You can deduct passive losses against nonpassive income only if you qualify for the rental real-estate-loss allowance.

▶ **Example 1:**   You're a physician and a partner in a partnership that rents a building to your practice. You report $150,000 income from your medical practice, $10,000 from investments, and a $10,000 loss from the partnership. The partnership loss is a passive loss, so you can't deduct it against your medical income or investment income.

▶ **Example 2:**   You're an attorney and you own a four-family apartment building you manage yourself. You report $80,000 in legal income, $5,000 in investment income, and a $12,000 loss from the apartment building. You can write off the $12,000 loss against your $85,000 nonpassive income.

◆ Amounts "at risk" are amounts that you can actually lose in an investment: cash contributions, your cost basis in property contributions, and loans for which you're personally responsible. You can deduct as much in expenses as you have income to offset. Beyond that, you can deduct only as much as you actually have "at risk" in the investment. You can carry forward losses disallowed by the at-risk rule to offset future income.

▶ **Example:**   Your adjusted gross income from your "day job" is $80,000, and you actively manage a four-family apartment. You've contributed $10,000 in cash and signed a $10,000 note for which you're personally responsible. In year one, the apartment venture takes in $36,000 and pays out $50,000, for a net loss of $14,000. You can deduct the full $14,000 as a rental real-estate loss allowance. In year two, the venture also loses $14,000. Since you've already deducted $14,000 of your $20,000 at risk, your rental real-estate-loss deduction is limited to $6,000. You can carry the disallowed $8,000 forward to offset next year's operating income, but not below zero.

BUYING AND OWNING RENTAL REAL ESTATE

❖ ❖ ❖

There are three main ways to own rental real estate: directly, through limited partnerships, and through real-estate-investment trusts (REITs). There are specific advantages and disadvantages to each.

1. Direct Ownership

With direct ownership, you assume responsibility to manage and maintain your property. This means all the headaches of being a landlord—the 3:00 A.M. phone calls, unexpected repairs, and deadbeat tenants. Of course, you can always hire a management firm to handle day-to-day chores for a cut of the income. Direct ownership also qualifies you for the rental real-estate-loss allowance.

144

Direct ownership may also be appropriate if you plan to retire to a popular locale—second-home prices have soared in resort locations such as Scottsdale, Arizona, and Hilton Head, South Carolina. If you can afford it, consider buying your retirement home now. If you can't afford to use it as a vacation home, hire a management company to rent it out. As long as you're involved in approving repairs and tenants, you'll be considered to actively participate to qualify for the rental real-estate-loss allowance.

> Direct ownership is best for hands-on investors willing to work as landlords (or hire a manager) in exchange for real estate's superior leverage and tax breaks.

2. Limited Partnerships

A limited partnership is an investment pool involving a general partner, who organizes and manages the investment, and limited partners, who contribute capital and generally don't participate in managing the investment. The limited partners' financial liability is limited to their actual investment—hence the name "limited partnership." Publicly offered limited partnerships are generally offered in units of $2,000 and up. These are regulated by the Securities and Exchange Commission (SEC) and come with a thick prospectus that nobody reads. (If you actually read it, you'll never invest.) Private partnerships are generally available for investments of $25,000 and up. These are often organized as blind pools, where the manager doesn't know what properties will be acquired. A limited partnership doesn't pay tax itself. Instead, income and expenses are "passed through" directly to the partners. A limited partnership thus gives investors much the same tax benefits of direct ownership.

Limited partnerships suffered the most in the 1986 tax reform. Those partnerships were set up to *lose* money, not make it. When Congress changed the law, investors could no longer write off partnership losses against their regular income. They could write off passive losses only against passive income. The problem is, none of their partnerships gave them passive income. These investors have piled up thousands of dollars in "suspended" passive losses. If you're stuck with old limited partnerships, there are two ways to take advantage of suspended passive losses.

- If you'd like to keep the partnership, you can use your passive losses to shelter income from passive-income generators, or PIGs. PIGs are investments that generate passive income for you. These can include profitable real-estate and limited-partnership investments, S corporations, and leasing arrangements. Buying passive-income generators lets you earn tax-free income because the passive losses will shelter your passive income.

- If you'd like to get rid of your partnership, you can "unlock" suspended losses by selling it (but not to a relative). You can then use your unlocked losses to offset passive income from PIGs, gain on the sale of the partnership interest, "portfolio" income (gains from investments), and up to $3,000 of regular income. If your losses exceed these totals, carry forward the balance until it's gone. Report your losses on Form 8582.

▶ **Example:** You're stuck with a limited partnership with a cost basis of $20,000 and suspended losses of $10,000. In 1998 you sell your partnership for $10,000. You now have a $20,000 loss ($10,000 of suspended losses and $10,000 from the loss on the sale) to offset this year's income. If this year's portfolio income totals $5,000, you can offset the full $5,000 of portfolio income, plus $3,000 of ordinary income, then carry the remaining $12,000 forward as long as it takes to erase the stench of that darned limited partnership.

The passive-loss and at-risk rules crushed real-estate prices by pulling the plug on demand. Limited-partnership prices fell below those shattered underlying values. In recent years a new breed of "vulture' investors has emerged to snatch them up on the cheap. In fact, many of these buyers have tendered offers to buy entire series of units. This secondary market has reinvigorated prices, and it may be possible to sell your units for a price that, combined with your tax savings from suspended losses, justifies exiting the deal. You'll also save a fortune on your tax-prep bill.

> Partnerships are best for investors who don't actually want to manage property. They offer most of the same breaks that you'd get with direct ownership.

3. Real-Estate-Investment Trusts

A real-estate-investment trust is a publicly traded company that buys and manages property and mortgages. There are equity REITs, which buy actual properties, mortgage REITs, which buy mortgages, and hybrid REITs, which buy both. There are even golf-course and trailer-park REITs. Investors who want to buy commercial property—office parks, industrial parks, shopping centers, and large apartment complexes—often can't invest enough to buy it directly themselves. What's more, these properties require a tremendous amount of specialized management expertise. REITs let you invest in these properties with many of the same advantages of mutual funds: professional management, instant liquidity, and better diversification than smaller investors could achieve on their own. Some REITs even pay tax-free income. Here's how they work:

◆ REITs must "pass through" at least 95% of their earnings to shareholders in order to avoid corporate income tax. This means most REITs pay high current income. Over the past ten years, REITs have returned just under 70% of their total return in current income. This figure varies from year to year, though, and in 1986 REITs paid just 17.2% of total return in current income.

◆ REITs pay income dividends, capital-gains dividends, and return-of-capital dividends. Income dividends are taxed as ordinary income. Capital-gains dividends are taxable at long-term capital gains regardless of how long you've held the REIT shares. Return-of-capital dividends are tax-free income that reduce your basis in the REIT.

♦ REITs that pay high current income may be the real estate best suited for tax-deferred accounts such as IRAs. Also, many variable life and annuity providers are adding REIT funds to their investment options.

> REITs don't give you the same direct leverage and tax breaks as direct ownership. But REITs' "pass-through" corporate structure lets them pay higher income than if they paid corporate income tax themselves. REITs are best for hands-off investors who want to include some real estate in their holdings.

TAX CREDITS FOR REAL-ESTATE INVESTORS

♦ ♦ ♦

Low-income housing and rehabilitation tax credits are special opportunities for real-estate investors. Tax credits are better than writeoffs because they cut your tax bill, not just your income. There's no material participation test to meet and no at-risk rules to worry about.

Low-Income-Housing Tax Credits

Congress created the low-income-housing tax credit in 1986 (at the same time it limited other real-estate investments) to encourage private development of low-income housing. These are usually suburban and small-town senior-citizen apartments—a far cry from the inner-city public housing most of us picture when we think of low-income housing. These investments are usually organized as limited partnerships. The manager buys or builds apartments to operate as low-income housing for 15 years under strict federal rules. The Treasury Department preallocates and prefunds 10 years of tax credits equal to nine cents for each dollar invested. Once the 15-year period expires, the manager's usual goal is to sell the property and split any appreciation with the investors.

Low-income-housing tax credits aren't comparable to the disastrous real-estate limited partnerships of the 1980s. Those partnerships were designed to throw off tax deductions, often equaling more than the original investment. Congress changed the rules in the middle of the game, denying deductions and lowering tax rates so the deductions were worth less. Low-income-housing tax credits, in contrast, are preallocated and prefunded, so Congress can't pull the plug. What's more, they don't depend on high tax rates for their value. Here's how they work:

You can use low-income-housing tax credits to shelter up to $25,000 in taxable income. That means investors in the 15% bracket can cut $3,750 off their total tax.

Investors in the 39.6% bracket can cut $9,900. Divide the amount of credit the partnership throws off by your marginal tax rate to figure how much you can invest. Of course, your income may change while you own the partnership. Excess credits are wasted, so don't buy more than you need to take the maximum credit.

> ▶ **Example:** You're a married couple with $100,000 taxable income. You'd like to buy a tax-credit partnership that pays an annual credit equal to 12% of your investment. The most that you can shelter is $7,000 (28% of $25,000). The most that you should invest is $58,333 (12% of $58,333 yields a $7,000 credit).

- ◆ You can't use low-income-housing tax credits to reduce your tax below the alternative minimum tax. (Corporations don't face this limit; they can shelter a virtually unlimited amount of income. In fact, corporations are the biggest tax-credit buyers. About two-thirds of the S&P 500 corporations own tax credits, often as much as tens of millions of dollars worth.)
- ◆ Tax-credit investments are limited to "qualified investors." Depending on state law, you may need a net worth of $150,000, excluding your home and personal property, or a net worth and annual income of $45,000.
- ◆ Married couples filing separately can't claim the credit.
- ◆ Tax credits cut your $25,000 rental real-estate loss allowance. For example, if you claim $2,000 in low-income-housing tax credits, you cut your $25,000 rental real-estate loss allowance to $23,000.
- ◆ Low-income-housing tax credits distributed by a partnership may also generate passive income and losses to offset other passive investments. This is usually the case when the manager uses leverage to boost the tax credit for each dollar invested. This is even more valuable if you have passive-income generators. The passive losses from the partnership can shelter your passive income, while the tax credits cut your tax on other income.

You can also buy low-income-housing tax-credit limited partnerships on a secondary exchange. (This can give you estate tax advantages as well. If you die owning a partnership, your estate-tax value can reflect the lower secondary-market price.)

Low-income-housing tax credits aren't easy to report. The bigger limited-partnership sponsors, to their credit, try to lay it out as simply as possible. But it can still send you running to a CPA. Your state housing authority will allocate the credit on Form 8609. Claim the credit itself on Form 8586.

Tax credits are particularly valuable if you're retired. If you've finished raising your kids and paid off your house, you might not have enough deductions to itemize. Since tax credits don't depend on writeoffs for their value, they are even more valuable for these investors. Also, tax credits, unlike municipal bonds, don't add to your "provisional income" for purposes of taxing your Social Security.

Rehabilitation Tax Credits

The rehabilitation tax credit is similar to the low-income-housing tax credit. It's available for certified historic structures and nonresidential pre-1936 buildings. The minimum rehabilitation expense is $5,000 or your adjusted basis in the building, whichever is greater. The credit itself is equal to 10% of rehabilitation expenses. Report rehabilitation expenses on Form 3468.

TEN

LIFE INSURANCE
AND ANNUITIES

LIFE INSURANCE AND ANNUITIES are two solutions to the financial problems of death. Life insurance protects you from dying too soon. Annuities protect you from living too long and outliving your income. Congress has favored both of these vehicles with tax advantages. Life-insurance and annuity cash values grow tax-deferred. We've seen how tax deferral fuels investment returns over time. Life insurance and annuities don't offer "pure" tax deferral like IRAs and retirement plans. In both cases, mortality expenses and contract administration charges eat away at investment returns. But both of them can be appropriate solutions for retirement income.

Life insurance and annuities offer two other benefits that few investments can match: state guarantees and asset protection. Each state operates a life-insurance guaranty fund, similar to the Federal Deposit Insurance Corporation for banks, that protects policyholders from insurance-company failure. Most states protect up to $100,000 of cash value and $300,000 of death benefit. And most states protect life-insurance and annuity cash values from creditor claims, usually up to $100,000. This protection isn't bulletproof. For example, a doctor who loses a malpractice suit can't just stash his fortune in an annuity. The transfer would be attacked as a fraudulent conveyance. But guaranty funds and creditor protection can still be valuable benefits.

You can exchange life-insurance and annuity contracts tax-free with a "1035 exchange," named for the section of the tax code that allows it. You can exchange a life policy for a life policy, an annuity for an annuity, and even a life policy for an annuity. (You can't exchange an annuity for a life policy.) This is useful to consolidate accounts, to switch to a more successful investment manager, or to update older fixed-annuities and whole-life policies to variable contracts.

At the same time, life insurance calls for a little extra homework before you buy. You need a company with strong financial strength to be sure you or your beneficiaries can collect when you need your benefits. Several independent agencies rate insurers for financial strength and claims-paying ability. These include A. M. Best, Standard & Poor's, Moody's, and Duff & Phelps. You can find more information at your public library.

LIFE INSURANCE

❖ ❖ ❖

Most of us would rather see a dentist than a life-insurance agent. That's too bad. Life insurance is a wonderful tax shelter, and if more investors knew just how to use it, they'd be asking how much they could get their hands on. But life insurance is a complicated purchase, and there are several conditions to satisfy before you buy. First, you should need the death protection, either to protect your family from the loss of your income or to protect your estate from taxes. Second, you should be healthy enough to qualify.

Third, you need to do some homework to find which policy is best for you. Still, when you've finished reading this chapter, you'll probably want to call your agent.

"Term" life is pure death protection, with no investment element. "Permanent" life combines death protection with an investment account designed to build cash value to help pay premiums down the road. Permanent life offers three strong tax advantages for investors who actually need the death protection: tax-deferred growth, tax-free death benefit, and tax-free income:

- Your cash value grows tax-deferred, just as in an IRA or a qualified retirement plan. There's no upfront deduction, of course, but your gain isn't taxed unless you let the policy lapse and cash out for more than you paid in. Your gain, or profit, equals your cash value minus premiums paid.

- When you die, your beneficiary receives the death benefit without paying income tax. Some policies let terminally ill insureds take "accelerated benefits" for payment of final expenses. These benefits are tax-free. Also, some states allow terminally ill patients to sell their death benefits in "viatical settlements." The patient sells the policy to an investor for an amount less than the policy's face value. When the patient dies, the investor collects the proceeds. The investor's profit equals the difference between the sale price and the face amount. These are also tax-free to the insured. Life-insurance proceeds may be included in the value of your estate, but there are ways to avoid that tax bite, too.

- You can take money out of your policy, tax-free, by withdrawing your original premiums and borrowing against the rest of the cash value. When you borrow from the policy, the insurance company will charge you interest, but it will credit the policy with earnings as well. Depending on the size of the loan, your net interest may cost nothing at all.

At the same time, there are two important considerations to keep in mind before buying life insurance.

- Insurance can be expensive, especially if you're in poor health or enjoy death-defying hobbies, such as scuba diving or parachuting. Commissions and mortality charges reduce your gain on your investment.

- If the policy lapses, you'll owe tax on any gain above your cumulative premiums paid. Your policy will lapse if there's not enough cash value to pay the insurance costs. This can happen if you don't pay enough premiums, or if your cash-value investments don't perform. To keep the policy from lapsing, you can add more premium dollars. You can also buy a no-lapse rider ensuring that this doesn't happen.

This is a book about taxes, not life insurance. Still, this chart should help you figure how much life insurance you need. That can help you decide if permanent life insurance is appropriate. And costs vary, particularly according to your age, your health, your driving record, and your death-defying hobbies. Underwriting, the decision to accept or reject a particular person, can make a big difference in the price you pay.

HOW MUCH INSURANCE DO YOU NEED?

1. Survivor annual living expenses
   (What your survivors would need without you)   _____

2. Survivor annual benefits
   Social Security   _____
   Survivor's pension   _____
   Survivor's income   _____
   Other income (investments, etc.)   _____
   Total   _____

3. Net survivor expense shortfall   _____
   (1 minus 2)

4. Lump sum required to produce Line 3   _____
   (What lump sum would you need to produce the income
   listed on Line 3? If you can earn 6% on your lump sum,
   divide Line 3 by .06. If you can earn 8%,
   divide Line 3 by .08, etc.)

5. Lump-sum expenses   _____
   (Funeral, medical costs, estate tax, mortgage cancellation,
   education fund, emergency fund)

6. Total capital required at death   _____
   (4 plus 5)

7. Present capital   _____
   (present assets)

8. Life insurance required   _____
   (6 minus 7)

For more information, see a life-insurance agent or a financial planner. Better yet, see several. Life-insurance prices vary from company to company, even for the same amount of coverage. And premium alone is not an accurate measure of price. You have to consider cash-value growth as well. In November 1997 *Investment Advisor* magazine presented a survey of 31 variable universal-life providers. They asked these insurers to project target premiums and 10-year cash values for a 45-year-old nonsmoker, assuming paid-up premiums and a 10% annual investment return. Target premiums ranged from $788 to $2,978, while cash values after 10 years ranged from $5,518 to $33,129. The lowest target premium doesn't necessarily indicate the best value, and a policy without enough cash value is more likely to "blow up" and require more money in case the investments fail to perform.

LIMITS ON LIFE-INSURANCE TAX BREAKS

It shouldn't surprise you that the insurance industry, like the real-estate industry, has one of the most powerful lobbies in Congress. That's why the industry has been able to preserve its tax breaks. In the 1970s, when universal and variable life appeared on the market, tax rates ranged as high as 70%. Life insurance became a tremendously popular tax shelter. Single-premium life was a particularly strong seller—a single upfront payment that guaranteed coverage for life and sheltered the entire cash value from taxes as long as the policyholder lived. But, like all parties, this one had to come to an end, and in 1988, Congress created the "seven-pay" test to weed out perceived abuses. The test is supposed to make sure that investors use the tax break to buy appropriate amounts of insurance, not shelter investment income.

Here's how the seven-pay test works. Be happy you didn't run across it in school. First, calculate how much money is needed to fully fund the policy, for life, at any point in the policy's first seven years. This amount is called the seven-pay premium. Then, compare the policy's actual contributions with the seven-pay premium. If, at any point in that seven-year period the cumulative premiums paid into the policy exceed the seven-pay premium, the policy will be deemed a "modified-endowment contract," or MEC, and lose much of its tax advantage. Loans and withdrawals will be taxed as ordinary income, up to the amount of gain in the contract. (Death proceeds will remain income-tax-free.) Naturally, single-premium policies are snared in the trap, since they're paid up from day one.

As coverage limits increase, so do MEC limits. This makes sense, since it takes increasingly larger amounts of cash to fund increasingly larger policies.

MEC rules are some of the most complicated in the tax code. Existing policies are grandfathered, unless the death benefit is raised or lowered, and there are all sorts of traps for unwary buyers. Since the seven-pay premium varies according to your age, health, and policy size, there's no easy way to calculate your seven-pay policy limit. For more information, see your agent.

WHAT TYPE OF POLICY IS BEST FOR YOU?

❖ ❖ ❖

Once you've decided how much insurance you need, it's time to decide what type of policy you want. There are three main types of permanent life insurance that build cash value. Here's how they work:

1. Whole Life

Whole life is the traditional form of cash-value life insurance. You pay a flat or increasing premium each year. Some of your premium goes directly toward paying for death protection. The rest goes into an investment fund and builds cash value. At some point, the cash value should grow large enough to pay the premium all by itself. At that point, you can keep your coverage without paying a premium.

With most whole-life policies, the company invests the cash value for you and guarantees a minimum investment return comparable to a bank CD or similarly conservative fixed-income investment. The company bears the risk if the investment return isn't enough to keep the coverage in force. The company will generally pass on some of the windfall if investment returns are greater than projected. This windfall is called a "dividend," although it's actually a return of your premium and not a traditional dividend you'd earn with a stock or mutual fund. (Life-insurance dividends are not taxed as income so long as the total amount of dividends paid out does not exceed the total amount of premiums you've paid into the policy.) You can take the dividend in cash or use it to buy more coverage.

Life-insurance critics oppose traditional whole life because of high fees and low returns. They argue that a taxable stock fund will return more over time than whole life's tax-deferred cash value. That's true, but it ignores the risk tolerance factor. If you've decided not to buy stocks, then whole life is a competitive alternative to taxable fixed-income investments. Insurance critics also point out that IRAs offer tax-deferred compounding. That's also true, but it ignores contribution limits. If your income is above the deductibility limit or you want to shelter more than $2,000 per year, then some form of permanent life insurance can be a competitive alternative to IRAs.

2. Universal Life

In the 1970s, the life-insurance industry introduced a new form of permanent insurance: universal life. Universal life enjoys the same tax advantages as whole life, but with two significant differences that made it a success. First, universal life pays a variable rate depending on current interest rates. Second, universal life gives the policyholder the flexibility to pay whatever premium he or she likes, including nothing at all, so long as there's sufficient cash value to keep the policy in force.

Universal life lost some credibility following the late 1970s and early 1980s. Many agents sold the policies based on projections that high current interest rates would last well into the future. These high rates would quickly build enough cash value to "vanish" current premiums. Of course, interest rates dropped. Thousands of policyholders were forced to pay huge extra premiums into supposedly paid-up policies, or lose their coverage. Universal life is an attractive option for buyers seeking flexibility and healthy current interest rates. Just be sure you buy it based on reasonable long-term interest projections.

3. Variable Life

In the mid-1970s, the life-insurance industry introduced the most sophisticated investment-oriented contract: variable life. Variable life extends life insurance's tax-advantaged wrapper to the stock market by letting the policyholder invest his or her cash value in a variety of investment subaccounts, just as mutual funds and variable annuities do. Most policies started out simply, with perhaps a stock account and bond account in addition to a traditional whole-life-style fixed account. But now, there is nearly as wide a choice of insurance subaccounts as there are mutual funds. In fact, many life-insurance subaccounts are "clones" of popular mutual funds. Life insurers have allied with top mutual-fund managers, and it's not unusual to find portfolios from a dozen managers in a single life-insurance or annuity contract.

Variable life is available as "variable ordinary life," with fixed premiums like traditional whole life, and "variable universal life," with the same flexible premium option as universal life. It can be a tremendous tool if you use it properly. You can accumulate cash for college and retirement while guaranteeing cash will be available for these needs if you die too soon. If you need money before age 59½, you'll avoid a 10% penalty tax on early withdrawals from IRAs and annuities.

Variable life may offer the highest returns over time. But if your investment choices don't perform, you'll have to add money to feed the policy. This is especially important if your cumulative withdrawals top your cumulative premiums. Remember, if you let the policy lapse, you'll owe tax on your cumulative gain.

PERMANENT LIFE VERSUS
"BUY TERM AND INVEST THE DIFFERENCE"
❖ ❖ ❖

Lots of advisers discourage investors from buying permanent life. Rather than mixing death protection and investments, they recommend you buy inexpensive term coverage and invest the difference outside your life insurance. This way, you avoid paying life-insurance commissions on investment dollars.

This advice made more sense when conservative whole life was the only life-insurance investment choice. But today's variable products can earn the same high returns as mutual funds and other investments. When you add in the life insurance's tax advantages, the case for permanent insurance can be compelling—so long as you need the insurance protection.

PERMANENT LIFE VS.
"BUY TERM AND INVEST THE DIFFERENCE"

Permanent Life	*"Buy Term and Invest the Difference"*
Cash values grow tax-deferred	No tax deferral on "the difference"
Tax-free withdrawals as long as policy remains in force	No tax-free withdrawals
Proceeds taxed as ordinary income if policy lapses	Capital-gains treatment available
Investment losses within variable contracts can't be used to offset other gains	Investment losses within "the difference" can be used to offset other gains
The cost of insurance is included in the policy's investment cost basis for purposes of figuring tax on gains—in essence, the death protection is "deductible"	Cost of term coverage not deductible

ANNUITIES
❖ ❖ ❖

An annuity is a contract with a life-insurance company that lets you take a guaranteed income for life. Annuities are designed as insurance against outliving your income. You can invest a portion of your portfolio, without ever having to worry about making it last.

Annuities are defined by three main characteristics.

◆ An *immediate* annuity begins paying an income immediately, while a *deferred* annuity accumulates earnings over time.

◆ A *single-premium* annuity lets you make a single investment. A *flexible-premium* annuity lets you make flexible investments over time.

◆ Finally, a *fixed* annuity pays a fixed interest rate over time, while a *variable* annuity ties your return to some underlying variable investment.

Any annuity is a combination of these three characteristics: a single-premium deferred-fixed annuity, perhaps, or a single-premium immediate-variable annuity.

IMMEDIATE ANNUITIES PAY TAX-ADVANTAGED INCOME
❖ ❖ ❖

Immediate annuities offer immediate income for a term as long as your life. The main attraction is an income you can't outlive. That makes them tremendously powerful retirement-income choices. Payout periods can range from a period of years to a joint lifetime, with optional "refund" guarantees to protect your heirs if you drop dead after getting a single payment. A typical immediate annuity might give you monthly payments for the lives of you and your spouse, with a 10-year "period-certain" guarantee that you'll get at least 10 years of payments, even if you and your spouse die before then. Immediate annuities are a surprisingly underappreciated choice for income investors.

When you buy an immediate annuity, the company takes your life expectancy (or the payout term) and its own current interest rate to figure an income it can pay over the course of your life. The process works like amortizing a mortgage in reverse. But the company guarantees that it will pay the income no matter how long you live. Immediate annuities are often described as a gamble—with you betting against the company that you'll outlive your life expectancy. In reality, immediate annuities are the exact opposite of a gamble—with you shifting the risk of outliving your money to the company.

Here are the basic tax rules for immediate annuities:

- Income from an immediate annuity is partially tax-free. That's because a portion of each payment is a return of your own principal. To figure the "exclusion ratio," or tax-free portion of the payment, first figure your investment in the contract. This will be your cost, minus the value of any refund feature. Next, divide that investment into the total income you expect to earn from the contract. Finally, multiply this percentage by the amount of each payment. Your result will be the tax-free portion of each payment. Your annuity provider will report the taxable part of each year's income on Form 1099-R at the end of the year. When your original investment is completely paid out, your remaining payments are fully taxable.

- If you die before you recover your cost, you can deduct your unrecovered cost on your final tax return. (Well, your executor can.) This is a miscellaneous itemized deduction *not* subject to the 2% floor.

- The longer you wait, the more your income grows. This is simply because you're getting older. The less time the insurance company figures it has to pay you, the more it can give you now with every payment.

- If you're in poor health, some providers offer "impaired risk" annuities that offer higher payouts based on your true life expectancy, considering your actual health, rather than your standard life expectancy based solely on your age.

- You can choose annuity payments from many employer-retirement plans. If you don't contribute to the cost of the annuity, or your only payments are deducted when you make them, every dollar you get is taxed as ordinary income. But if you've made after-tax contributions to the plan, use this simplified method to figure how much of every payment isn't taxed. Figure your after-tax investment in the contract. Then divide that investment by the number of monthly payments shown in the table. The result is the tax-free portion of every payment.

RETIREMENT ANNUITY PAYOUT CALCULATIONS

Single Life

Age at Start Date	Number of Payments
55 and under	360
56–60	310
61–65	260
66–70	210
71 and over	160

Joint Lives

Combined Age at Start Date	Number of Payments
110 and under	410
111–120	360
121–130	310
131–140	260
141 and over	210

- Depending on state law, immediate annuities can also help protect your assets if you or your spouse accept Medicaid for nursing-home costs. Medicaid rules require you to spend all but a specified portion of your assets on nursing-home costs before the state steps in to pick up the tab. Immediate annuities let you convert a portion of those assets into an income stream that Medicaid can't take. This is a tricky, constantly changing area. Consult a qualified expert before making any specific moves.

Most immediate annuities offer a fixed payment for life. These "plain-vanilla" contracts grow less valuable over time as inflation eats away at your purchasing power. But a new breed of "variable-immediate" annuities has expanded retirement-income options. These contracts pay out a fixed number of "accumulation units," similar to a regular immediate annuity. The difference is, the dollar value of these accumulation units fluctuates with the value of the underlying investment. So, rather than accepting the insurance company's own declared interest rate, your income over time can rise (or fall) with the value of the underlying accumulation units. Some of these contracts let you take loans or withdrawals against your principal as well.

Split Annuities

A "split annuity" is a way to earn tax-advantaged income now, without locking your money up for the future. Let's say you have $100,000 to invest. You need to make $6,000 for each of the next five years. You could simply buy a bond that pays you 6%. But you'll owe tax on what you earn unless you buy a muni bond. Instead, you buy an immediate annuity large enough to pay you $6,000 for each of the next five years. Then you take the rest of your $100,000 and buy a fixed or variable deferred annuity. At the end of the five-year period, the deferred annuity replaces your original $100,000 principal. How is this different from merely buying a 6% bond? Most of your income for the five-year period is tax-free return of your original principal. You save what you otherwise would have paid in taxes.

FIXED ANNUITIES FOR TAX-DEFERRED GROWTH

◆ ◆ ◆

A fixed annuity resembles a bank CD in a tax-deferred wrapper. The insurance company guarantees a fixed interest rate for a specified period of time. At the end of that period, the company renews the contract for a new period at a new rate. Fixed annuities are a popular choice for older, conservative investors who don't need current income. They're also popular estate-planning choices for investors looking to bypass probate.

Fixed annuities carry no up-front sales loads or commissions. Instead, the company levies a contingent deferred sales charge on withdrawals within a specified period, much like the familiar "penalty for early withdrawal" you'd face with a bank CD. Surrender periods range from as low as four years to as long as 12. Actual charges range from 4% to 12%. Most companies will let you withdraw 10% of the contract value or 100% of the annual earnings without penalty. There may also be a "market-value adjustment" on withdrawals within a specified period to protect the company from the effect of interest-rate changes during the contract term.

Here are the rules for fixed annuities:

◆ You can invest as much as you want no matter how much you make. There are no contribution limits or income-eligibility limits.

◆ Money in the annuity grows tax-deferred until you withdraw it.

◆ Withdrawals are taxed as income first until all earnings are withdrawn from the contract.

◆ There is usually a 10% penalty for withdrawals before age 59½. The main exceptions are for payments to a beneficiary, payments due to disability, and payments you take when you annuitize the contract.

◆ At your death, the contract passes to your named beneficiary free from probate. There's no stepped-up basis for gains held at death. Instead, your beneficiaries will owe ordinary income tax (at their rate) on any gain they take from the contract.

Be sure to shop around before you buy a fixed annuity. Many companies offer one-time interest "bonuses" and teaser rates. These up-front incentives occasionally mask unconscionably high and long surrender charges. The agent's commission can sometimes be more than the buyer's first-year income. And make sure you buy from a strong company. Fixed-annuity assets are held as a part of the company's general-asset account. So the company's credit rating is a crucial consideration.

If you like the thought of a tax-deferred CD, but don't like the long surrender periods of some fixed annuity contracts, consider a variable annuity instead. Variable annuities can have lower commissions, lower expenses, and generally shorter surrender periods than their fixed counterparts. But variable annuities generally offer a fixed-account option similar to a fixed annuity. And variable annuities let you switch your money, tax-free, into other investments if rates drop. Most accounts offer money-market and bond funds that may also be appropriate for fixed-annuity investors.

Variable Annuities for Extra Retirement Savings

◆ ◆ ◆

A variable annuity is an insurance contract offering a family of "subaccounts" resembling mutual funds in a tax-deferred wrapper. In fact, many variable-annuity-investment subaccounts are "clones" of popular mutual funds. Variable annuities offer anywhere from a dozen to over 100 of these portfolios for your money. There will generally be a fixed account, a money-market account, and various stock-and-bond options, perhaps including international and emerging-markets choices as well. Your investment buys "accumulation units" in one or more of these subaccounts. You can transfer amounts from subaccount to subaccount, generally at any time. During this "accumulation period," your money grows tax-deferred. When you're ready to take your money, you can withdraw any number of accumulation units in cash. Or you can convert the entire contract to an income stream.

Variable-annuity sales have exploded in recent years as aging baby boomers seek tax-sheltered retirement savings. There are no up-front commissions with variable annuities. Instead, the company imposes a back-end surrender charge on early contract withdrawals. A typical surrender charge begins at 7% for surrenders during the first contract year, then declines 1% each year until reaching 0% in the eighth year. Most companies will let you withdraw up to 10% per year with no penalty. Also, some states protect variable annuities against creditors as they do with IRAs. This is particularly valuable for doctors, lawyers, and other high-risk professionals. Finally, some new contracts let you pick and choose the features you want, such as death benefits, payout options, and nursing-home and disability waivers.

Here are the basics tax rules for variable annuities:

◆ You can invest as much as you want no matter how much you make. There are no contribution limits or income-eligibility limits.

◆ Your money grows tax-deferred until you withdraw it from the contract.

◆ You can switch money from one subaccount to another with no tax on the transfer. Many annuities now offer automatic portfolio rebalancing, switching funds every quarter or year to maintain a predetermined allocation. There's no tax on rebalancing as there would be with taxable mutual funds.

◆ The insurance company provides a guaranteed death benefit, regardless of how your accounts perform. Some annuities guarantee at least your original contributions. Others increase by a certain percentage each year, or "reset" at each year's "high-water" mark as your account balance grows.

♦ Withdrawals are taxed first as income until all earnings are withdrawn from the contract. Only after you pay tax on earnings can you withdraw contributions tax-free.

♦ All income is taxed at ordinary income rates. There's no favorable capital-gains treatment, even if you invest for more than 18 months or choose stock investments that would otherwise offer favorable capital-gains treatment.

♦ Withdrawals before age 59½ generally carry a 10% penalty tax. The main exceptions are for payments to a beneficiary, payments due to disability, and payments when you annuitize.

♦ At your death, the contract passes to your named beneficiary outside probate. There's no stepped-up basis for earnings in the account. Instead, your beneficiaries will owe ordinary income tax (at their rates) on any gain they withdraw from the contract.

You should exhaust your employer-retirement plan and IRA opportunities before you buy a variable annuity. Retirement plans give you up-front tax deductions and possible employer matches as well. IRAs give you an up-front tax deduction or tax-free earnings, depending on which kind of IRA you choose. Even a nondeductible traditional IRA avoids the higher expenses of variable annuities.

Also, it makes no sense to put a variable annuity in a qualified plan or IRA if all you want is the tax deferral. Variable annuities have higher expenses and longer surrender periods than comparable mutual funds. There's no need to pay these charges in a qualified plan or IRA since the account itself gives you tax deferral. However, variable annuities offer more than just tax deferral. These features may make them attractive in a retirement plan. These include the fixed-account investment option (which offers you the return of an intermediate-term bond fund without the price volatility), tax-free transfers between funds, and the guaranteed death benefit. Annuities also offer a guaranteed annuitization option based on current life expectancies. As medical science improves, life expectancy should climb even higher. So today's guaranteed rates may provide a higher income than tomorrow's uncertain future.

FIVE QUESTIONS TO ASK
BEFORE YOU BUY A VARIABLE ANNUITY

♦ ♦ ♦

We've seen that there are two main strategies for cutting tax on investments: tax deferral and capital gains. Variable annuities give you tax deferral, at the expense of capital gains. This tradeoff is particularly important after the Taxpayer Relief Act of 1997 cut capital-gains rates. The question is, which is worth more for you? Does annuity tax deferral outweigh mutual-fund capital gains? It counts even more if you're considering an investment that's available both in a fund or an annuity.

The National Association of Variable Annuities, an industry trade group, commissioned the accounting firm of Price Waterhouse to study whether variable annuities still make sense after the Taxpayer Relief Act of 1997. Specifically, the controversial study calculated how long it would take for a variable annuity's higher expenses and tax defer-ral to "break even" with a taxable mutual fund's lower expenses and capital-gains treat-ment. It concluded that variable annuities remain attractive vehicles for retirement sav-ings, even after the new, lower capital-gains rates. Although some factors come down to numbers, most depend on your own psychology and investing style.

Price Waterhouse considered these main factors:

- Load type (no-load, front-load, and back-load)
- Investment objective (growth, balanced, bond, and "specialty" sector funds)
- Gross returns (ranging from 8.9% for back-load bond funds to 19% for front-load specialty funds)
- Each category's percentage of return from dividends and short-term capital gains, long-term capital gains, and unrealized gains
- Historical expense ratios for both funds and annuities
- Holding periods (fund holders were assumed to transfer 20% of their holdings per year from one fund into another)
- Tax brackets of 32.32% during the accumulation period and 20.1% during the pay-out period (equivalent to 28% federal and 6% state rates during the accumulation period and 15% federal and 6% state rates during the payout period)
- Four types of distribution (lump-sum, 10-year term certain, variable annuitization for life, and 20-year systematic withdrawal)

The "base case" found break-even periods ranging from one year for most bond-fund scenarios to as long as 20 years for some growth-fund scenarios. Although each investor's case is different, the study is a useful starting point for examining the factors that go into the decision. Let's look at how each of these factors affect your results.

1. What Kind of Load and Expenses Would You Pay?

Annuities' back-end surrender charges contrast with the three categories of funds: (1) no-load funds, which levy no sales load; (2) front-load funds, which levy an up-front sales charge on all deposits; and (3) back-load funds (and level-load funds), which levy smaller back-end sales loads and charge higher annual expenses (in order to pay bro-kers). Variable annuities generally cost more than funds. The average fund costs 1% per year, while the average annuity costs 1.87%. These extra expenses eat into returns, whether earnings are tax-deferred or not.

The study found that variable annuities compare best against back-load funds. That's because back-load funds' higher expenses compare closest to variable annuities. Annuities also compare well against front-load funds. That's because the funds' front-end commission means less money goes to work for you when you invest. Variable annuities compare worst against no-load funds because of higher expenses. The study didn't specifically address level-load, or "C share" funds. However, these funds have high expenses similar to back-load funds. Variable annuities should compare as well against "C shares" as they do against back-load shares.

2. What Kind of Investment Would You Buy?

Choosing which investments to buy is a crucial issue in making the most of annuities. Tax deferral is more effective with cash and bonds than with stock. Cash and bonds pay current income that benefits more from tax deferral. Holding cash and bonds in a tax-deferred wrapper lets you delay the tax bill without costing you the chance to benefit from lower capital-gains rates. Stocks pay at least a portion of total return in lower-taxed capital gains. Holding growth stocks in a tax-deferred wrapper converts those capital gains into higher-taxed ordinary income.

The study found that variable annuities' tax deferral is worth more with bond funds than with growth funds. This confirms advice to favor bond funds and balanced funds before growth funds within an annuity.

3. How Long Do You Hold Your Funds?

The longer you hold an investment, the more it grows before you hit it with taxes. This is especially true with stocks, which defer tax on most of their gains until you choose to sell. Holding period plays a huge role in determining your final returns. The more whacks you take at your capital gains, the less your returns will compound over time. The study found that the average load-fund investor holds a fund four years, while the average no-load investor holds just three years.

The study assumed that investors switch 20% of their funds each year into a different fund. This works out to an average holding period of five years. The study didn't specifically research the effects of different holding periods. Clearly, longer holding periods increase the annuity's break-even period. And furious trading makes the annuity more valuable. How long do you hold your funds? Do you switch funds often to take advantage of short-term trends or time the market? Or do you buy and hold, looking for long-term gains over time? If you trade often, lean toward a variable annuity. You'll avoid whacking your profits with frequent sales. What's more, your shorter holding periods might not even qualify for lower long-term capital-gains rates. If you buy and hold, lean toward taxable funds. The lower taxes you pay when you take out your money will make up for current taxes on current-income dividends. This is especially true with index investing. You probably can't live long enough for a variable annuity to beat an index fund's low expenses, tax efficiency, and capital-gains treatment.

This is a question you can't answer with numbers. It's more of a "gut check" of your own investing psyche. And this is where a lot of traditional tax planning falls apart. Buying an S&P 500 index fund—and holding it, through thick and thin—is a more tax-efficient way to harness the growth of the U.S. stock market than buying a variable annuity. It's easy to read this here on paper. It's harder to execute out on the field. Do you really have the discipline to do it? If so, great! Buy the index fund and be done with it. If not, don't worry about bucking conventional wisdom. Buy the annuity, safe in knowing that you can panic without whacking your profits. You can't just look at the numbers. You have to consider the real world of your own investing psyche.

4. What Are Your Tax Rates, Today and Tomorrow?

This is the hardest question to answer, especially over time, because you don't know where your tax rates will be when you take your gains. You don't know what your tax rates will be in retirement. Even if you're retired now, you can count on tax-rate changes to come. And you can't even assume that your rates will be lower. Plenty of retirees who've paid off their houses and finished raising their kids find that losing their deductions pushes them into *higher* brackets.

The study chose a 28% federal rate during accumulation and 15% during payout because these are the typical rates for today's owners. The study also assumed a 6% state tax rate during both periods. (A married couple, filing jointly and taking the standard deduction, needs to earn nearly $55,000 before hitting the 28% federal rate.) The study found that variable annuities' tax deferral is worth more as your tax rate goes up during the accumulation period. That's because tax deferral is more valuable for investors in higher brackets. Also, variable annuities' tax deferral is worth more if your tax bracket drops at withdrawal. That's because tax deferral delays your gains until you avoid the higher bracket entirely.

5. How Would You Take Your Gains?

Fewer than 1% of annuity owners ever "annuitize" their contract, or convert it into a guaranteed income. And few owners simply surrender their contracts, paying tax in a lump sum. Most take out money as needed, compounding earnings and delaying tax as long as possible. The choice you make plays a large role in choosing whether annuities make more sense. The study found that most periodic withdrawals increase the annuity break-even period against most fund categories. That's because annuity withdrawals are taxed as income first, while a portion of each mutual-fund sale is a return of your own capital.

You can always "annuitize" yourself, withdrawing income as you need it without converting to a fixed income. This strategy lets you continue compounding your annuity earnings at the underlying subaccounts' rates, rather than accepting the low rates most companies credit to fixed-annuity payouts. Or, if you want the guaranteed lifetime income of an immediate annuity, you can choose a variable payout. This lets your principal earn more interest, with the risk that your income could temporarily fall, but still gives you a guaranteed income for life.

What should you conclude from these questions and answers? Generally, variable annuities are still attractive options for retirement savings once you've made the most of your employer-retirement plan and IRA opportunities. Here's a review of the conclusions:

◆ Variable annuities grow more valuable, relative to taxable funds, the longer you hold the contract.

◆ Variable annuities are better for sheltering bond funds and balanced funds, with higher immediate incomes, than they are at sheltering stock funds with their built-in capital-gains advantage. Use variable annuities to shelter the fixed-income portion of your portfolio before investing in stock subaccounts.

- ◆ If you trade frequently, however, consider doing so inside an annuity to avoid a tax whack every time you trade.

- ◆ Variable annuities are best for money you intend to spend rather than leave to your heirs. There's no stepped-up basis for gains you leave to your beneficiaries. Nor are there "stretchout" options as there are for IRAs. So plan on spending your variable annuity gains first, before tapping any more than your required minimums from IRAs.

- ◆ Variable-annuity growth doesn't add to your adjusted gross income. So variable annuities may be better than funds if you need to keep down adjusted gross income, to preserve your deductions and adjustments to income, or to qualify for tax credits or the rental real-estate-loss allowance.

Several annuity providers offer computer programs that purport to calculate exactly which choice is better, funds or annuities. These, like any other programs, are based on current assumptions. Tax rates change, expenses and investment results vary, and personal circumstances change. Don't put too much faith into projections based on assumptions you know will change. These programs are most useful when they show truly dramatic differences. If you do choose to "crunch the numbers," run several comparisons using different future tax rates to see how changing assumptions affect your results.

Finally, do your homework, just as you would with any other investment. Shop around. Make sure your contract offers experienced investment managers, plus reasonable expenses and a fair surrender charge. Also make sure the issuer has a respectable credit rating. These aren't as important with variable annuities as they are with other insurance products. But fixed-account assets are still a part of the insurer's general assets, and if you eventually choose to annuitize, your income stream will depend on that company's safety.

EQUITY-INDEX ANNUITIES—NO PAIN, NO GAIN

◆ ◆ ◆

Equity-index annuities are a new hybrid of fixed and variable annuities. It's still unclear whether they'll be regulated as "insurance" or as a "security." Equity-index annuities offer a return tied to an equity index—almost always the S&P 500—or a guaranteed return if the index loses money. These contracts promise "no pain"—no chance of losing—but offer "no gain" compared to what you can make in the market yourself.

Different companies have different ways of figuring your gains. There will be a "participation rate," which tells you how much of the index's gain you earn, and a "crediting method," which tells you how the company calculates the gain itself. The company might promise you something like this: "90% of the price appreciation of the S&P 500 *or* 3% per year of 90% of the initial investment." The company invests the bulk of your money in its own general account to cover the minimum-guaranteed return, then puts the rest into options and futures to capture the index return.

Equity-index annuities are taxed like any other annuity. You can invest an unlimited amount; your money grows tax-deferred until withdrawal; you'll pay tax at ordinary rates when you do withdraw your money; and your heirs will owe gain at their ordinary rate at your death. You can make a "1035 exchange" from one equity-index contract to another, or from an equity-index contract to a fixed or variable annuity.

Are equity-index annuities worth the tradeoffs? Your mother always told you that you don't get something for nothing. This time she was right. Equity-index annuities give you *some* of the index's growth (but not necessarily 100%, and no dividends) or *some* of the fixed guarantee (but not as much as you could earn in a straight-fixed annuity). The hidden cost is what you might have earned somewhere else. Which is more important, safety or growth? If one is substantially more valuable than the other, choose an investment designed to deliver it, not an equity-index annuity designed to deliver weak doses of both.

LIFE INSURANCE VERSUS ANNUITIES

❖ ❖ ❖

Variable-annuity sales have exploded in recent years. By some estimates, Americans have poured over $300 billion into these tax-deferred contracts. Are they really that appropriate for that many investors? Just how valuable is tax deferral, particularly when it means converting capital gains to ordinary income? Life insurance offers tax deferral as well, along with tax-free income and a tax-free death benefit.

In many cases, variable-annuity buyers who also need life-insurance protection would be better off investing their annuity dollars in a variable-universal-life policy. The difference turns mostly on whether you plan to spend your gains during your lifetime, or plan to leave your gains to your heirs.

This chart compares the most important factors between the two.

INSURANCE VS. ANNUITIES

Annuities	*Life Insurance*
No underwriting required	Underwriting usually required
Contract fees include minimal expenses for death benefit	Contract fees include substantial expenses for death benefit
10% penalty for withdrawals before 59½	No penalty for withdrawals before 59½
Withdrawals taxed as ordinary income	Withdrawals up to total premiums available tax-free; loans available to access earnings tax-free as long as policy stays in force
Heirs taxed on gains at death	Heirs pay no tax on death benefits
Death proceeds included in owner's estate	Death benefits can be excluded from estate

Finally, lots of annuity owners who don't need current income from their contracts are realizing that their tax-deferred gain may actually be a "tax time bomb" for their beneficiaries, who will owe huge amounts of tax at the owners' deaths. Many of them are trading their annuities for insurance to give their beneficiaries a tax-free death benefit. The main drawback is that they owe tax at the time of the exchange on the accumulated gain in the annuity. If you've bought an annuity and you aren't likely to need the money, should you exchange the annuity for life insurance?

The answer depends on two factors. First, how much are your heirs likely to receive, after taxes at their marginal rates? Second, how much life insurance can you buy after surrendering your annuity? If your after-tax-annuity proceeds can buy more death benefit, then by all means dump the annuity. Not only will you do better for your heirs, but you'll be able to reach your cash without paying tax.

> ▶ **Example:** At age 60, you bought an annuity paying 8%. Now you're 69, and the annuity is worth $100,000. Your life expectancy is 12.6 years, and at your death, the annuity is likely to be worth $263,717. Your heirs are in the 28% bracket, so their net inheritance will be $217,876 ($263,717 minus 28% of the $163,717 gain). If you can buy more than $217,876 worth of coverage, your heirs win.

ELEVEN

INVESTING FOR COLLEGE

Do you want to give your kids a tax problem? Send them to the best college you can. Their years of extra earnings will make you proud and make the IRS happy too.

Saving for college is one of the most intimidating tasks a family faces. First, there's a built-in deadline. Once your child is born, the clock starts ticking. You can't push it off the way you can other financial goals. And second, college itself is a daunting expense. Just compare what you paid yourself with today's astronomical tabs. The most expensive colleges cost north of $30,000 per year. What will college cost when your child starts? You'll probably need to sock away $1,000 a month to bank it all by a newborn baby's eighteenth birthday.

College saving is even harder for families looking for need-based financial aid. That's because there are two, sometimes mutually contradictory, sets of rules. One set governs taxes on your college-savings plans. The other governs how much you qualify for need-based financial aid. It's important to make sure steps you take to save taxes don't compromise your eligibility for aid.

Fortunately, the problem isn't as bad as it first appears. For starters, your child probably won't go to Harvard. As bright as he or she may be, there's still a fierce competition for spots at the top private colleges. And the nation's "public Ivies"—the universities of California, Virginia, Michigan, and North Carolina, among others—offer outstanding educations at less intimidating prices. Second, there's a whole host of loan opportunities available for even the wealthiest families. Third, you can tap your own resources not specifically earmarked for college, including home equity, life insurance, and retirement accounts.

The Taxpayer Relief Act of 1997 threw nervous parents a whole new bag of college-savings bones. These new opportunities include tax credits for college costs, educational IRAs, and penalty-free IRA withdrawals for college costs. These join the classic college-saving strategies of custodial accounts, prepaid-tuition programs, life insurance, and even tax-free earnings on U.S. Savings Bonds used to pay for college costs. This chapter gives you strategies for saving money while your children grow. You also learn how to take advantage of college tax credits and even how to deduct student loan interest after graduation.

NINE TAX-ADVANTAGED COLLEGE-SAVINGS STRATEGIES

❖ ❖ ❖

1. College IRAs

College IRAs are the most obvious new college-saving strategies. Contributions aren't tax-deductible. But earnings grow tax-deferred, and withdrawals are tax-free if you use them for "qualified college costs." Unfortunately, College IRAs are the least valuable tax-advantaged college-savings strategies. Frankly, they stink. You can't contribute enough to make a real difference. And the rules force you to choose between the College IRA and other, more valuable breaks. Here's how they work:

♦ Each child can accept $500 per year until age 18.

♦ The child can accept money from donors with "modified-adjusted gross incomes" between $95,000 and $110,000 ($150,000 and $160,000 for joint filers). "Modified-adjusted gross income" equals regular adjusted gross income, plus foreign income excluded from your regular taxable income. If you can't contribute yourself, an aunt, uncle, or grandparent with lower income can. If you can't *find* a relative with lower income, you don't need the tax savings.

♦ You can't put money into a College IRA in any year when the child receives a contribution to a qualified state tuition program.

♦ You can take out as much as you need to pay your child's college costs, including reasonable room and board, tax-free. If you take out more than your child's college costs, your child will pay tax on whatever portion of the IRA's earnings equal the percentage of the withdrawal used for college costs. Let's say you contribute $5,000 to your child's College IRA. The account grows to $10,000, and you withdraw the money in a year when your child's college costs are just $8,000. Eighty percent of the withdrawal is attributable to college costs ($8,000 of the $10,000 withdrawal), so your child will pay tax on $4,000 (80% of the $5,000 earnings). This actually appears to be a mistake in the law. It makes more sense to tax you on the percentage of the excess withdrawal you *don't* use for college than on the percentage you do.

♦ If the child dies, you'll have to distribute the account balance to his or her estate within 30 days of his or her death.

♦ If your child doesn't use the money by his or her thirtieth birthday, the funds must be distributed and taxed, along with a 10% penalty, or rolled over into another family member's College IRA. This rule was accidentally left out of the law but included in the Congressional "Conference Committee" report used to interpret the law. It should be added in the future.

College IRAs sound like a great idea. But the $500 annual contribution limit—just $9,000 over 18 years—really cripples their value. Five hundred dollars a year isn't enough to make a difference. Invest it for 18 years at 10.5% (the historical long-term stock-market return), and you'll have just $26,483, far less than a single year's tuition by the time your child gets to school. What's more, the tax deferral doesn't save that much. Let's say you invest the same $500 per year in a taxable stock fund earning the same 10.5%. Two percent of the return comes from income dividends, taxed at 28%, and 3% comes from long-term capital gains, taxed at 20%, for an overall tax rate of 10.66%. Your after-tax return will be $23,452—just $3,030 less than in the College IRA. The College IRA does let you shift assets out of stocks and into more conservative investments as college grows closer. But there's still more sizzle than steak in these accounts.

What's more, you can't claim the Hope Scholarship Credit or Lifetime Learning Credit in any year you take money from one of these accounts (see "Claim the College Tax Credits" on p. 175). That's no problem if your adjusted gross income is too high to qualify for the credit. But it poses a real dilemma if you can choose between the two.

At this point, it looks as if the new college credits will be worth more than the College IRA. The maximum credit is $2,000 per year. If you're in the 28% bracket, that equals the tax you'd save on $7,142 in income. If you're in the 15% bracket, it equals the tax you'd save on $13,333 of income. (If you're in a higher bracket, you won't qualify for the credits.) The credit is worth more than the tax you'd save with the College IRA. What's more, the credit amounts and phaseout thresholds are indexed for inflation, while College IRA contributions and income thresholds aren't.

Here's a final problem with the new College IRAs. At the time this book went to press, it wasn't clear what their effect would be on federal financial-aid formulas. We can be sure that colleges will consider College IRAs to be 100% fair game, either the first year or over the course of the student's education. But just what effect will they have on traditional loans and scholarships? Putting money into a College IRA will cost your child more than investing it in any other place. And a grandparent's well-intentioned gift could wind up hurting your child's ability to qualify for need-based assistance.

2. U.S. Savings Bonds

U.S. Savings Bonds aren't the most exciting investment available. But they offer one significant break for parents saving for college. Interest on Series EE Savings Bonds redeemed to pay for college may be partially or fully tax-free. The bonds must be issued in your name or jointly with the child, and you must use the proceeds the year of redemption for college or vocational tuition and fees. Figure the tax-free amount on Form 8815.

- Reduce your total educational costs by any tax-free scholarships, benefits from qualified state-tuition plans, and expenses for which you claim the Hope Scholarship and Lifetime Learning credits.

- If the redemption amount exceeds the eligible educational expenses, the tax-free amount equals the percentage of educational expenses divided by the redemption amount.

- The interest exclusion is available for unmarried filers with modified adjusted-gross incomes below $65,850 (phased out for incomes between $50,851 and $65,850) and joint filers with modified adjusted-gross incomes below $106,250 (phased out for incomes between $76,250 and $106,250). Married couples filing separately don't qualify. Modified adjusted-gross income generally equals regular adjusted-gross income plus the interest on the redeemed savings bonds and any foreign income excluded from your income.

> ▸ **Example:** You're a single mother with a $45,000 income. In 1998 you redeem $8,000 of bonds to pay for your daughter's college tuition. Of this, $3,000 is interest. Your daughter's eligible tuition totals $6,000. Dividing $6,000 of tuition by $8,000 of redemption gives you a 75% excludable percentage; 75% of the $3,000 interest is $2,250, so $2,250 is excludable. If your income had been $55,850, or one-third of the way through the phaseout range, just two-thirds of that amount, or $1,500, would be excludable.

Phaseout figures are indexed for inflation; these numbers are for the 1997 tax year. For general information on savings bonds, see Chapter 7, Investment Securities.

> Series EE bonds won't give you the long-term growth you need to pay for college. But they make good sense for last-minute savings as your child approaches college. They're also good for holding money you've shifted out of stocks in preparation for paying tuition costs.

3. Custodial Accounts

Investing in your child's name with trusts or custodial accounts lets you manage investments and pay the bulk of the taxes at their low rates. If a child under age 14 has investment income over $1,300, you'll owe "kiddie tax" on the excess at your marginal rate. But custodial accounts can shelter income on thousands of dollars of savings. And once the child reaches age 14, the gate opens even wider. For more information, see "Tax Breaks for Your Kids," in Chapter 2.

> If you apply for college financial aid, the college will expect your children to use 35% of their assets to finance college. In contrast, they'll expect you to use just 5.6% of your assets. Putting money in your child's name can hurt you when you apply for financial aid. However, most financial aid comes in the form of loans, not grants, so at worst, you'll hurt your child's chance to qualify for loans. Also, money in a child's name won't be affected by a parent's divorce or bankruptcy.

4. Prepaid-Tuition Programs

"Qualified state-tuition programs" let you pay for tomorrow's tuition at today's price. Currently, over 30 states make this offer. Although each state's plan is different, they generally agree to pay a future unit of costs—a credit hour, a course, or even an entire year's worth of tuition—at any participating college in the state. The programs make three valuable promises.

- ◆ Your purchasing power keeps pace with college costs, no matter how fast they rise. That's especially important because college costs have climbed so much faster than general inflation.
- ◆ Your money grows tax-deferred until your child redeems it for tuition.
- ◆ There's no conflict with the new college credits as there is with the College IRA.

Of course, nothing in life is free. The main drawback of these programs is what happens if your child chooses not to go to college. Some programs just give back your original investment. Others give you a slight return on your money, but certainly not as much as if you'd invested it on your own.

Here are the tax rules for these programs:

♦ Withdrawals are treated first as return of capital, with no tax due until total withdrawals top the parents' investment in the program.

♦ Withdrawals are taxed to the student at the student's presumably lower rate.

♦ Parents are taxed only if they get a refund exceeding their initial investment.

♦ Contributions are considered complete gifts for gift-tax purposes.

5. Individual Retirement Accounts

The Taxpayer Relief Act of 1997 lets you take money from an IRA for "qualified tuition expenses." The money is still taxable, but there's no 10% penalty if you take it out before age 59½. Qualified students include yourself, your spouse, your children, and your grandchildren. Qualified expenses include tuition, room and board, books, fees, supplies, and equipment. For more information on IRA withdrawals, including rules for reporting them, see Chapter 12, Investing for Retirement.

6. Permanent Life Insurance

If you have children you plan to send to college, you need life insurance. Life insurance can finish financing your kids' education if you're not around to do it yourself. But permanent life insurance—including whole life, universal life, and variable life—has strong tax advantages you can harness to finance your kids' education. For general information on life insurance, see Chapter 10, Life Insurance and Annuities. Here are specific pluses for college savers:

♦ You can take tax-free income for tuition in the form of withdrawals and loans.

♦ There's no conflict with state prepaid-tuition programs, as there is with College IRA contributions.

♦ There's no conflict with the Hope Scholarship and Lifetime Learning tax credits, as there is with College IRA withdrawals.

♦ There's no penalty for withdrawals before age 59½.

♦ Life-insurance and annuity cash values are not fully included as assets when calculating the family's expected contribution under most financial-aid formulas.

7. Gifts of Appreciated Property

If you have investments that have appreciated over time, you can sell them, pay tax, and use the proceeds to pay for college. Or, you can give them to your children, who then sell them, pay *less* tax, and use more of the proceeds for college.

You can give up to $10,000 per year to a child (or anyone else, for that matter), without paying gift tax on the gift. If your spouse joins you in making the gift, you can give up to $20,000. If you give your children appreciated securities, they take over your original basis. But when they go to sell the securities, they pay tax on the appreciation at their lower rate.

This strategy also keeps down your adjusted gross income, preserving your eligibility for deductions, credits, and other income-based breaks.

> ▶ **Example:** You buy shares in the College Savers' Growth Fund for $5,000. Your shares are now worth $10,000, and your daughter plans to attend Hamilton in the fall. You're in the 31% tax bracket; she makes $8 an hour at the mall. If you sell the shares yourself you'll pay $1,550 on the gain. If you give her the shares to sell she pays just $750. The gift of shares gives her $800 more for tuition.

U.S. T-bills aren't taxed until maturity. If you want to defer income, consider buying your child a T-bill maturing after December 31 of the year you make the purchase. Income won't be taxable until the following calendar year.

8. Employer Retirement Accounts

Tapping your own retirement savings isn't the best way to pay for college, unless your kids plan to make enough money to support you in your retirement. However, you can consider a loan or hardship withdrawal from your employer-retirement plan. For more information, see the next chapter.

9. Buy a Home for Your College Student

Housing is hardly the largest part of most students' expenses. But once your kid hits college, you can cut this significant cost, and give yourself a tax break, by buying off-campus housing. Here's how it works: You buy an off-campus house, apartment, or condominium. You can treat it as a second home and write off the mortgage and taxes. This should be enough to convert what would have been worthless rent receipts into valuable deductions. Or, you can choose to treat the home as rental property. Hire your kid to manage the place and rent to a bunch of friends. Assuming they don't destroy the place, you'll get to write off depreciation as well as the management fee. Either way, you'll get the leveraged appreciation from owning the house. You can also buy the house in the child's name, and co-sign the mortgage. This will give him or her the appreciation, to be taxed at the student's low rate. It will also help build a credit rating.

CLAIM THE COLLEGE TAX CREDITS

❖ ❖ ❖

The Hope Scholarship and Lifetime Learning Tax Credits are more valuable breaks for middle-income parents of college students. These are credits for parents of students (if the parents claim the student as a dependent) or credits for students themselves (if they can't be declared as someone else's dependents). Tax credits are more valuable than deductions because they cut your actual tax, not just your income.

Here are the rules:

♦ Hope Scholarship credits are available for qualifying tuition and related expenses of you, your spouse, or your dependent enrolled at least half-time in the first two years of postsecondary education. This generally includes any accredited school offering credit toward a bachelor's degree, associate's degree, or other recognized postsecondary credential. Lifetime Learning credits are available for any year of postsecondary or graduate education, plus any course of instruction at an eligible institution to acquire or improve job skills.

♦ You can claim the credits for more than one qualifying student at a time.

♦ The Hope Scholarship credit is equal to 100% of the first $1,000 of costs, plus 50% of the next $1,000 of costs, for a maximum credit of $1,500 per year. The Lifetime Learning credit is equal to 20% of qualifying expenses up to $5,000, for a maximum credit per student of $1,000. Beginning in 2003, the Lifetime Learning credit will rise to 20% of qualifying expenses up to $10,000, for a maximum credit of $2,000.

♦ The credits phase out for taxpayers with adjusted gross incomes between $40,000 and $50,000 ($80,000 and $100,000 for joint filers). These amounts will be indexed for inflation beginning in 2002.

♦ You can't claim the credits during any year in which you withdraw money from a College IRA account for that particular student.

♦ The credits aren't available for married couples filing separately.

DEDUCT STUDENT-LOAN INTEREST

❖ ❖ ❖

The Taxpayer Relief Act of 1997 made student-loan interest deductible. You take this deduction "above the line"—before you figure adjusted gross income. This makes the deduction more valuable because it's not limited as a percentage of adjusted gross income. Here's how to claim it:

♦ The deduction is available for interest paid on "qualified education loans"—generally, loans you take to pay for tuition, room and board, and related expenses.

♦ The maximum deduction is $1,500 in 1999, $2,000 in 2000, and $2,500 in 2001 and later.

♦ The deduction is phased out for taxpayers with "modified adjusted gross incomes" between $40,000 and $55,000 ($60,000 and 75,000 for joint filers). These amounts will be indexed for inflation starting in 2003. Modified adjusted gross income generally equals regular adjusted gross income plus U.S. Savings Bond redeemed to pay tuition, employer-provided adoption assistance, and foreign-earned income and allowances.

- ◆ The deduction is available for interest you pay during the first 60 months for which interest is required.
- ◆ No deduction is allowed for taxpayers who can still be claimed as dependents

Report the deduction as an adjustment to income on Form 1040.

TWELVE

INVESTING FOR RETIREMENT

YOU CAN'T SUCCESSFULLY save for retirement without the tax man on your side. How many of us will be able to retire, without working at all during retirement, with sufficient income to fund the lifestyle we want? How many more of us will fund our dream of early retirement? Your retirement will be longer, and healthier, than any generation before. This will all take money—and lots of it.

The U.S. Department of Health and Human Services reported in 1992 that out of 100 people starting a career, at age 65:

- Twenty will be dead. This honestly suggests you enjoy life now rather than obsessing over a retirement that may never come.

- 14 will have incomes under $12,000. These are the workers who didn't save, or couldn't save for retirement, eking out modest lives on Social Security.

- 31 will have incomes between $12,000 and $30,000. These employees might have saved, but started late or just didn't try hard enough.

- Finally, 35 will have incomes of $30,000 or more.

Retirees can make $35,000 go farther than the rest of us can. The house is paid off, the kids are gone, and the days of buying "things" are largely over. Of course, a Florida condo would be nice, the kids still have their hands out, and grandchildren need "things." But these are still depressing figures, especially if retirement looms near.

Bookstores and magazines are full of hopeful stories on "How to Retire Rich," and even "How To Retire Tomorrow." These are fine for families willing to make a supernatural commitment to saving. But most of us have kids to raise, houses to buy, and college to pay for. Retirement savings too easily take a back seat to more pressing needs. Fortunately, help is on the way . . . and from the IRS! The tax law guarantees help for retirement in ways that no hot mutual fund ever can. Qualified retirement plans (the kind your employer sponsors) and Individual Retirement Accounts (IRAs) arm you with the most powerful weapon in your financial arsenal: tax-deferred compounding. Tax-advantaged retirement plans are the basic building block of successful retirement planning. You can turn your retirement savings accounts into real money if you treat them right. Million-dollar and multimillion-dollar accounts are common enough that the Congress once imposed a special "success tax" to penalize excess accumulations.

This is the most technical part of the *Sixty-Minute Tax Planner*. Congress authorizes qualified plans and IRAs to encourage retirement savings, and there are some tough rules intended to keep investors from abusing the tax advantages. But stick with it. Even if you hire a professional to crunch the numbers, you learn how to harness the awesome power of tax-deferred compounding. You learn where to put your money to make the most of available tax breaks. You learn how to withdraw funds before age 59½ without paying the usual 10% penalty, and how to minimize required annual withdrawals at age 70½ to preserve your principal. Finally, you learn how to "stretch out" your retirement savings for years and even decades of tax-deferred compounding past your death.

MAKE THE MOST OF EMPLOYER RETIREMENT PLANS

❖ ❖ ❖

A qualified retirement plan is a savings and investment plan that your employer maintains that qualifies for special tax treatment. "Defined-benefit" plans promise a predetermined annual benefit, usually based on your salary and length of service. These are the traditional "pension plans" maintained by governments and large corporations. "Defined-contribution" plans, such as today's popular 401(k)s, promise no defined benefit, and future benefits will depend on how much you and your employer contribute to the plan. Employers are shifting away from traditional defined-benefit plans and shifting the responsibility for accumulating and managing retirement savings onto employees themselves. Clearly, this is cheaper for your employer. It also takes the employer off the hook for employee investment performance (They still remain liable for selecting investment options offered by the plan.)

The qualified-plan tax break costs the government around $70 billion per year, according to the congressional Joint Tax Committee. Of course, the IRS eventually collects that much and more when employees take out their savings.

This is a book about taxes, not about retirement planning. But if you're responsible for funding your own retirement plan, you'll get immediate tax benefits to turbocharge your retirement savings over time. When you put money into your plan, you get to deduct your contributions from your taxable income the year you make the contribution. (Your employer will deduct your contributions from the amount reported to you on your W-2.) Your money grows tax-deferred until you pull it out at retirement. Even then there are strategies for taking money early.

Most employees who fund their own plans get some sort of match from their employer. Your employer's match increases your account balance even faster. Contribute as much as it takes to maximize that match. The combination of immediate tax savings, employer matches, and tax deferrals is the next best thing to a knock on the door from Publisher's Clearinghouse.

> ▶ **Example:** You make $50,000 per year, and you're in the 28% tax bracket. Your employer offers a 401(k) and matches contributions 50% up to 4% of salary. You'd like to save $2,000 per year toward retirement in a stock account earning 10.5% per year. Should you contribute to the 401(k), open an IRA, or buy taxable mutual funds?

- ❖ If you contribute to the 401(k), you'll get an immediate $560 tax saving, plus an extra $1,000 from your employer. You'll invest $3,000, at a cost of just $1,440. Over 20 years, you'll invest $28,800 and your account will grows to $200,991.
- ❖ If you contribute to the IRA, you'll get an immediate $560 tax saving, but no employer match. You'll invest $2,000, at a cost of $1,440. Over 20 years, you'll invest $28,800 and your account will grow to $133,994.

♦ If you buy a taxable mutual fund, you'll get no immediate tax saving and no employer match. You'll invest $2,000 at a cost of $2,000. Over 20 years, you'll invest $40,000 and your account will grow to $93,774.

WHAT IF YOU NEED YOUR MONEY BEFORE RETIREMENT?

❖ ❖ ❖

Qualified-retirement plans are intended for long-term retirement savings. That's why Congress gives away such generous tax breaks. But many people are reluctant to contribute as much as they can. They worry about locking up money they might need for a down payment on a house, or perhaps for medical emergencies. Fortunately, some plans give you escape hatches in the form of loans, hardship withdrawals, and in-service withdrawals.

Some plans let you borrow against your account. Loans let you tap your money without giving up tax-deferral. They also let you reach age 59½ without paying a 10% early-withdrawal penalty. You can generally borrow $50,000 or 50% of your vested account balance, whichever is less. (If your plan is particularly flexible, you can borrow up to 100% of your plan balance by putting up extra security, such as your house.) You have to repay your loan within five years (unless you use it to buy a primary residence), with substantially level installments paid at least quarterly. If you leave your job before you repay the loan, you'll owe tax on the unpaid balance unless you pay the loan with funds from another source. Plan loan interest isn't tax deductible—you'll repay the loan with after-tax dollars, then pay tax again when you withdraw your money from the plan. But plan loans are the easiest way to access your money before retirement. For more information, see your plan administrator.

Some 401(k) and 403(b) plans also let you take a "hardship withdrawal" of your own contributions (but not employer contributions or earnings) for an "immediate and heavy" financial need. Some plans limit these to medical bills, a down payment on a house, college costs, and payment of any amount needed to prevent eviction or foreclosure on your primary residence. Other plans make hardship withdrawals available for any other reason creating an immediate and heavy financial need. If your plan allows both loans and hardship withdrawals, you have to borrow the maximum amount available before taking a hardship withdrawal. And, if you do take a hardship withdrawal, you can't contribute to the plan for the next year. For more information, see your plan administrator.

Finally, some plans let you make "in-service withdrawals" while you still work for the company. You can take the withdrawal in cash (after you pay tax and a 10% penalty, if applicable), or you can roll the withdrawal into an IRA. (You can use an in-service withdrawal to roll money into an IRA if you don't like your plan's investment options.) Again, for more information, see your plan administrator.

By some estimates, at least one-third of 401(k) participants have loans against their accounts, with an average loan balance of $6,000. It's true that borrowing from your plan is easier and cheaper than borrowing from someplace else. There's no approval process, and rates are generally at or near the prime rate. But borrowing from your plan costs you the chance to earn a higher return in the market. And borrowing from your plan forces you to pay tax twice on the interest you pay—once when you earn it before you put it in the plan, then again when you withdraw it from the plan. So, think of loans and hardship withdrawals as emergency "escape hatches." They aren't intended to help you buy a car or a bass boat. But they should give you some comfort that you can take money out in case of emergency. This should give you the confidence to make the most of your employer retirement plan.

WHAT TO DO WHEN YOU LEAVE YOUR JOB

❖ ❖ ❖

What to do with your qualified plan balance may be the single largest financial decision you ever make. If you've successfully invested over the course of your career, your qualified-plan balance can reach millions of dollars. In 1997 Baltimore mutual-fund giant T. Rowe Price reported over $300 million-dollar balances among its 401(k) accounts under management.

When you leave your job, whether you move on to another job or retire completely, you have several choices for your qualified-plan balance. These choices can make a huge difference in your future retirement income. There are five basic choices: (1) leave the money in the current plan; (2) move it into your new employer's plan; (3) roll it into an IRA; (4) take the account balance in cash; or (5) at retirement, take an annuity. The following table summarizes each of these options:

WHAT TO DO WHEN YOU LEAVE YOUR JOB

Option	Tax Consequences	Investment Choice	Access
Leave Balance in Current Plan	Funds not taxed until withdrawn	Limited to current plan options	Loans
Roll Balance into New Plan	Funds not taxed until withdrawn	Limited to new plan options	Loans
Roll Balance into IRA	Funds not taxed until withdrawn (trustee-to-trustee transfer)	Greater flexibility	Unlimited access (taxes and penalties may apply)
Take Cash	Taxed immediately (forward averaging may be available)	Unlimited flexibility	Unlimited access
Annuitize	Distributions taxed as you receive them	No flexibility	No unscheduled access to funds

1. Leave Your Balance in Your Current Plan

This choice is generally available if your plan balance is greater than $5,000. If you like your current employer's plan and your investment choices, it may make sense just to leave your money where it is. Traditionally, employers resent paying ongoing administrative fees for terminated employees. But as total plan assets grow, employers find themselves better able to negotiate fee discounts, and terminated employees' account balances give them extra bargaining power.

2. Roll Your Balance into Your New Employer's Plan

If your new employer allows it, you can roll your balance into the new employer's plan. Currently, more than 80% of qualified plans accept rollovers. You'll enjoy the same investment choices as existing employees have. Another advantage of rolling your account into your new employer's plan is that you can continue to borrow against your account, a privilege you lose if you roll into an IRA.

You may have to "park" your old balance in a "conduit IRA" until you're eligible to participate in the new employer's plan. If so, don't put any more money into that account. Commingling any other money will disqualify the entire balance from rolling into the new plan. The only amounts you can roll into the new plan are the original qualified-plan balance plus earnings on that balance.

3. Roll Your Balance into an IRA

If you roll your account balance into an IRA, you can manage your account just like any other IRA (see the following). You'll enjoy the full range of investment options your IRA sponsor provides.

There are two ways to transfer money from your employer plan into an IRA:

♦ You can have your old employer transfer the money directly to your IRA. This is called a trustee-to-trustee transfer. There will be no tax on the amount you transfer.

♦ You can take the money directly, then deposit the payment into an IRA. If you take the money yourself, your employer will withhold 20% of the balance for tax. You can replace that 20% with funds from other sources within 60 days of when you take your money. If you do, at the end of the year, the IRS will refund the 20% withheld. But this strategy is risky. If, for any reason, you don't replace that 20%, you'll owe tax on the amount withheld. Sure, you'll get a refund on whatever part of the 20% you don't need to pay that tax. But you'll still owe a hefty tax, and you'll lose your tax-deferred compounding on that part of your account. This is playing with fire if there's any chance you can't replace that 20%.

> ▶ **Example:** You switch jobs with $40,000 in your employer-plan account. You can choose to roll the $40,000 directly into an IRA. You can also take the money directly. You'll get $32,000, and your employer will withhold $8,000. You can deposit the $32,000 into an IRA yourself. But if you don't add $8,000 more, you'll owe tax on that amount because it didn't make it into the IRA. If you're in the 28% tax bracket, that failure will cost you $2,240.

If you choose to roll your account into an IRA, have your employer transfer your account directly to your IRA custodian, not to you.

If your qualified-plan balance includes employer stock, it may not make sense to roll that stock into an IRA. Employer stock gets special treatment that lets you take advantage of lower capital-gains rates. This can be valuable whether you choose to hold your employer stock or sell some to diversify your portfolio.

Presumably, your stock has gained value since it was contributed to the plan and will continue to gain value in the future. If you roll the stock into an IRA, you'll pay no tax now, and you'll pay ordinary income rates on the entire value when you withdraw the funds.

However, you can choose to take your employer stock outright. You'll pay ordinary tax now on the stock's value at the time it was contributed to the plan. When you eventually sell the stock, you'll pay lower capital-gains tax on the appreciation since the date of contribution. It may make sense to take a small tax hit now in exchange for capital-gains rate savings down the road:

- If you plan to keep some stock and sell the rest to diversify, it makes sense to roll the portion you plan to sell into an IRA. You'll avoid immediate tax on the portion of stock you sell.
- If you plan to sell stock to raise cash, take the stock outright. You'll benefit from lower capital-gains rates on the portion of stock you sell. Also, you can take stock outright and use it to secure a loan to raise cash without selling at all. For more information, see "Tax Breaks for Capital Gains," in Chapter 6.

If you've acquired stock at different values over the course of your employment, you can pick and choose which shares to take now and which to roll into the IRA. That way, you can take advantage of capital-gains rates on older shares with a lower cost basis, while rolling the rest into your IRA.

(If your stock's value now is lower than when it was contributed to the plan, you'll pay ordinary income rates on the full value at the time you take the distribution.)

4. Take Your Balance in Cash

You can simply take your balance in cash. If you're under age 59½, this is a lousy choice. Your employer will withhold 20% of your account balance in tax. You'll owe ordinary income tax on the entire balance, and you'll owe an extra 10% penalty for the withdrawal before age 59½. If you truly need the money now, roll it into an IRA. Even if you pull it out immediately, you'll avoid the 20% withholding. For better choices, see "Avoid Penalties on Early Withdrawals," page 198.

Special Averaging

If you're over 59½, it might make sense to take your balance. Special averaging cuts your tax by letting you pay as if you had taken the income over a series ten years. This amount may be less than if you take the same balance out of an IRA. If your spouse dies, you can choose special averaging if your spouse would have been able; your age doesn't matter. Special averaging is especially beneficial for distributions under $70,000 because a portion of the distribution, called the "minimum-distribution allowance," is tax-free.

To elect special averaging, file Form 4972 with your return for the year you receive the distribution. If you choose not to use special averaging the year you take the distribution, you can change your mind by filing an amended return. For more information, see Chapter 13, Put Cash in Your Next Paycheck.

Ten-year averaging is available for lump-sum distributions if you were born before 1936. You have to have participated in the plan for at least five years, and you have to choose ten-year averaging for all distributions you take that year. Here's how it works:

+ Take your account balance in a lump sum, free from withholding.

+ Subtract any nontaxable amounts included in the distribution (nondeductible contributions to the employer plan, one-year-term costs of life insurance included in the plan, any other employer contributions you've already paid tax on, and any plan loan balances included in your regular income).

+ Subtract a "minimum-distribution allowance," which won't be included as part of the taxable distribution. The allowance equals $10,000 *or* one-half of the total distribution, whichever is less, reduced by 20% of the amount by which the distribu-

TEN-YEAR FORWARD-AVERAGING RATES

If One-Tenth of the Taxable Amount Is:	*Ten-Year Averaging Tax Is 10 Times:*
Over 0 but not over $1,190	$0 + 11% of excess over $0
Over $1,190 but not over $2,270	$130.90 + 12% of excess over $1,190
Over $2,270 but not over $4,530	$260.50 + 14% of excess over $2,270
Over $4,530 but not over $6,690	$576.90 + 15% of excess over $4,530
Over $6,690 but not over $9,170	$900.90 + 16% of excess over $6,690
Over $9,170 but not over $11,440	$1,297.70 + 18% of excess over $9,170
Over $11,440 but not over $13,710	$1,706.30 + 20% of excess over $11,440
Over $13,710 but not over $17,160	$2,160.30 + 23% of excess over $13,710
Over $17,160 but not over $22,880	$2,953.80 + 26% of excess over $17,160
Over $22,880 but not over $28,600	$4,441.00 + 30% of excess over $22,880
Over $28,600 but not over $34,320	$6,157.00 + 34% of excess over $28,600
Over $34,320 but not over $42,300	$8,101.80 + 38% of excess over $34,320
Over $42,300 but not over $57,190	$11,134.20 + 42% of excess over $42,300
Over $57,190 but not over $85,790	$17,388.00 + 48% of excess over $57,190
Over $85,790	$31,116.00 + 50% of excess over $85,790

tion exceeds $20,000. For example, if the distribution is $50,000, the allowance is $4,000 ($10,000, minus 20% of $30,000). If the distribution is $70,000 or more, there's no minimum distribution allowance.

♦ Pay a flat 20% on the portion of your account attributable to pre-1974 contributions.

♦ Finally, pay ordinary tax on the rest according to the rates in the previous table. You can also choose ten-year averaging on the entire account balance. This makes sense for distributions less than $114,400.

▶ **Example:** In 1998, you take a $250,000 lump-sum distribution that qualifies for 10-year averaging. One-tenth of the taxable amount is $25,000. Your tax is 10 times ($4,441 plus 30% of the excess over $22,880), or $50,770.

Special averaging cuts your tax when you take your full distribution in cash. But special averaging still costs more than if you choose an IRA rollover. And special averaging kills your tax deferral. It's best for small distributions, generally $70,000 or less.

5. Annuitize

When you retire, you can choose a guaranteed-income annuity. In some cases, this will be the only choice you have. This won't give you the highest rate of return on your plan balance. Other investments will pay you higher rates than an insurance company will guarantee with an annuity. But it might be the best choice for conservative investors who want a guaranteed income. The insurance company providing the annuity will offer a variety of choices, including income for life, income for the joint lives of you and your spouse, and various guarantee periods to make sure you don't lose your entire account balance if you and your spouse both drop dead after cashing three payments. For more information, see Chapter 10, Life Insurance and Annuities.

MAKE THE MOST OF IRAS

◆ ◆ ◆

Congress established IRAs in 1974 to encourage retirement savings. Since then account balances have soared past the trillion-dollar mark. Congress sharply limited the deduction for IRA contributions in 1986. But millions of Americans still contribute faithfully each year. What's more, tax-law changes have spawned a whole zoo of IRAs. There are now regular-deductible IRAs, nondeductible IRAs, spousal IRAs, Roth IRAs, rollover

Form 4972

Department of the Treasury
Internal Revenue Service (O)

Tax on Lump-Sum Distributions

From Qualified Retirement Plans

▶ Attach to Form 1040 or Form 1041.   ▶ See separate instructions.

OMB No. 1545-0193

1998

Attachment
Sequence No. **28**

Name of recipient of distribution

Identifying number

Part I	**Complete this part to see if you qualify to use Form 4972**		
		Yes	**No**
1	Was this a distribution of a plan participant's entire balance from all of an employer's qualified plans of one kind (pension, profit-sharing, or stock bonus)? If "No," do not use this form **1**		
2	Did you roll over any part of the distribution? If "Yes," do not use this form **2**		
3	Was this distribution paid to you as a beneficiary of a plan participant who died after reaching age 59½ (or who had been born before 1936)? **3**		
4	Were you a plan participant who received this distribution after reaching age 59½ **and** having been in the plan for at least 5 years before the year of the distribution? **4**		
	If you answered "No" to both questions 3 **and** 4, do not use this form.		
5a	Did you use Form 4972 after 1986 for a previous distribution from your own plan? If "Yes," do not use this form for a 1998 distribution from your own plan **5a**		
b	If you are receiving this distribution as a beneficiary of a plan participant who died, did you use Form 4972 for a previous distribution received for that plan participant after 1986? If "Yes," you may not use the form for this distribution **5b**		

Part II	**Complete this part to choose the 20% capital gain election** (See instructions.) Do not complete this part unless the participant was born **before** 1936.	
6	Capital gain part from box 3 of Form 1099-R **6**	
7	Multiply line 6 by 20% (.20) **7**	
	If you also choose to use Part III, go to line 8. Otherwise, include the amount from line 7 in the total on Form 1040, line 40, or Form 1041, Schedule G, line 1b, whichever applies.	

Part III	**Complete this part to choose the 5- or 10-year tax option** (See instructions.)	
8	Ordinary income from Form 1099-R, box 2a minus box 3. If you did not complete Part II, enter the taxable amount from box 2a of Form 1099-R **8**	
9	Death benefit exclusion for a beneficiary of a plan participant who died before August 21, 1996 **9**	
10	Total taxable amount. Subtract line 9 from line 8 . . . . **10**	
11	Current actuarial value of annuity (from Form 1099-R, box 8) **11**	
12	Adjusted total taxable amount. Add lines 10 and 11. If this amount is $70,000 or more, **skip** lines 13 through 16, and enter this amount on line 17 . . . . **12**	
13	Multiply line 12 by 50% (.50), but **do not** enter more than $10,000 **13**	
14	Subtract $20,000 from line 12. If the result is less than zero, enter -0- **14**	
15	Multiply line 14 by 20% (.20) **15**	
16	Minimum distribution allowance. Subtract line 15 from line 13 . . . . **16**	
17	Subtract line 16 from line 12 . . . . **17**	
18	Federal estate tax attributable to lump-sum distribution **18**	
19	Subtract line 18 from line 17 . . . . **19**	
	If line 11 is blank, skip lines 20 through 22 and go to line 23.	
20	Divide line 11 by line 12 and enter the result as a decimal (rounded to at least four places) . . **20**	
21	Multiply line 16 by the decimal on line 20 . . . . **21**	
22	Subtract line 21 from line 11 . . . . **22**	

For Paperwork Reduction Act Notice, see separate instructions.   Cat. No. 13187U   Form **4972** (1998)

Form 4972 (1998)   Page **2**

Part III   5- or 10-year tax option—CONTINUED

23	Multiply line 19 by 20% (.20)	**23**		
24	Tax on amount on line 23. Use the Tax Rate Schedule for the 5-Year Tax Option in the instructions	**24**		
25	Multiply line 24 by five (5). If line 11 is blank, skip lines 26 through 28, and enter this amount on line 29	**25**		
26	Multiply line 22 by 20% (.20)	**26**		
27	Tax on amount on line 26. Use the Tax Rate Schedule for the 5-Year Tax Option in the instructions	**27**		
28	Multiply line 27 by five (5)	**28**		
29	Subtract line 28 from line 25. (Multiple recipients, see page 2 of the instructions.) . . .	**29**		

5-year tax option (side label for lines 23–29)

Note: *Complete lines 30 through 36 ONLY if the participant was born before 1936. Otherwise, enter the amount from line 29 on line 37.*

30	Multiply line 19 by 10% (.10)	**30**		
31	Tax on amount on line 30. Use the Tax Rate Schedule for the 10-Year Tax Option in the instructions	**31**		
32	Multiply line 31 by ten (10). If line 11 is blank, skip lines 33 through 35, and enter this amount on line 36	**32**		
33	Multiply line 22 by 10% (.10)	**33**		
34	Tax on amount on line 33. Use the Tax Rate Schedule for the 10-Year Tax Option in the instructions	**34**		
35	Multiply line 34 by ten (10)	**35**		
36	Subtract line 35 from line 32. (Multiple recipients, see page 2 of the instructions.) . . .	**36**		
37	Compare lines 29 and 36. Generally, you should enter the **smaller** amount here (see instructions) . . . . ▶	**37**		
38	Tax on lump-sum distribution. Add lines 7 and 37. Also, include this amount in the total on Form 1040, line 40, or Form 1041, Schedule G, line 1b, whichever applies . . . . . ▶	**38**		

10-year tax option (side label for lines 30–36)

IRAs, conduit IRAs, and even College IRAs. IRAs gives you the same tax-deferred growth as an employer retirement plan. But there's even more flexibility to manage your account because you aren't limited to your employer's investment choices.

You'll want to strap on a helmet for some of this ride. There are excellent books that talk about nothing more than taking cash from your IRA. But this discussion will give you what you need to chart a course. You'll learn how to choose the right IRA, how to withdraw money without penalties, how to withdraw your money during retirement, and how to preserve your tax breaks long past your death.

If you're self-employed and you'd like to save more than the $2,000 annual IRA limit, be sure to see "Set Up Your Own Retirement Plan," in Chapter 4.

Congress turned IRA rules upside down with The Taxpayer Relief Act of 1997 and the introduction of new Roth IRAs and College IRAs. Here are the basic rules for the most common choices, regular-deductible IRAs and Roth IRAs.

OPEN AN ORDINARY IRA FOR UP-FRONT DEDUCTIONS

◆ ◆ ◆

Ordinary IRAs let you deduct your contribution (subject to certain qualifications) and compound your earnings tax-deferred for retirement.

◆ Anyone with earned income (salary, self-employment income, and so forth) can contribute to an IRA.

◆ You can contribute 100% of your earned income up to $2,000.

◆ If you don't actively participate in an employer retirement plan, you can deduct your contribution as an adjustment to income regardless of how much you make.

IRA DEDUCTION PHASEOUTS

Year	Phaseout Range (Single Filers)	Phaseout Range (Joint Filers)
1999	$31,000–$41,000	$51,000–$61,000
2000	$32,000–$42,000	$52,000–$62,000
2001	$33,000–$43,000	$53,000–$64,000
2002	$34,000–$44,000	$54,000–$64,000
2003	$40,000–$50,000	$60,000–$70,000
2004	$45,000–$55,000	$65,000–$75,000
2005	$50,000–$60,000	$70,000–$80,000
2006	$50,000–$60,000	$75,000–$85,000
2007	$50,000–$60,000	$80,000–$100,000

If you do participate in an employer retirement plan, you can deduct your contribution if your adjusted gross income falls within these limits:

♦ You have to contribute cash; you can't transfer securities from another account.

♦ You can buy almost any investment inside an IRA: bank deposits, stocks, bonds, mutual funds, real estate, mortgages and other loans, private placements, even limited partnerships. About the only things you can't buy are most collectibles (rugs, wine, stamps, and the like), and certain options and futures investments.

♦ It pays to contribute early. You can put your money in as early as January 1 or as late as April 15 of the following year. If you contribute on January 1 and earn a steady 10.5% return, your contribution will already be worth $2,276 by the April 15 contribution deadline.

♦ If you take out money before age 59½, you'll owe ordinary income tax plus a 10% penalty tax on withdrawals. (See "Avoid Penalties on Early Withdrawals," page 198, for exceptions to this rule.)

♦ Once you reach age 59½ you can withdraw money as ordinary income. Your trustee will report your withdrawals on Form 1099-R. The entire withdrawal is taxed as ordinary income, unless you've made nondeductible contributions (see the following section).

♦ You have to start taking money out by April 1 of the year after you reach age 70½.

♦ When you die, your IRA passes to your designated beneficiary and avoids probate.

♦ You can deduct your IRA account fee as a miscellaneous itemized deduction if you pay it separately by check, rather than from plan assets.

Don't overlook the power of that $2,000 annual deduction. If you're in the 28% tax bracket, your $2,000 annual contribution saves you $560 in federal income tax. In effect, your $2,000 contribution costs just $1,440.

IRA sponsors report contributions to the IRS, so if you fail to make your contribution by the April 15th deadline, don't just take the deduction and hope for the best. IRS computers can cross-check your return against contributions to verify the deduction.

The most important choice you make when you set up your account is your beneficiary. If you're married, it should almost always be your spouse.

Nondeductible IRAs

If you actively participate in an employer retirement plan and your income exceeds these limits, you can still contribute to a nondeductible IRA and get tax-deferred compounding without the up-front deduction. Use Form 8606 to report these contributions.

Keep a copy of each Form 8606 you file over the years. When you start taking money out, each withdrawal will include a nontaxable portion of your total nondeductible contribution. To figure this tax-free portion, divide the amount of nondeductible contributions by the total of all your IRA account balances. Each year, as you withdraw money, your "nondeductible balance" will shrink by the tax-free portions of each year's withdrawals. To figure future tax-free portions, divide the total of unrecovered nondeductible contributions.

> ▶ **Example:** In 1990, 1991, and 1992 you make a total of $6,000 in nondeductible contributions. Now the account is worth $20,000 and you'd like to take out $2,000. Since $6,000 of the $20,000 balance, or 30%, is from nondeductible contributions, 30% of your $2,000 withdrawal, or $600, is tax-free.
>
> Let's assume that next year, your account grows back to $20,000. You'd like to take out another $2,000. Since just $5,400 of your $20,000 balance, or 27%, remains from nondeductible contributions, 27% of your $2,000 withdrawal, or $540, is tax-free.

If it seems like a lot of work to keep track of nondeductible balances, you're right. Some advisers discourage nondeductible contributions for this reason. The answer depends on how organized you are. If you've still got your tax returns from waitressing in college, don't let the thought of a lifetime's worth of record keeping scare you off.

Spousal IRAs

Nonworking spouses can put up to $2,000 into a "spousal IRA." The couple's combined income, minus the working spouse's own IRA, is enough to cover the nonworking-spouse contribution. If the working spouse doesn't actively participate in an employer retirement plan, the nonworking spouse can contribute $2,000 regardless of the couple's income. If the working spouse does participate in an employer retirement plan, the nonworking spouse can contribute so long as the couple's adjusted gross income is $150,000 or less. Otherwise, the rules are the same as with ordinary IRAs.

OPEN A ROTH IRA FOR TAX-FREE INCOME

◆ ◆ ◆

Roth IRAs are a new form of IRA with a "back-end" tax advantage: Contributions aren't deductible, but withdrawals are tax-free if earnings are held in the account for at least five years and you have reached age 59½. Here's how they work:

◆ You can contribute to a Roth IRA, regardless of whether you participate in an employer plan, if you have earned income and your adjusted gross income is less than $110,000 ($160,000 for joint filers). Contributions are phased out between $95,000 and $110,000 ($150,000 and $160,000 for joint filers).

◆ You may contribute up to $2,000 of earned income to a Roth IRA.

◆ Roth IRA contributions are not deductible.

◆ You must contribute cash; you can't transfer securities from another account.

◆ You can, however, buy almost any investment into an IRA: bank deposits, stocks, bonds, mutual funds, real estate, mortgages and other loans, private placements, even limited partnerships. About the only things you can't buy are most collectibles (rugs, wine, stamps, and the like), and certain options and futures investments.

◆ It pays to contribute early. You can contribute as early as January 1 or as late as April 15 of the following year. If you contribute on January 1 and earn a steady 10.5% return, your contribution will already be worth $2,276 by the April 15 deadline.

◆ You can withdraw funds without taxes or penalties once you've reached age 59½ and held the funds in the Roth IRA for five *tax* years after the year in which you make your initial contribution.

▶ **Example:** On April 15, 2000, you open a Roth IRA for the 1999 tax year. The five-year period expires January 1, 2004, even though five calendar years haven't passed.

◆ Withdrawals within the five-year period are treated first as original deposits, then earnings. That means you can withdraw your original deposits without paying any tax. Once you start withdrawing earnings, you'll owe ordinary income tax plus the usual 10% penalty if you're under age 59½.

▶ **Example:** You contribute $2,000 per year for three years, and your account grows to $7,000. You can withdraw $6,000 (your original contribution) tax- and penalty-free. If you withdraw the $1,000 growth, you'll owe ordinary tax on that amount (because the account is less than five years old), plus the 10% penalty if you're under 59½.

◆ There are no required distributions from a Roth IRA as there are for a regular deductible IRA, nondeductible IRA, or spousal IRA. You can continue contributing to a Roth IRA even after reaching age 70½, as long as you have earned income.

◆ At death, your Roth IRA passes to your designated beneficiaries without passing through probate. Your beneficiaries can withdraw the entire balance, tax-free. Or they can leave the balance in the account up to five years or withdraw the money, tax-free, over their own life expectancies.

◆ Withdrawals from Roth IRAs should be tax-free in the majority of states that structure their tax code after the federal code, as well as those with no state income tax. However, some states will tax Roth IRA withdrawals as income, and some states may even tax the annual gain in the account. Many states may change their laws to permit the new accounts. But before you open an account, make sure your state tax law doesn't eliminate the advantage of the Roth account.

♦ Roth IRAs do not enjoy the same protection from creditors as ordinary IRAs. This may be important for business owners, high-risk professionals, or anyone else at risk of being sued.

CHOOSE THE RIGHT IRA

♦ ♦ ♦

Which IRA is best for you, the ordinary IRA with the up-front deduction or the Roth IRA with the tax-free income? The following table summarizes the main differences between the two. But choosing which account to fund depends on two questions: First, what is your tax rate now, compared to where it will be when you need the money? And sec-

IRA COMPARISON

	Deductible IRAs	**Roth IRA**
Highlights	♦ Up-front deduction ♦ Earnings grow tax-deferred ♦ Withdrawals taxed as ordinary income	♦ After-tax contributions ♦ Earnings grow tax-deferred ♦ Tax-free withdrawals
Eligibility	♦ Anyone not actively participating in a retirement plan ♦ Retirement-plan participants with AGIs under specified limits	♦ Anyone with AGI under $110,000 ($160,000 for joint filers)
Contributions	Up to $2,000	Up to $2,000
Withdrawals	Taxed as ordinary income at: ♦ Age 59½ ♦ Age 55 and retired ♦ Death ♦ Disability ♦ First-time home buyer ♦ Postsecondary education ♦ Medical expenses ♦ Annuitized withdrawals *10% penalty tax for:* ♦ Withdrawals before age 59½ (unless annuitized)	Tax free at: ♦ Age 59½ and earnings held in account for five tax years ♦ First-time home purchase ♦ College tuition ♦ Death ♦ Disability *10% penalty tax for:* ♦ Withdrawals before age 59½

ond, what will you do with the taxes you save if you take your deduction up front? The choice is easy if you don't qualify for a tax-deductible ordinary IRA. In that case, choose the Roth IRA if you can. But if you don't actively participate in an employer retirement plan, or if your income allows you to choose between an ordinary IRA and a Roth IRA, you have a dilemma.

Surprisingly, you'll net the same amount with identical investments whether you pay the tax now, as with a Roth IRA, or later, as with an ordinary IRA. Let's say you're in the 28% tax bracket and you have $2,000 to invest. You can invest the full $2,000, then pay tax on your withdrawal. Or you can pay $560 in tax, invest the remaining $1,440, then pay no tax on your withdrawal. Either way you'll net the same amount down the road. That's because you pay the same 28% on your principal today, with the Roth IRA, as you would on the future growth, as with the ordinary IRA.

The picture changes depending on what you do with your IRA tax savings. If you can afford to invest your savings, you'll have more money down the road by choosing the deductible IRA and stuffing your savings into a side fund. Let's say you have $2,000 of income to invest. You can invest the full $2,000 in an ordinary IRA, or $1,440 in a Roth IRA. But if you choose the deductible IRA, you'll have $560 in tax savings. If you can invest the tax savings in a side fund, you'll have more down the road with that choice. The after-tax withdrawal from the ordinary IRA gives you the same meat-and-potatoes as the tax-free withdrawal from the Roth IRA. The side fund gives you extra gravy, even invested in a taxable account.

Now let's say that you can afford to invest the full $2,000 in either account. This is an easy case. Your $2,000 investment grows to the same amount in either IRA. At the end, though, you'll owe tax on whatever you have in the ordinary IRA. There's no tax on whatever you have in the Roth IRA. Clearly, the Roth IRA wins. It wins even if you invest your $560 tax savings in a side fund. That's because most side funds will pay ordinary taxes. You could possibly even the race by investing your side fund in a tax-deferred vehicle such as a variable annuity. Still, the Roth IRA will almost always leave you with more.

The Roth IRA nets you more because it actually lets you invest more of your income. This is true even though the limit for both contributions is $2,000. Here's why. Let's say you're in the 28% tax bracket. If you contribute $2,000 to an ordinary IRA, it costs you just $1,440. That's because you get a $560 tax deduction. If you invest your tax savings as well, you get to invest $2,560. But it costs you just $2,000 of pretax income to make that $2,560 contribution.

Now let's say you contribute to a Roth IRA. Your contribution is the same $2,000 as with the ordinary IRA. But how much of your pretax income does it actually cost you to make that $2,000 contribution? In other words, how much do you have to earn, before tax, to make that $2,000 after-tax contribution? In the 28% tax bracket, it costs you $2,777.77. Of that amount $777.77 goes to taxes; the rest goes in the Roth IRA. We discussed earlier how your after-tax results are the same if your tax rates on *identical* investments are the same going in and going out. But here you have *different* investments. With the ordinary IRA, your investment pot is $2,560. With the Roth IRA, your pot is $2,777.77. Since taxes take the same percentage of both pots, the $2,777.77 pot naturally wins.

The picture also changes if your tax rates are different going in and going out. If your future tax rate will be lower, you'll be better off taking the high deduction now and paying the lower tax later. Take the deduction now when it's worth more. It makes no sense to pass up 28% now to save 15% down the road. Similarly, if your future tax rate will be higher, you'll wind up better forgoing a low deduction now and saving the higher tax later. Save the tax break for then. It makes no sense to save 15% now and then pay 28% down the road.

What's more, your money going in may get you a deduction now at your highest rate. But your money coming out will likely be taxed at your average rate. That's because your future withdrawals will make up a larger portion of your total income than your contributions today. Your $2,000 contribution today probably saves tax at your highest rate. It's not large enough to lower your tax bracket. But when you take money out down the road, you'll get the advantage of deductions, exemptions, and moving up through the brackets *before* you finally pay tax at your highest rate. So don't just look at your likely marginal rate for taking money out. Look at your likely *average* rate for a more realistic comparison.

Plenty of financial-services companies have created IRA "calculators" purporting to show you, down to the dollar, which choice is best for you. These are available for computers, as well as for plain old pencils and paper. The problem, of course, is that nobody knows what his or her future tax rate will be. Even if you're retired now, you can count on future tax-rate changes. These calculators are useful only when they show a dramatic difference in results. If you do choose to "crunch the numbers," run several comparisons using different future tax rates to see how changing assumptions affect your results.

> If your tax rate in retirement will be lower than your tax rate today, choose a deductible IRA for immediate tax savings. If your rate in retirement will be the same as your rate today, choose a deductible IRA if you can afford to invest your tax savings in a side fund. Finally, if your tax rate in retirement will be higher than it is today, choose the Roth IRA for tax-free income.

Convert Ordinary IRAs to Roth IRAs?

You can convert your existing IRA into a Roth IRA if your adjusted gross income is under $100,000. If you convert, you'll have to declare the value of your account on the date of conversion (minus any nondeductible contributions) as taxable income the year you convert. Should you take the offer? The answer here depends on the same issues as the choice between IRAs for new money. First, what will your tax bracket be when you take out the money, compared to what it is now? And second, where will you find the money to pay the tax?

First, let's see what happens if your tax rate stays the same. Let's assume your tax rate now is 28%. Down the road your withdrawals from an ordinary IRA will also be taxed at 28%. If you use part of your IRA balance to pay the tax you'll owe on conversion, there's no difference whether you pay tax now to convert, or wait until retirement. Remember, as long as the tax you pay now is the same as the tax you avoid in the future, it doesn't matter when you actually pay. Your after-tax total remains the same.

But if you can pay the tax from somewhere else, you'll have more money down the road by converting to a Roth IRA and paying your taxes from the outside source. Paying the tax from the outside source is like investing your tax savings in a side fund. It has the same effect as contributing that amount to the IRA now. Let's say you have $100,000 to convert. Your tax on the conversion will be $28,000. Paying the tax from an outside source will give you the same result down the road as if you had dumped that $28,000 into the IRA itself, then paid 28% tax on withdrawals down the road.

The picture changes again if your tax rates are different today and tomorrow. If your tax rate now is higher than it will be down the road, then don't convert. Why pay a high tax now to save a low tax down the road? And if your tax rate down the road will be higher, then do convert. Why not pay 15% now to save 28% later?

Unfortunately, you can't just look at marginal rates today versus tomorrow. There are two reasons for this.

♦ First, the amount you convert will probably be taxed at a *higher* rate than today's marginal rate. That's because you add the amount you convert to your regular taxable income. This extra income may be enough to push you into an even higher tax bracket. Why convert an enormous account, and add it to this year's income, if it means paying 39.6% today to save 28% or 31% down the road? The extra income might also be enough to phase out deductions and credits, or subject your Social Security benefits to tax. You might want to convert just part of your account each year, or wait for a year when you have less income elsewhere.

♦ Second, the future income you take from an ordinary IRA will probably be taxed at a *lower* rate than tomorrow's marginal rate. Remember, your IRA will grow over time. Your future withdrawals will make up a larger portion of your total income than your contributions today. Your $2,000 annual contribution probably saves tax at your highest rate. It's not enough to lower your tax bracket. But your future withdrawals won't all be taxed at your highest rate. If they make up a substantial portion of your total income, some will be taxed at less than your highest rate. So you need to know what your *average* rate will be when you take out your money.

Remember to consider these adjustments when you think about converting. Even if your present and future rates appear the same, they probably aren't. This means that conversion isn't as compelling as it appeared to be when the Roth IRA first appeared. And most Roth IRA "conversion calculators" are ill-equipped to consider these important adjustments.

Here are some final points to consider, clarified by the 1998 IRS restructuring act:

+ If you're under age 59½ and you withdraw money from your IRA account to pay the tax on the conversion, you'll owe the usual 10% penalty tax on that withdrawal.

+ If you're above age 70½, you'll have to include this year's required minimum distribution when calculating whether your adjusted gross income falls under the $100,000 limit. This will no longer be the case beginning in 2003.

+ If you could convert an ordinary IRA into a Roth IRA before age 59½ and immediately withdraw the converted amount balance as "principal," you still owe the usual 10% penalty tax on premature withdrawals of "earnings."

+ If you convert in 1998 and spread the tax bill over four years, then withdraw funds from the amount within that four-year period, you'll accelerate tax on the converted funds when you take your withdrawal.

> Consider converting your IRA if: (1) the tax you would pay on the conversion is less than the tax you would pay on an ordinary IRA withdrawal when you retire; (2) the income you report by converting doesn't significantly increase the tax you pay today; and (3) you can pay the tax with funds from outside the IRA itself. Also consider converting if you're rich enough that you'll never spend the money. Converting saves more for your heirs.

AVOID PENALTIES ON EARLY WITHDRAWALS

IRAs are intended as long-term retirement accounts, not merely tax-deferred savings accounts, so the IRS imposes a 10% penalty on most withdrawals before age 59½. Fortunately, there are several ways to access funds from your IRA without paying the 10% penalty.

+ There's no penalty to withdraw money at death or (more importantly for you) disability.

+ There's no penalty to withdraw money from a regular IRA (but not a Roth IRA) to pay for unreimbursed medical expenses (up to the amount allowed as a medical-expense deduction).

   This sounds like an attractive loophole, but it's really quite impractical. The medical-expense deduction is limited to medical expenses over 7.5% of adjusted gross income. But how do you know what your medical costs will be? And how do you know what your adjusted gross income will be? Don't forget, the amount you withdraw from the IRA is included in adjusted gross income, cutting your medical-expense deduction even further.

♦ There's no penalty for withdrawals of up to $10,000 (lifetime maximum) used within 120 days of the withdrawal for qualified acquisition costs of a first-time homebuyer's principal residence. For more information, see Chapter 3, Buying, Owning, and Selling Your Home.

♦ There's no penalty to withdraw money for higher-education expenses (including tuition, room and board, fees, books, supplies, supplies, and required equipment).

♦ There's no penalty to withdraw money if you're retired and over age 55.

♦ There's no penalty or tax to transfer money to a divorcing spouse under a qualified domestic-relation order. (For more information, see "Divorce," in Chapter 2.)

If you need money for just a short time, take it from your IRA and deposit it in a *different* IRA within 60 days. The redeposit qualifies as a rollover, and there will be no tax due at all. You can use this strategy once within a 12-month period.

Annuitize Your Account

If you need to withdraw funds from a regular IRA (but not a Roth IRA), you can avoid the 10% penalty if you "annuitize," or take the funds in a series of substantially equal payments over your life expectancy. You'll still owe ordinary tax on the withdrawals, but you'll avoid the 10% penalty. The biggest catch is that you have to keep withdrawing funds for five years or until you reach age 59½, whichever is longer.

There are three ways to calculate your withdrawal.

1. Life-Expectancy Method

To use this method, divide the balance of your IRA account by your life expectancy or the joint and last survivor expectancy of you and your designated beneficiary. You can recalculate this amount each year, or reduce your life expectancy by one for each year you make withdrawals. This method yields the smallest annual payment because it doesn't consider future earnings in the account.

> ♦ **Example:** You are 50 years old and your IRA balance is $100,000. Your life expectancy is 33.1 years. You may withdraw $3,021.15 without penalty.

2. Amortization Method

Amortize your IRA like a mortgage (using your single-life expectancy or the joint-and-last-survivor life expectancy of you and your designated beneficiary) and a reasonable long-term interest rate. This method yields larger withdrawals because it includes future earnings in the account (the interest rate selected).

> ♦ **Example:** You are 50 years old, your IRA balance is $100,000, and you set an 8% interest rate for amortization. One hundred thousand dollars amortized at 8% for 33.1 years yields $8,679 per year. You may withdraw $8,679 without penalty.

3. Annuity-Factor Method

This method works the same as the aforementioned amortization method, but lets you use insurance mortality tables showing a shorter life expectancy to withdraw an even larger amount per year.

Obviously, the amortization method and annuity-factor method require more work than the life-expectancy method. The point is, you can in fact withdraw substantial funds from your IRA before age 59½ without paying the 10% penalty. It's easier to do as you approach age 59½ because you can withdraw larger amounts for a shorter time. But the strategy is available for everyone.

Finally, if you own your home and you need more money than you can get with the annuitization method, you can combine early withdrawals with a home-equity loan to leverage your early withdrawals. Here's how it works: Take out a home-equity loan or line of credit and use the annuitization method to pay off the loan with IRA withdrawals. You'll avoid a huge up-front withdrawal, and your IRA will continue compounding tax-free. You'll pay ordinary income tax on your annual withdrawals. But interest up to $100,000 of your home-equity indebtedness may be tax deductible, offsetting the tax. See Chapter 3, Buying, Owning, and Selling Your Home.

> ▶ **Example:**   You're 50 years old with a $100,000 rollover from your 401(k), you've just been "downsized" from a management position with a large corporation, and you need $50,000 to buy a print-shop franchise. If you take out a 10-year home-equity loan at 8%, your annual payments will be $7,279.68. You can easily cover the payments by annuitizing your IRA under the aforementioned amortization method. The bulk of your IRA continues compounding for long-term growth, and you avoid a $5,000 penalty for a $50,000 early withdrawal.

If you take an early distribution subject to the 10% penalty and your IRA custodian or employer retirement plan administrator enters distribution code "1" on Box 7 of your 1099-R, report the income as a retirement plan distribution on your Form 1040 and enter 10% of the distribution as an additional tax where indicated. If your custodian or administrator reports a protected distribution and enters distribution code "2," "3," or "4" on Box 7 of your 1099-R, then report the distribution as ordinary income on your Form 1040. However, if your custodian or administrator does not enter distribution code "1," for a taxable early distribution, or does not enter distribution code "2," "3," or "4," for a protected distribution, file Form 5329 and attach it to your Form 1040 for that year.

START WITHDRAWALS BY AGE 70½

◆ ◆ ◆

Since IRAs are intended as retirement accounts, the IRS requires you to start withdrawing money from your regular deductible IRA, nondeductible IRA, or Spousal IRA by April 1 of the year after you reach age 70½. This date is called the "required beginning date."

LIFE EXPECTANCIES FOR ANNUITIES
AND MINIMUM REQUIRED DISTRIBUTIONS (SINGLE LIVES)

Age	Unisex Expectancy	Age	Unisex Expectancy
40	42.5	70	16.0
41	41.5	71	15.3
42	40.6	72	14.6
43	39.6	73	13.9
44	38.7	74	13.2
45	37.7	75	12.5
46	36.8	76	11.9
47	35.9	77	11.2
48	34.9	78	10.6
49	34.0	79	10.0
50	33.1	80	9.5
51	32.2	81	8.9
52	31.3	82	8.4
53	30.4	83	7.9
54	29.5	84	7.4
55	28.6	85	6.9
56	27.7	86	6.5
57	26.8	87	6.1
58	25.9	88	5.7
59	25.0	89	5.3
60	24.2	90	5.0
61	23.3	91	4.7
62	22.5	92	4.4
63	21.6	93	4.1
64	20.8	94	3.9
65	20.0	95	3.7
66	19.2	96	3.4
67	18.4	97	3.2
68	17.6	98	3.0
69	16.8	99	2.8

(Roth IRAs have no required minimum distributions.) Your minimum distribution depends on your account balance and life expectancy. You can certainly withdraw more, but many investors prefer to withdraw the minimum to preserve their principal for longer tax-deferred compounding. You can read entire books on taking money out of IRAs. This discussion will help you choose which method best suits your need for current income and your wishes regarding your heirs.

Calculating Your First Required Distribution

To calculate your minimum required distribution, start with the account balance as of December 31 of the year you reach age 70½. Then take your life expectancy (or the joint-and-last-survivor life expectancy of you and your beneficiary), as determined by your ages on your birthdays in the year *you* reach age 70½. (If your beneficiary is not your spouse, you may treat the beneficiary as being no more than ten years younger than you, even if the beneficiary is a child or grandchild.) Finally, divide the account balance by the life expectancy. If you have more than one IRA, you must calculate a required minimum distribution for each separate account. However, you can withdraw the required total from a single account.

You must take your first distribution by April 1 of the year after the year in which you reach age 70½. That distribution counts for the calendar year in which you reach age 70½. You must take your next distribution by December 31 of the same year. That second distribution is based on the same December 31 account balance, *minus* the amount of your first distribution.

> ▶ **Example:** Husband reaches age 70½ on August 1, 1998, and rings out the old year with $100,000 in his IRA. Husband's life expectancy at age 70 is 16.0 years. Husband must withdraw ¹⁄₁₆.₀ of his December 31, 1998, account balance, or $8,264, by April 1, 1999. His December 31, 1999, withdrawal will be based on a $91,736 account balance.

You can also take your required minimum distribution over your *joint* life expectancies of yourself and your designated beneficiary. The process works the same as the preceding example, except that you use your joint life expectancy to figure your withdrawals.

> ▶ **Example:** Husband reaches age 70½ on August 1, 1998. Wife turns 68 that same year. They ring out the old year with $100,000 in husband's IRA. Their joint life expectancy is 19.2 years. Husband must withdraw ¹⁄₁₉.₂ of his account, or $5,208, by April 1, 1999.

You can choose someone beside your spouse to figure your distributions. But if your nonspouse beneficiary is more than ten years younger, you have calculate your joint life expectancy as if your designated beneficiary were no more than ten years younger. This "Minimum Distribution Incidental Benefit" rule is supposed to make sure you use the IRA for your own retirement income, and not for estate planning.

If you've got more than one beneficiary, use the one with the shortest life expectancy to figure your joint life expectancy.

If you wait until the required beginning date to take money from your account, you'll have to take your second minimum distribution by December 31 of the *same* year. This will raise your adjusted gross income for figuring deductions and credits and may bump you into a higher tax bracket. If this will be the case, consider taking your required minimum distribution in the actual year in which you reach age 70½, rather than waiting until the next year's required beginning date.

Calculating Your Next Required Distributions

There are two ways to calculate withdrawals in later years.

◆ With the "straight-line" method, you (or you and your beneficiary) subtract one year from your life expectancy for each year. Using the joint life example above, husband must withdraw ¹⁄₁₉.₂ of his December 31, 1998, account balance by April 1, 1999. He must withdraw ¹⁄₁₈.₂ of his December 31, 1998, account balance (minus the first withdrawal) by December 31, 1999; ¹⁄₁₇.₂ of his December 31, 1999, account balance by December 31, 2000; and so on.

◆ With the "recalc" method, you (or you and your beneficiary) recalculate your life expectancy each year. Using the same example, husband and wife have joint life expectancies of 19.2 years in 1998, 18.5 years in 1999, and 17.8 years in 2000. Husband must withdraw ¹⁄₁₉.₂ of his December 31, 1998, account balance by April 1, 1999. He must withdraw ¹⁄₁₈.₅ of his December 31, 1998, account balance (minus the first withdrawal) by December 31, 1999; ¹⁄₁₇.₈ of his December 31, 1999, account balance by December 31, 2000; and so on.

◆ If you're really ambitious, you can use the straight-line method for one spouse and the recalc method for the other. This will make sure you don't run out of money during your lifetime.

If you don't withdraw the required minimum, you'll owe a penalty equal to 50% of how much you didn't withdraw. Let's say you're 72 years old. Your IRA balance requires you to take $20,000. If you take just $12,000, you'll owe $3,000 tax on the $6,000 more you should have taken out.

The "recalc" method lets you make smaller withdrawals now. But the difference isn't dramatic, especially in the early years. And the recalc method has one big problem: *The year after you die, your life expectancy drops to zero.* This is a big problem if you want to leave as much as you can to your heirs.

PRESERVE YOUR TAX DEFERRAL BEYOND THE GRAVE

❖ ❖ ❖

When you die, your IRA passes to your designated beneficiary without passing through probate. Your tax consequences depend on whether you've reached the required beginning date and whom you've named as your beneficiary.

If you die before the required beginning date and:

- If you haven't named a beneficiary, your entire account must be distributed by the end of the fifth calendar year after the calendar year of your death.

- If you've named a beneficiary, he or she has to start taking money by the end of the first calendar year after your death. Some plans require the beneficiary to take the entire amount by the end of the fifth year after the year of death. Other plans let the beneficiary take the balance over the beneficiary's life expectancy.

- If your beneficiary is your spouse, he or she can treat the account as his or her own. Distributions can wait until April 1 of the year after the year your spouse reaches age 70½.

- If the account is a Roth IRA, your designated beneficiaries can withdraw the entire balance tax-free, leave it in the account for five years, or withdraw the account balance over their own life expectancies. If the beneficiary is your spouse, he or she can choose to treat the account as his or her own and choose new beneficiaries.

If you die after the required beginning date, distributions after your death have to continue at least as quickly as they would have during your life.

- If you chose the straight-line method for figuring distributions, your beneficiary continues to take distributions according to your original individual or joint life expectancy.

- If you chose the recalc method, the year after you die, *your* life expectancy drops to zero. If you took distributions over your individual life expectancy, the entire account must be distributed (and taxed) by the end of the year after the year you die. If you and your beneficiary took distributions over your joint life expectancy, your beneficiary continues taking distributions according to your beneficiary's individual life expectancy. Your beneficiary cannot name a new beneficiary and extend the payout period (except for your spouse).

- If you chose your spouse as your beneficiary, your spouse may treat the entire account as his or her own IRA. This works whether your spouse has reached the required beginning date, and even works if you (but not your spouse) have chosen the recalc method for taking withdrawals.

For maximum tax deferral, strap on your helmet. Here's how to create a "stretchout" IRA for generations of tax-deferred compounding:

- Designate your spouse as beneficiary.

- When you begin taking withdrawals, calculate your joint life expectancy using the straight-line method. (You can use the recalc method for the spouse likeliest to die first and the straight-line method for the spouse likeliest to die last. This can ensure that you don't run out of money during your lifetime. But it can backfire if the wrong spouse dies first.)

- At the first death, surviving spouse takes over the IRA but keeps the account in the decedent's name as "Spouse, deceased, for benefit of surviving Spouse."

- Surviving spouse then selects a new beneficiary, most likely a child or grandchild, and calculates new withdrawals based on their joint life expectancy (remember, you can treat the new beneficiary as only ten years younger).

- When surviving spouse dies, new beneficiary starts withdrawing money according to the true joint life expectancy, minus the number of payments already taken. The account continues compounding tax-deferred until new beneficiary dies.

▶ **Example:**   Husband, age 70, and wife, age 68, begin withdrawing funds over their joint life expectancy of 19.2 years. They take $\frac{1}{19.2}$ of the account balance for the first year and $\frac{1}{18.2}$ of the account balance for the next year. Husband dies. Wife takes over the account as "Husband, deceased, for benefit of Wife." Wife chooses 42-year-old son as her beneficiary. Their true joint life expectancy is 33.4 years. But wife can treat son as being only ten years younger, so they calculate their joint life expectancy at 22.0 years. The first year, they withdraw $\frac{1}{22}$ of the account balance. The next year, they withdraw $\frac{1}{21}$ of the account balance, and so on. Wife dies at age 80 after eight years of withdrawals. Son takes over the account in his name. Son's life expectancy for purposes of this account equals 33.4 years (the true joint life expectancy at the time wife [his mother] designated him beneficiary) minus 8 years (the number of payments already taken), or 23.4 years. His first withdrawal is $\frac{1}{23.4}$ of the account balance, and he can continue compounding tax-deferred until he's in his seventies.

If you don't have a spouse, designate your children or other heirs as beneficiaries and calculate withdrawals over your joint life expectancies (with a maximum age difference of ten years). At your death, the beneficiary takes over the account and continues withdrawing funds at the true joint life expectancy minus the number of payments already taken. This can also yield decades of tax-deferred compounding.

This "stretchout IRA" may be the single most profitable strategy in the entire *Tax Planner*. A $100,000 IRA compounding at 10.5% per year can balloon to $542,000 over the next 40 years of your children's lives. That same $100,000 "blown up" at death and compounding at 10.5% outside the IRA grows to just $326,000. This single choice can mean literally hundreds of thousands of dollars for your family. Of course, $100,000 40 years from now isn't the same as $100,000 today. But it's still an important consideration.

If Your Beneficiary Is a Trust or Charity

These strategies all depend on designating a beneficiary with an ascertainable life expectancy. What if your one of your beneficiaries is a trust or charity with no life expectancy? If you're not careful, taxes will be due at death and these strategies will fail.

You can designate a trust as IRA beneficiary without blowing up the account. It's usually done to take advantage of the full unified credit exemption equivalent ($625,000 in 1998) in estates consisting largely of an IRA (by leaving the IRA to the marital deduction bypass trust). You can designate an irrevocable trust as beneficiary if it meets these five requirements:

+ The trust must be valid under state law.
+ It must be irrevocable as of April 1 following the year the owner reaches 70½.
+ It must have only people as beneficiaries, not corporations, estates, other trusts, or charities.
+ The individual beneficiaries must be specifically identifiable from the trust document.
+ Finally, the IRA sponsor must have a copy of the trust document.

You can also designate a revocable trust as a beneficiary as long as the trust becomes irrevocable at the beneficiary's death. These trusts include the popular living trusts that so many taxpayers have adopted to avoid probate.

If you plan to leave just a part of your account to charity, you can split your IRA into separate accounts, leaving one to charity and additional accounts to individual beneficiaries.

Obviously, it's important to make sure your IRA custodian permits multiple accounts and stretchout IRAs. Also, some financial advisers (and many mutual-fund customer service reps at the other end of the "800" number) aren't familiar with these strategies. Make sure that your advisers are.

MANAGING YOUR NEST EGG

❖ ❖ ❖

Congratulations! You've worked hard, lived a clean life, and built up a hell of a nest egg. Now it's time to reward yourself. Whether you dream of golf in the sun, a condo on the beach, or getting big in the grandchild business, your tax and investment choices play a big part in your quality of retirement.

Managing your nest egg means more than simply choosing how much to take from your IRA. It means holding appropriate investments in appropriate accounts, considering the effect that your income has on Social Security benefits, and making sure your money lasts as long as you need it to. If you want to leave a ton for your heirs, then managing your nest egg means considering them as well. If you're interested in spending it all, then you want to make sure your last check bounces—the day *after* you die.

If most of your savings are in your retirement accounts, there's not much choice where you'll find your retirement income. You'll pay ordinary tax on your withdrawals, regardless of what investments are in your account. But if you have funds invested outside tax-deferred accounts, from additional savings or an inheritance, you'll have to choose which funds to tap first. Here are some guidelines:

◆ If you want to make your savings last as long as possible, spend your taxable funds first. Tax deferral means that your tax-deferred accounts will grow larger than your taxable accounts. Once you start taking money out of your tax-deferred accounts, you'll pay more tax than if you had raised the same amount of tax by liquidating principal from a taxable account. But tax deferral will make your money last longer.

◆ If you want to maximize the amount you leave to your heirs, consider tapping tax-deferred accounts first. At your death, your heirs will receive your taxable property with a stepped-up basis equal to its value at your date of death. Retirement plans and tax-deferred annuities get no stepped-up basis. However, if you use stretchout IRAs, as described later, and you can trust your heirs not to raid the cookie jar, the additional years of tax deferral can justify spending down your taxable accounts.

◆ If your taxable account consists of individual stocks you plan to hold forever, spend down your tax-deferred funds. Your individual stocks grow tax-deferred until you sell them. Since you pay no current tax on the gain, the only disadvantage relative to taxable accounts is the tax you'll pay on the dividends. When you die, your heirs will enjoy the stepped-up basis your tax-deferred accounts can't give.

This strategy carries its own risks if you have to sell your stocks unexpectedly. Most investment experts will tell you there's no such thing as a "one-decision" stock you can hold forever. All companies go through lean periods when their stock lags alternative investments. You might be able to earn a higher after-tax return by transferring assets elsewhere. Remember, the point of investing is to earn the highest after-tax return.

◆ If your retirement income is high enough to phase out your Social Security income, consider consuming principal from your taxable accounts to generate cash while preserving your Social Security. Yes, your mother told you never to spend your principal. But if she's so smart, how come she isn't rich?

◆ If your 97-year-old grandma's still around to warn you against outliving your money, invest a part of your nest egg in an immediate annuity. This will insure that there's income available no matter how long you live. Today's contracts offer far more flexibility than the plain-vanilla contracts of yesterday.

Make the Most of Social Security
◆ ◆ ◆

Social Security has evolved from an old-age insurance program into a mainstream retirement-income supplement. Today it provides a modest retirement income that increases with the cost of living. It won't pay for a life of luxury, but it can boost your income enough to make a difference. For most taxpayers, Social Security presents these questions: First, when should you start collecting benefits? Second, how can you hold down tax on those benefits?

For that matter, should you count on Social Security at all? It's fashionably cynical to dismiss Social Security as a dinosaur, doomed to collapse under demographic weight. This view holds that the system can't possibly support all the baby boomers due to retire. These skeptics ignore two important political facts: (1) old people vote, and (2) Washington knows it. And, in fact, Social Security is far sounder than the skeptics realize. The system is now expected to start running out of money in 2029. But four simple reforms can keep it running well over 75 years.

- Raise the retirement age and index it to life expectancy.
- Add the contributions of state and local employees not currently covered by the system.
- Raise the wage base (from its current $68,400 to perhaps $90,000) and adjust benefits for high-income earners to reflect their higher contributions.
- Tax beneficiaries on all income once the person's original contribution is recovered.

What's more, any attempt to convert the program from "pay as you go" would force current workers to perform the impossible feat of saving more for their own retirement while supporting today's retirees.

When Should You Start Collecting Benefits?

You can start collecting Social Security any time after you reach age 62. At age 65, you become eligible for "full" benefits, and you can increase your benefit even further by waiting until age 70. When should you start collecting benefits to make the most of your Social Security?

Actuarially, it makes sense to start collecting benefits as soon as you can. Take the money and sock it away, then start paying yourself when you actually retire. Even at reduced rates, the money you get for the extra years can more than make up for the percentage you lose after age 65. And what if you don't live long enough to collect the extra benefits? Not all of us will live to see age 90. If you start collecting at age 62, you'll get 80% of what your benefit would be at age 65. If you wait until age 65, it will take 12 years before the extra 20% per year exceeds the benefit you receive between ages 62 and 65. When you consider the time value of money—the fact that a dollar of benefit paid today is worth more than a dollar of benefit paid sometime down the road—it generally takes until age 80 before you break even waiting to collect the full benefit at age 65. (This age is scheduled to begin increasing to 67 in 2002.)

However, there's a special tax penalty you'll pay if you're under age 70 and you still work while you collect Social Security. You'll need to consider this penalty if you plan to work while you collect benefits. There's no penalty for investment or pension income. You can draw $1 million from your IRA without docking your Social Security. The penalty applies to earned income from wages, salaries, commissions, and self-employment income. If you're between ages 65 and 70, you'll lose $1 in benefits for every $3 your earnings exceed the limit. If you're under age 65, you'll lose $1 in earnings for every $2 in earnings. The penalty can wipe out the advantage of starting early, particularly if you work between ages 62 and 65.

SOCIAL SECURITY EARNINGS LIMITS

Year	1999	2000	2001	2002 and beyond
Earnings Limit	$15,500	$17,000	$25,000	$30,000

There are several strategies you can use to hold down earned income if you own your own business. You can pay yourself in the form of loans, rents, or equipment leases, rather than straight earned income. You can create a special class of stock, or consider selling shares back to the business. However, the Social Security Administration may ask you to file a Self-Employment Corporate Officer Questionnaire to verify that you're actually retired and not simply dodging the penalty.

If you plan to earn income while you receive benefits, be sure to include this benefit reduction in your plans. It's actually possible to *lose* money by working while you collect benefits.

Avoid Tax on Your Benefits

Social Security is intended as a "backup" retirement income along with pension plans and personal savings. You don't owe tax on your benefits unless your "provisional income" exceeds certain limits. Provisional income includes regular taxable income, tax-exempt interest income, and 50% of your Social Security benefits. You'll owe tax on 50% of your benefits if your provisional income exceeds $25,000 ($32,000 for joint filers). You'll owe tax on 85% of your benefits if your provisional income exceeds $34,000 ($44,000 for joint filers). This extra tax can be a real blow to your income, as well as artificially spiking your tax bracket. A single dollar of income can mean $1.85 in extra taxable income. If your federal and state combined rate is 33%, you'll owe 61 cents tax on that extra dollar of income.

These worksheets, adapted from IRS Publication 915, will help you figure how much of your Social Security benefit is taxable:

PROVISIONAL INCOME

1. Income: From Form 1040, add Lines 7, 8a, 8b, 9–14,
   15b, 16b, 17–19, and 21   _____

2. Exclusions: tax-free foreign earned income and
   housing, qualifying U.S. Savings Bond interest used
   for tuition, employer-provided adoption benefits,
   and income earned as a bona fide resident of
   Puerto Rico or American Samoa   _____

3. Add Line 1 and Line 2   _____

4. Adjustments from Form 1040, Line 31
   (other than foreign housing)   _____

5. Subtract Line 4 from Line 3   _____

6. 50% of Social Security income   _____

7. Provisional income: Lines 5 and 6   _____

TAXABLE BENEFITS

Check one:

___ A. Single, head of household, or qualifying widow(er)

___ B. Married/Joint

___ C. Married/Separate and LIVED WITH your spouse at ANY TIME during the year

___ D. Married/Separate and LIVED APART from your spouse FOR ALL of the year

1. Provisional income   _____

2. Base amount 1   _____
    A: $25,000   B: $32,000   C: $0   D: $25,000

3. Subtract Line 2 from Line 1   _____
    If zero or less, your Social Security isn't taxable.

4. 50% of Line 3   _____

5. 50% of Social Security income   _____

6. Base amount 2   _____
    A: $34,000   B: $44,000   C: $0   D: $34,000

7. Subtract Line 6 from Line 1   _____
    If zero or less, go to Line 13 now.

8. Base amount 3   _____
    A: $4,500   B: $6,000   C: $0   D: $4,500

9. Enter the smallest of Lines 4, 5, and 8   _____

10. Multiply Line 7 by 85% (.85)   _____

11. Add Lines 9 and 10   _____

12. 85% of Social Security income   _____

13. Taxable Social Security: _____
    If Line 7 is zero, enter the smaller of Line 4 and Line 5.
    If Line 7 is more than zero, enter the smaller of Line 11 and Line 12.
    Enter your net Social Security income and taxable amount on Form 1040.

If your provisional income clearly tops these thresholds, these steps just make your taxes more complicated. If you're close to the threshold, though, there are strategies you can use to cut your provisional income and preserve your benefits from tax. The answer is to take your income from sources that don't increase your provisional income:

- ◆ Immediate annuities pay tax-advantaged income because a portion of each payment consists of return of principal. Only the taxable part of your payment adds to your provisional income. For more information, see Chapter 10, Life Insurance and Annuities.

- ◆ Fixed and variable annuities grow tax-deferred until you take your gains from the contract. Fixed annuities resemble bank CDs in a tax-deferred wrapper; variable annuities resemble a family of mutual funds, also in a tax-deferred wrapper. But annuity growth doesn't add to provisional income unless you withdraw your gains from the contract.

- ◆ Roth IRA distributions are completely tax-free unless you withdraw funds before the five-year holding period or age 59½. Roth IRA distributions don't add to your provisional income. This makes Roth IRAs more valuable than regular IRAs if your provisional income is near the tax threshold. It can also make sense to convert some or all of your regular IRA to a Roth IRA, even if the income "spike" in the year you convert subjects all of that year's benefits to tax. For more information, see the preceding discussion of Roth IRAs.

- ◆ You can draw income from a home-equity line of credit or margin account without realizing taxable income. The interest you pay may be less than the Social Security you forfeit.

- ◆ Low-income housing tax credits boost your spendable income without increasing provisional income. For more information, see Chapter 9, Real Estate.

If you're right on the edge at the end of the year, consider liquidating principal or use the strategies for avoiding tax on capital gains rather than drawing taxable income. For more information, see Chapter 6, Tax-Advantaged Investments to Meet Your Needs.

THIRTEEN

PUT CASH
IN YOUR NEXT PAYCHECK

NOW THAT YOU'VE LEARNED how to cut your tax to the bone, it's time to claim your savings. Why wait for your money when you can put extra cash in your paycheck? The average taxpayer's biggest mistake is letting the IRS withhold too much. Two-thirds of taxpayers wind up with refunds averaging over $1,300. Sure, you get the money back when you finally file your return. But you lose the chance to use the money throughout the course of the year. You can earn extra income if you invest that money monthly. Or you can save yourself a ton of credit-card interest.

Some people use their tax refund as a way to force themselves to save. But this is lousy discipline because the IRS gets the "float." Consider "paying yourself first" and writing a regular check to an investment account. If that's too hard, most mutual funds will set up monthly transfers out of your checking account. Every month the fund will take your "overpayment" and put it to work. If you record your paycheck deposits minus that monthly investment, you'll never see it and never miss it.

This chapter teaches you how to file a new Form W-4 with your employer to adjust your withholding and start seeing those tax savings in your paycheck. If you file quarterly estimates, you learn how to adjust your quarterly estimates. Finally, if you've learned something you could have used to cut your taxes in *previous* years, you learn how to file an amended return to claim those old overpayments.

PUT CASH IN YOUR NEXT PAYCHECK

◆ ◆ ◆

If taxpayers actually had to write checks for their tax bills, the revolt would make the Boston Tea Party look like—well, a tea party. The vast majority of us pay our taxes through employer withholding. Our employer thoughtfully deducts taxes from our pay and sends them directly to the IRS, cutting out the middleman. Yes, that makes us the "middleman" for spending our own pay. Withholding is actually an efficient way to collect taxes. It cuts down on time and paperwork, it ensures that tax deposits are filed regularly and timely, and it saves us the time and effort of filing our payments. It also gives rise to the annual "refund" for taxpayers who send in too much.

Withholding began during World War II, when the government needed cash to finance the war. Before withholding, taxpayers calculated their tax at the close of the year, then sent in their tax in a single check. As the war effort grew, the government needed a quick source of cash. Economists hit upon withholding to provide a fast, steady source of cash.

Tax withholding is now a familiar burden. Can you forget receiving your first paycheck—and wincing, if not crying, when you saw how much you lost to taxes? (And what the heck is FICA, anyway?) Still, most taxpayers are surprised to learn just how much control they have over withholding. Employers withhold according to IRS tables according to filing status. But *you* tell your employer how much to withhold.

Withholding tells your employer how much you intend to report in taxable income. Each personal exemption cuts your tax by the same amount as that much in deductions. Your employer already knows how much you make. Extra income from spouses, investments, and sideline jobs increase your final figure. Deductions, losses, and credits cut your bill. Your goal when you file your W-4 is to tell them how much you'll really pay tax on. Start with your salary. Then add or subtract whatever number of $2,700 "exemption equivalents" it takes to reach your taxable income. Your employer then withholds however much it takes to pay your bill. If your income is substantially higher than what your employer pays, you have two choices. You can direct your employer to withhold whatever extra it takes to pay your bill. Or you can make additional quarterly payments.

Don't underestimate the power of that $2,700 exemption. If you're in the 28% bracket, a single additional exemption will save you $63 per month. That's cash that you can spend—or invest—as soon as you earn it, without waiting months for an IRS refund.

Of course, you can't just wipe out your withholding throughout the year. You'll need to make sure you deposit a certain amount by the end of the tax year to avoid penalties for underwithholding. Here are the safe-harbor amounts:

◆ If your adjusted gross income is $150,000 or less, you'll need to withhold 100% of this year's tax or 90% of last year's.

◆ If your adjusted gross income is $150,000 or more, you'll need to withhold 100% of this year's tax or 110% of last year's.

If you overstate deductions and credits, or understate your income, you can wind up owing a $500 civil penalty. If you supply false information, there's a $1,000 criminal penalty, plus possible jail time. So you want to do this right. Do what it takes to avoid a refund. But don't get greedy.

You should review your withholding any time your tax picture changes.

◆ If you have a baby (or adopt a child), file a new W-4 with an additional exemption as early as possible in the year the child will be born.

◆ If you or your spouse take a new job, complete the worksheets to file a correct W-4 to reflect the additional income.

◆ If you or your spouse receive a significant salary raise, review your situation to see if enough tax will be withheld.

◆ If there will be a significant change in your itemized deductions, such as purchase of a new house, check to see if your withholding will be enough.

◆ If you get a divorce, file a new W-4 as soon as possible in the year your filing status changes.

◆ If there's a death in the family, you should file a new W-4 for the *following* tax year.

Your employer has to make your new W-4 effective by the start of the first payroll period ending on or after the thirtieth day after you submit your form.

The following worksheets, adapted from IRS Publication 919, "Is My Withholding Correct?", will help you calculate your most accurate withholding. If you file a joint return, enter combined amounts for all items. Worksheet 1 will help calculate your tax. Worksheet 2 will help calculate proper withholding for your particular tax bill. Worksheets 3 through 5 will make necessary adjustments for itemized-deduction and personal-exemption phaseouts, net capital gains, and self-employment tax. If your income includes a significant amount of capital gains, consult Publication 919.

Worksheet 1. 1999 Tax Worksheet *(Note: Enter combined amounts if married filing joint return.)*

1. Enter amount of Adjusted Gross Income (AGI) you expect in 1999. (AGI means wages, interest, dividends, alimony received, and all other income **minus** adjustments to income, such as alimony paid, interest on education loans, and deductible contributions to an IRA.) **1**	
2. • If you plan to itemize deductions, enter the estimated total of your deductions allowable after applying any limits, such as the 7.5% limit on medical expenses. **(Caution:** If the amount on line 1 is more than $126,600 ($63,300 if married filing separately), use Worksheet 4 to figure the amount to enter here.) • If you do not plan to itemize deductions, enter the amount of your standard deduction from the *1999 Standard Deduction Tables*, later **2**	
3. Subtract line 2 from line 1. Enter the difference here. (If zero or less, enter zero.) **3**	
4. Exemptions. Multiply $2,750 by the number of exemptions you plan to claim. If you can be claimed as a dependent on another person's return, you cannot claim an exemption for yourself.* **(Caution:** If the amount on line 1 is more than the amount shown below for your 1999 filing status, use Worksheet 5 to figure the amount to enter here.) . . . . **4** • Single, $126,600 • Married filing jointly or Qualifying widow(er), $189,950 • Head of household, $158,300 • Married filing separately, $94,975 * *This applies even if the other person will not claim your exemption or the exemption will be reduced or eliminated under the exemption phaseout rule.*	
5. Subtract line 4 from line 3. (If zero or less, enter zero.). **5**	
6. Tax. Figure your tax on the amount on line 5 by using the 1999 Tax Rate Schedules later in this publication. DO NOT use the Tax Table or Tax Rate Schedules in the 1998 tax return instructions. **(Caution:** If the amount on line 1 includes a net capital gain, you have to use Worksheet 6 to figure the amount to enter here.). **6**	
7. Enter additional taxes (those figured on Forms 8814 and 4972) **7**	
8. Add lines 6 and 7 . . . . **8**	
9. Credits (includes child tax credit, higher education credits (Hope and lifetime learning), credit for child and dependent care expenses, credit for the elderly or disabled, credit for foreign taxes, etc.) See *Tax Credits* **9**	
10. Subtract line 9 from line 8. (If zero or less, enter zero.). **10**	
11. Self-employment tax. Estimate of 1999 self-employment income $ _____ Multiply self-employment income by .153 (15.3%). **(Caution:** If the estimated total of wages and self-employment income is more than $72,600, use Worksheet 7 to figure the amount to enter here.) **11**	
12. Other taxes (includes tax on early distributions from an IRA, alternative minimum tax, etc.) **12**	
13. Total taxes. Add lines 10 through 12. Enter the total here and on line 1 of Worksheet 2 below **13**	

Worksheet 2. 1999 Withholding Worksheet *(Note: Enter combined amounts if married filing joint return.)*

1. Enter your total taxes from line 13 of Worksheet 1 . . . . **1**	
2. Total federal income tax withheld to date in 1999 (include all jobs). **2**	
3. Tax withholding expected for the rest of 1999: For each job, multiply the amount of federal income tax now being withheld each payday by the number of paydays remaining in 1999 and enter the combined amount for all jobs . **3**	
4. Total expected tax withholding for all paydays in 1999. Add lines 2 and 3 . . . . . . **4**	
5. Subtract line 4 from line 1. If the result is positive, too little tax is being withheld. Go to line 6. If the result is negative, too much tax may be being withheld. Stop here and see *Too much tax withheld?* . **5**	
6. Divide line 5 by the number of paydays remaining in 1999 and enter the result. This is the additional amount you should have withheld from your pay each payday. **6**	

Worksheet 3. **Worksheet for Tax Credits**

Child Tax Credit

1. Enter the number of children eligible for the Child Tax Credit	**1**	
2. Multiply the number on line 1 by $500		**2**
3. Enter your modified adjusted gross income (see page 3)	**3**	
4. Enter: – $ 75,000 if you file as "single" or "head of household"		
– $110,000 if you are "married filing jointly" or		
– $ 55,000 if you are "married filing separately"	**4**	
5. Subtract line 4 from line 3. If less than zero, enter zero	**5**	
6. Divide line 5 by $1,000. Increase any fraction to the next larger whole number	**6**	
7. Multiply line 6 by $50		**7**
8. Subtract line 7 from line 2. If less than zero, enter zero		**8**

Higher Education Credits: Hope Credit

Note: *Complete lines 9 through 13 for each student and enter the total for all students on line 14.*

9. Enter the eligible amount paid in 1999	**9**	
10. Enter the lesser of line 9 or $2,000	**10**	

Note: *If the amount on line 10 is $2,000, skip lines 11 through 13, and enter $1,500 on line 14.*

11. Enter the lesser of $1,000 or the amount on line 10	**11**	
12. Subtract line 11 from line 10	**12**	
13. Multiply the amount on line 12 by 50%	**13**	
14. Add lines 11 and 13	**14**	

Higher Education Credits: Lifetime Learning Credit

15. Enter the eligible amount paid in 1999	**15**	
16. Enter the lesser of line 15 or $5,000	**16**	
17. Multiply the amount on line 16 by 20%	**17**	

Allowable Education Credits

18. Add lines 14 and 17	**18**	
19. Enter: $100,000 if married filing jointly; $50,000 if single, head of household, or qualifying widow(er)	**19**	
20. Enter your modified AGI	**20**	
21. Subtract line 20 from line 19. If line 20 is equal to or more than line 19, **stop;** you cannot take any education credits	**21**	
22. Enter $20,000 if married filing jointly; $10,000 if single, head of household, or qualifying widow(er)	**22**	
23. If line 21 is equal to or more than line 22, enter the amount from line 18 on line 24 and go to line 25. If line 21 is less than line 22, divide line 21 by line 22. Enter the result as a decimal (rounded to at least three places)	**23**	
24. Multiply line 8 by line 23	**24**	
25. Enter your expected tax	**25**	
26. Enter the total, if any, of your credits for child and dependent care expenses and for the elderly or the disabled	**26**	
27. Subtract line 26 from line 25. If line 26 is equal to or more than line 25, **stop;** you cannot take any education credits	**27**	
28. Education credits. Enter the **smaller** of line 24 or line 27 ▶	**28**	

Other Credits

29. Enter the estimated amount of your other tax credits, including the child and dependent care credit, the earned income tax credit, the credit for the elderly and disabled, the adoption credit, and the foreign tax credit	**29**	

TOTALS

30. Total estimated tax credits. Add lines 8, 28 and 29	**30**	
31. Enter the appropriate number from one of the credit tables on page 5:		
– Use the table which matches your filing status		
– Find the line in the table that matches your total income		
– Then, enter here the amount shown next to your income	**31**	
32. Multiply line 30 by line 31. Enter the result here and include it in the total on Form W-4, page 2, Deductions and Adjustments Worksheet, Line 5	**32**	

1999 Tax Rate Schedules

Caution: *Do not use these Tax Rate Schedules to figure your 1998 taxes. Use only to figure your 1999 estimated taxes.*

Single—Schedule X

If line 5 is: Over—	But not over—	The tax is:		of the amount over—
$0	$25,750	.... 15%		$0
25,750	62,450	$3,862.50 +	28%	25,750
62,450	130,250	14,138.50 +	31%	62,450
130,250	283,150	35,156.50 +	36%	130,250
283,150	....	90,200.50 +	39.6%	283,150

Head of household—Schedule Z

If line 5 is: Over—	But not over—	The tax is:		of the amount over—
$0	$34,550	.... 15%		$0
34,550	89,150	$5,182.50 +	28%	34,550
89,150	144,400	20,470.50 +	31%	89,150
144,400	283,150	37,598.00 +	36%	144,400
283,150	....	87,548.00 +	39.6%	283,150

Married filing jointly or Qualifying widow(er)—Schedule Y-1

If line 5 is: Over—	But not over—	The tax is:		of the amount over—
$0	$43,050	.... 15%		$0
43,050	104,050	$6,457.50 +	28%	43,050
104,050	158,550	23,537.50 +	31%	104,050
158,550	283,150	40,432.50 +	36%	158,550
283,150	....	85,288.50 +	39.6%	283,150

Married filing separately—Schedule Y-2

If line 5 is: Over—	But not over—	The tax is:		of the amount over—
$0	$21,525	.... 15%		$0
21,525	52,025	$3,228.75 +	28%	21,525
52,025	79,275	11,768.75 +	31%	52,025
79,275	141,575	20,216.25 +	36%	79,275
141,575	....	42,644.25 +	39.6%	141,575

Worksheet 4 — Itemized Deductions Limit

Use this worksheet to figure the amount to enter on line 2 of Worksheet 1 — 1999 Tax Worksheet.

1. Enter the estimated total of your itemized deductions allowable after applying any limits . . . . _____
2. Enter the amount included in line 1 for medical and dental expenses, investment interest, casualty and theft losses, and gambling losses . . . . _____
3. Subtract line 2 from line 1 . . . . . . _____

Note. *If the amount on line 3 is zero, stop here and enter on line 2 of Worksheet 1 the larger of the amount from line 1 of this worksheet or your standard deduction.*

4. Multiply the amount on line 3 by .80 . . _____
5. Enter the amount from line 1 of Worksheet 1 . . . . _____
6. Enter $126,600 ($63,300 if married filing separately) . . . . _____
7. Subtract line 6 from line 5 . . . . . . _____

Note. *If the amount on line 7 is zero or less, stop here and enter on line 2 of Worksheet 1 the larger of the amount from line 1 of this worksheet or your standard deduction.*

8. Multiply the amount on line 7 by .03 . . _____
9. Enter the smaller of line 4 or line 8 . . . _____
10. Subtract line 9 from line 1. Enter the result here and on line 2 of Worksheet 1 . . . _____

Worksheet 5 — Exemptions Phaseout

Use this worksheet to figure the amount to enter on line 4 of Worksheet 1 — 1999 Tax Worksheet.

1. Multiply $2,750 by the number of exemptions you plan to claim. . . . . _____
2. Enter the amount from line 1 of Worksheet 1 . . . . _____
3. Enter:
   $126,600 if single
   $189,950 if married filing jointly or qualifying widow(er)
   $94,975 if married filing separately
   $158,300 if head of household . . . _____
4. Subtract line 3 from line 2. If zero or less, do not use this worksheet. See the instructions on line 4 of Worksheet 1 . _____

Note: *If line 4 is more than $122,500 (more than $61,250 if married filing separately),* **stop;** *you* **cannot** *take a deduction for exemptions. Enter -0- on line 4 of Worksheet 1.*

5. Divide the amount on line 4 by $2,500 ($1,250 if married filing separately). If the result is not a whole number, increase it to the next whole number . . . . _____
6. Multiply the number on line 5 by .02. Enter the result as a decimal, but not more than 1. . . . . _____
7. Multiply the amount on line 1 by the decimal on line 6 . . . . _____
8. Subtract line 7 from line 1. Enter the result here and on line 4 of Worksheet 1 . _____

Worksheet 6 — For Figuring Tax If You Have Capital Gain

Use this worksheet to figure the amount to enter on line 6 of Worksheet 1 — 1999 Tax Worksheet only if the amount on line 1 of that worksheet includes capital gain.

1. Enter your expected net long-term capital gain or (loss) for 1999 . . . . _____
2. Enter your expected net short-term capital gain or loss for 1999. . . . . _____
3. Combine lines 1 and 2. If a loss, or if line 1 is a loss, none of your gains are subject to the maximum capital gains rates. Figure your tax using the instructions on line 6 of your 1999 Tax Worksheet, and do not use the rest of this worksheet. If a gain, continue using this worksheet . . . . _____
4. Enter the amount from line 5 of Worksheet 1 . . . . _____
5. Enter the smaller of line 1 or line 3 . . . _____
6. Enter the amount of net capital gain from the disposition of property held for investment that you elect to include in investment income for purposes of figuring the limit on investment interest. Do not include more than the total net gain from the disposition of property held for investment . . . . _____
7. Subtract line 6 from line 5. If zero or less, enter -0-. . . . . _____
8. Enter the total of your 28% rate gain or (loss). This includes all collectibles gains and losses. It also includes part or all of the eligible gain on qualified small business stock. (To see what small business stock qualifies, see *Gains on Qualified Small Business Stock,* in Publication 550.). . . _____
9. Combine lines 2 and 8. If zero or less, enter -0-. . . . . _____
10. Enter the smaller of line 8 or line 9, but not less than zero . . . . _____
11. Enter your unrecaptured section 1250 gain, if any (see page D-7 of the 1998 Schedule D (Form 1040) instructions for guidance on how to figure this amount). . . . . . _____
12. Add lines 10 and 11 . . . . _____
13. Subtract line 12 from line 7. If zero or less, enter -0-. . . . . _____
14. Subtract line 13 from line 4. If zero or less, enter -0-. . . . . _____
15. Enter the smaller of line 4 or $43,050 ($25,750 if single; $21,525 if married filing separately; $34,550 if head of household). _____
16. Enter the smaller of line 14 or line 15 . . _____
17. Subtract line 7 from line 4. If zero or less, enter -0-. . . . . _____
18. Enter the larger of line 16 or line 17. . . _____
19. Figure the tax on the amount on line 18. Use the 1999 Tax Rate Schedules . . . _____
20. Enter the amount from line 15 . . . . _____

21. Enter the amount from line 14 . . . . . _____
22. Subtract line 21 from line 20. If zero or less, enter -0-. . . . . _____
23. Multiply line 22 by 10% (.10) . . . . . _____
24. Enter the smaller of line 4 or line 13 . . _____
25. Enter the amount from line 22 . . . . . _____
26. Subtract line 25 from line 24. If zero or less, enter -0-. . . . . _____
27. Multiply line 26 by 20% (.20) . . . . . _____
28. Enter the smaller of line 7 or line 11 . . _____
29. Add lines 7 and 18 . . . . _____
30. Enter the amount from line 4 . . . . . _____
31. Subtract line 30 from line 29. If zero or less, enter -0-. . . . . _____
32. Subtract line 31 from line 28. If zero or less, enter -0-. . . . . _____
33. Multiply line 32 by 25% (.25) . . . . . _____
34. Enter the amount from line 4 . . . . . _____
35. Add lines 18, 22, 26, and 32 . . . . . _____
36. Subtract line 35 from line 34 . . . . . _____
37. Multiply line 36 by 28% (.28) . . . . . _____
38. Add lines 19, 23, 27, 33, and 37. . . . _____
39. Figure the tax on the amount on line 4. Use the 1999 Tax Rate Schedule . . . . . _____
40. **Tax.** Enter the smaller of line 38 or line 39 here and on line 6 of the 1999 Tax Worksheet . . . . _____

Worksheet 7 — Self-Employment Tax

Use this worksheet to figure the amount to enter on line 11 of Worksheet 1 — 1999 Tax Worksheet. If you are married filing a joint return and you are both self-employed, complete the self-employment tax calculation separately for each spouse, and combine the amounts on line 11 of Worksheet 1.

1. Enter estimated self-employment income for 1999 . . . . _____
2. Multiply the amount on line 1 by .9235. . _____

Note. *If the total of line 2 and your estimated wages is $72,600 or less, do not use this worksheet. See the instructions on line 11 of Worksheet 1.*

3. Multiply the amount on line 2 by .029 . . _____
4. Social security tax maximum income . . $72,600
5. Enter estimated wages for 1999 . . . . _____
6. Subtract line 5 from line 4 . . . . . . _____

Note. *If line 6 is zero or less, stop here and enter the amount from line 3 on line 11 of Worksheet 1.*

7. Enter the smaller of line 2 or line 6 . . . _____
8. Multiply the amount on line 7 by .124 . . _____
9. Add line 3 and line 8. Enter the result here and on line 11 of Worksheet 1 . . . . _____

1999 Standard Deduction Tables

Caution: If you are married filing a separate return and your spouse itemizes deductions, or if you are a dual-status alien, you cannot take the standard deduction even if you were 65 or older or blind.

Table 1. Standard Deduction Chart for Most People*

If Your Filing Status is:	Your Standard Deduction is:
Single	$4,300
Married filing joint return or Qualifying widow(er) with dependent child	7,200
Married filing separately	3,600
Head of household	6,350

*DO NOT use this chart if you were 65 or older or blind, OR if someone can claim you (or your spouse if married filing jointly) as a dependent.

Table 2. Standard Deduction Chart for People Age 65 or Older or Blind*

Check the correct number of boxes below. Then go to the chart.

You   65 or older ☐   Blind ☐

Your spouse, if claiming spouse's exemption   65 or older ☐   Blind ☐

Total number of boxes you checked ☐

If Your Filing Status is:	And the Number in the Box Above is:	Your Standard Deduction is:
Single	1	$5,350
	2	6,400
Married filing jointly or Qualifying widow(er) with dependent child	1	8,050
	2	8,900
	3	9,750
	4	10,600
Married filing separately	1	4,450
	2	5,300
	3	6,150
	4	7,000
Head of household	1	7,400
	2	8,450

*If someone can claim you (or your spouse if married filing jointly) as a dependent, use the worksheet in Table 3, instead.

Table 3. Standard Deduction Worksheet for Dependents*

If you were 65 or older or blind, check the correct number of boxes below. Then go to the worksheet.

You   65 or older ☐   Blind ☐

Your spouse, if claiming spouse's exemption   65 or older ☐   Blind ☐

Total number of boxes you checked ☐

1. Enter your **earned income** (defined below) plus $250.	1.	_____
2. Minimum amount.	2.	$700
3. Compare the amounts on lines 1 and 2. Enter the **larger** of the two amounts here.	3.	_____
4. Enter on line 4 the amount shown below for your filing status. • Single, enter $4,300 • Married filing separate return, enter $3,600 • Married filing jointly or Qualifying widow(er) with dependent child, enter $7,200 • Head of household, enter $6,350	4.	_____
5. **Standard deduction.** a. Compare the amounts on lines 3 and 4. Enter the **smaller** of the two amounts here. If under 65 and not blind, stop here. This is your standard deduction. Otherwise, go on to line 5b.	5a.	_____
b. If 65 or older or blind, multiply $1,050 ($850 if married or qualifying widow(er) with dependent child) by the number in the box above. Enter the result.	5b.	_____
c. Add lines 5a and 5b. This is your standard deduction for 1999.	5c.	_____

Earned income *includes wages, salaries, tips, professional fees, and other compensation received for personal services you performed. It also includes any amount received as a scholarship that you must include in your income.*

*Use Table 3 ONLY if someone can claim you (or your spouse if married filing jointly) as a dependent.

Form W-4 (1999)

Purpose. Complete Form W-4 so your employer can withhold the correct Federal income tax from your pay. Because your tax situation may change, you may want to refigure your withholding each year.

Exemption from withholding. If you are exempt, complete only lines 1, 2, 3, 4, and 7, and sign the form to validate it. Your exemption for 1999 expires February 16, 2000.

Note: *You cannot claim exemption from withholding if (1) your income exceeds $700 and includes more than $250 of unearned income (e.g., interest and dividends) and (2) another person can claim you as a dependent on their tax return.*

Basic instructions. If you are not exempt, complete the Personal Allowances Worksheet. The worksheets on page 2 adjust your withholding allowances based on itemized deductions, adjustments to income, or two-earner/two-job situations. Complete all worksheets that apply. They will help you figure the number of withholding allowances you are entitled to claim. **However, you may claim fewer allowances.**

Child tax and higher education credits. For details on adjusting withholding for these and other credits, see **Pub. 919,** Is My Withholding Correct for 1999?

Head of household. Generally, you may claim head of household filing status on your tax return only if you are unmarried and pay more than 50% of the costs of keeping up a home for yourself and your dependent(s) or other qualifying individuals. See line **E** below.

Nonwage income. If you have a large amount of nonwage income, such as interest or dividends, you should consider making estimated tax payments using Form 1040-ES. Otherwise, you may owe additional tax.

Two earners/two jobs. If you have a working spouse or more than one job, figure the total number of allowances you are entitled to claim on all jobs using worksheets from only one Form W-4. Your withholding will usually be most accurate when all allowances are claimed on the Form W-4 prepared for the highest paying job and zero allowances are claimed on the others.

Check your withholding. After your Form W-4 takes effect, use Pub. 919 to see how the dollar amount you are having withheld compares to your estimated total annual tax. Get Pub. 919 especially if you used the Two-Earner/Two-Job Worksheet and your earnings exceed $150,000 (Single) or $200,000 (Married).

Recent name change? If your name on line 1 differs from that shown on your social security card, call 1-800-772-1213 for a new social security card.

Personal Allowances Worksheet

A Enter "1" for **yourself** if no one else can claim you as a dependent . . . . **A** ____

B Enter "1" if:
- You are single and have only one job; or
- You are married, have only one job, and your spouse does not work; or
- Your wages from a second job or your spouse's wages (or the total of both) are $1,000 or less.

. . **B** ____

C Enter "1" for your **spouse.** But, you may choose to enter -0- if you are married and have either a working spouse or more than one job. (This may help you avoid having too little tax withheld.). . . . . **C** ____

D Enter number of **dependents** (other than your spouse or yourself) you will claim on your tax return . . . . **D** ____

E Enter "1" if you will file as **head of household** on your tax return (see conditions under **Head of household** above) . **E** ____

F Enter "1" if you have at least $1,500 of **child or dependent care expenses** for which you plan to claim a credit . . **F** ____

G **Child Tax Credit:** • If your total income will be between $20,000 and $50,000 ($23,000 and $63,000 if married), enter "1" for each eligible child. • If your total income will be between $50,000 and $80,000 ($63,000 and $115,000 if married), enter "1" if you have two eligible children, enter "2" if you have three or four eligible children, or enter "3" if you have five or more eligible children . . **G** ____

H Add lines A through G and enter total here. **Note:** This amount may be different from the number of exemptions you claim on your return. ▶ **H** ____

For accuracy, complete all worksheets that apply.
- If you plan to **itemize or claim adjustments to income** and want to reduce your withholding, see the Deductions and Adjustments Worksheet on page 2.
- If you are **single,** have **more than one job** and your combined earnings from all jobs exceed $32,000, OR if you are **married** and have a **working spouse or more than one job** and the combined earnings from all jobs exceed $55,000, see the Two-Earner/Two-Job Worksheet on page 2 to avoid having too little tax withheld.
- If **neither** of the above situations applies, **stop here** and enter the number from line H on line 5 of Form W-4 below.

· · · · · · · · · · · · · · · · **Cut here and give the certificate to your employer. Keep the top part for your records.** · · · · · · · · · · · · · · · ·

Form **W-4**	**Employee's Withholding Allowance Certificate**	OMB No. 1545-0010
Department of the Treasury Internal Revenue Service	▶ **For Privacy Act and Paperwork Reduction Act Notice, see page 2.**	19**99**

1 Type or print your first name and middle initial	Last name	**2** Your social security number

Home address (number and street or rural route)	**3** ☐ Single ☐ Married ☐ Married, but withhold at higher Single rate.
	Note: *If married, but legally separated, or spouse is a nonresident alien, check the Single box.*
City or town, state, and ZIP code	**4** If your last name differs from that on your social security card, check here. **You** must call 1-800-772-1213 for a new card . . ▶ ☐

5 Total number of allowances you are claiming (from line H above or from the worksheets on page 2 if they apply) . | **5** ____

6 Additional amount, if any, you want withheld from each paycheck . . . . | **6** $ ____

7 I claim exemption from withholding for 1999, and I certify that I meet **BOTH** of the following conditions for exemption:
- Last year I had a right to a refund of **ALL** Federal income tax withheld because I had **NO** tax liability **AND**
- This year I expect a refund of **ALL** Federal income tax withheld because I expect to have **NO** tax liability.

If you meet both conditions, write "EXEMPT" here . . . . ▶ | **7** ____

Under penalties of perjury, I certify that I am entitled to the number of withholding allowances claimed on this certificate, or I am entitled to claim exempt status.

Employee's signature
(Form is not valid unless you sign it) ▶ _____ Date ▶ _____

8 Employer's name and address (Employer: Complete 8 and 10 only if sending to the IRS)	**9** Office code (optional)	**10** Employer identification number

Cat. No. 10220Q

Form W-4 (1999)   Page **2**

Deductions and Adjustments Worksheet

Note: *Use this worksheet only if you plan to itemize deductions or claim adjustments to income on your 1999 tax return.*

1. Enter an estimate of your 1999 itemized deductions. These include qualifying home mortgage interest, charitable contributions, state and local taxes (but not sales taxes), medical expenses in excess of 7.5% of your income, and miscellaneous deductions. (For 1999, you may have to reduce your itemized deductions if your income is over $126,600 ($63,300 if married filing separately). Get Pub. 919 for details.)   **1** $ _____

2. Enter:
   - $7,200 if married filing jointly or qualifying widow(er)
   - $6,350 if head of household
   - $4,300 if single
   - $3,600 if married filing separately
     2 $ _____

3. **Subtract** line 2 from line 1. If line 2 is greater than line 1, enter -0-   **3** $ _____
4. Enter an estimate of your 1999 adjustments to income, including alimony, deductible IRA contributions, and student loan interest   **4** $ _____
5. **Add** lines 3 and 4 and enter the total . . . .   **5** $ _____
6. Enter an estimate of your 1999 nonwage income (such as dividends or interest) . . . .   **6** $ _____
7. **Subtract** line 6 from line 5. Enter the result, but not less than -0- . . . .   **7** $ _____
8. **Divide** the amount on line 7 by $3,000 and enter the result here. Drop any fraction . . . .   **8** _____
9. Enter the number from Personal Allowances Worksheet, line H, on page 1 . . . .   **9** _____
10. **Add** lines 8 and 9 and enter the total here. If you plan to use the Two-Earner/Two-Job Worksheet, also enter this total on line 1 below. Otherwise, **stop here** and enter this total on Form W-4, line 5, on page 1 . . . . .   **10** _____

Two-Earner/Two-Job Worksheet

Note: *Use this worksheet only if the instructions for line H on page 1 direct you here.*

1. Enter the number from line H on page 1 (or from line 10 above if you used the Deductions and Adjustments Worksheet)   **1** _____
2. Find the number in **Table 1** below that applies to the **LOWEST** paying job and enter it here . . . .   **2** _____
3. If line 1 is **GREATER THAN OR EQUAL TO** line 2, subtract line 2 from line 1. Enter the result here (if zero, enter -0-) and on Form W-4, line 5, on page 1. **DO NOT** use the rest of this worksheet . . . . . .   **3** _____

Note: *If line 1 is **LESS THAN** line 2, enter -0- on Form W-4, line 5, on page 1. Complete lines 4–9 to calculate the additional withholding amount necessary to avoid a year end tax bill.*

4. Enter the number from line 2 of this worksheet . . . . **4** _____
5. Enter the number from line 1 of this worksheet . . . . **5** _____
6. **Subtract** line 5 from line 4 . . . .   **6** _____
7. Find the amount in **Table 2** below that applies to the **HIGHEST** paying job and enter it here . . . .   **7** $ _____
8. **Multiply** line 7 by line 6 and enter the result here. This is the additional annual withholding amount needed   **8** $ _____
9. Divide line 8 by the number of pay periods remaining in 1999. (For example, divide by 26 if you are paid every other week and you complete this form in December 1998.) Enter the result here and on Form W-4, line 6, page 1. This is the additional amount to be withheld from each paycheck . . . .   **9** $ _____

Table 1: Two-Earner/Two-Job Worksheet

Married Filing Jointly				All Others			
If wages from **LOWEST** paying job are—	Enter on line 2 above	If wages from **LOWEST** paying job are—	Enter on line 2 above	If wages from **LOWEST** paying job are—	Enter on line 2 above	If wages from **LOWEST** paying job are—	Enter on line 2 above
$0 - $4,000	0	40,001 - 45,000	8	$0 - $5,000	0	65,001 - 80,000	8
4,001 - 7,000	1	45,001 - 54,000	9	5,001 - 11,000	1	80,001 - 100,000	9
7,001 - 12,000	2	54,001 - 62,000	10	11,001 - 16,000	2	100,001 and over	10
12,001 - 18,000	3	62,001 - 70,000	11	16,001 - 21,000	3		
18,001 - 24,000	4	70,001 - 85,000	12	21,001 - 25,000	4		
24,001 - 28,000	5	85,001 - 100,000	13	25,001 - 40,000	5		
28,001 - 35,000	6	100,001 - 110,000	14	40,001 - 50,000	6		
35,001 - 40,000	7	110,001 and over	15	50,001 - 65,000	7		

Table 2: Two-Earner/Two-Job Worksheet

Married Filing Jointly		All Others	
If wages from **HIGHEST** paying job are—	Enter on line 7 above	If wages from **HIGHEST** paying job are—	Enter on line 7 above
$0 - $50,000	$400	$0 - $30,000	$400
50,001 - 100,000	770	30,001 - 60,000	770
100,001 - 130,000	850	60,001 - 120,000	850
130,001 - 240,000	1,000	120,001 - 250,000	1,000
240,001 and over	1,100	250,001 and over	1,100

Cut Your Next Quarterly Estimate

❖ ❖ ❖

If you don't get a regular paycheck, you pay taxes with quarterly estimates. These are even more painful than withholding because you actually write those checks. You might also file quarterly estimates for income not subject to withholding. The quarterly-estimate system works a bit like withholding, but with more precision. To figure your quarterly estimates, take a "dry run" at figuring your final bill. Then divide the total by four and send your checks to the IRS.

Quarterly estimates are more complex than withholding because you need to pay specific percentages by specific dates.

- 22½% by April 15
- 45% by June 15
- 67½% by September 15
- 90% by January 15

If the right amounts aren't in by the right dates, you can face a penalty even if the total estimates for the year are enough.

This worksheet from Form 1040-ES lets you estimate your next year's tax bill.

FORM 1040-ES

1998 Estimated Tax Worksheet (keep for your records)

1	Enter amount of adjusted gross income you expect in 1998 (see instructions)	**1**
2	• If you plan to itemize deductions, enter the estimated total of your itemized deductions. Caution: If line 1 above is over $124,500 ($62,250 if married filing separately), your deduction may be reduced. See Pub. 505 for details. • If you do not plan to itemize deductions, see **Standard Deduction for 1998** on page 3, and enter your standard deduction here.	**2**
3	Subtract line 2 from line 1	**3**
4	Exemptions. Multiply $2,700 by the number of personal exemptions. If you can be claimed as a dependent on another person's 1998 return, your personal exemption is not allowed. **Caution:** If line 1 above is over $186,800 ($155,650 if head of household; $124,500 if single; $93,400 if married filing separately), see Pub. 505 to figure the amount to enter	**4**
5	Subtract line 4 from line 3	**5**
6	**Tax.** Figure your tax on the amount on line 5 by using the 1998 Tax Rate Schedules on page 2. DO NOT use the Tax Table or the Tax Rate Schedules in the 1997 Form 1040 or Form 1040A instructions. **Caution:** If you have a net capital gain, see Pub. 505 to figure the tax.	**6**
7	Additional taxes (see instructions)	**7**
8	Add lines 6 and 7	**8**
9	Credits (see instructions). Do not include any income tax withholding on this line	**9**
10	Subtract line 9 from line 8. Enter the result, but not less than zero	**10**
11	Self-employment tax (see instructions). Estimate of 1998 net earnings from self-employment $...................... ; if **$68,400 or less,** multiply the amount by 15.3%; if **more than $68,400,** multiply the amount by 2.9%, add $8,481.60 to the result, and enter the total. **Caution:** If you also have wages subject to social security tax, see Pub. 505 to figure the amount to enter . .	**11**
12	Other taxes (see instructions)	**12**
13a	Add lines 10 through 12	**13a**
b	Earned income credit and credit from **Form 4136**	**13b**
c	Subtract line 13b from line 13a. Enter the result, but not less than zero. **THIS IS YOUR TOTAL 1998 ESTIMATED TAX** . . . . ▶	**13c**

14a	Multiply line 13c by 90% (66⅔% for farmers and fishermen) . . .	**14a**	
b	Enter the tax shown on your 1997 tax return.	**14b**	

c	Enter the **smaller** of line 14a or 14b. **THIS IS YOUR REQUIRED ANNUAL PAYMENT TO AVOID A PENALTY** . . . . ▶	**14c**
	Caution: Generally, if you do not prepay (through income tax withholding and estimated tax payments) at least the amount on line 14c, you may owe a penalty for not paying enough estimated tax. To avoid a penalty, make sure your estimate on line 13c is as accurate as possible. Even if you pay the required annual payment, you may still owe tax when you file your return. If you prefer, you may pay the amount shown on line 13c. For more details, see Pub. 505.	
15	Income tax withheld and estimated to be withheld during 1998 (including income tax withholding on pensions, annuities, certain deferred income, etc.)	**15**
16	Subtract line 15 from line 14c. **(Note:** *If zero or less, or line 13c minus line 15 is less than $1,000, stop here. You are not required to make estimated tax payments.)*	**16**
17	If the first payment you are required to make is due April 15, 1998, enter ¼ of line 16 (minus any 1997 overpayment that you are applying to this installment) here and on your payment voucher(s)	**17**

Find Gold in Old Returns

❖ ❖ ❖

Over the course of this book—especially in the next chapter—you'll find tax breaks you previously overlooked. Maybe you didn't know you could deduct job-hunting expenses. Perhaps you forgot to deduct your childrens' braces. Is it too late to claim credit for these expenses? No!

You can file an amended return up to three years after you file your original return. An amended return, Form 1040-X, lets you claim deductions, credits, and other forgotten breaks from previous years, then take your savings with a check today.

You can file an amended return within three years of the original filing date, or two years of when you actually paid the tax, whichever is later. If you've moved since you filed the original return, file it with the IRS service center where you *currently* live.

Finally, if you amend your federal return, make sure to amend your state return as well.

Here are candidates for filing amended returns:

- ◆ Missed deductions
- ◆ Missed credits
- ◆ Social Security overpayments (If you paid twice, file to collect the overpayment.)
- ◆ Lump-sum distributions (If you took a distribution from a pension plan and find you qualify for forward averaging, use Form 1040-X to make the change. For more information, see Chapter 12, Investing for Retirement.)
- ◆ Joint returns versus separate returns (If you filed separately, you can amend to file a joint return, but not the other way around.)
- ◆ Bad debts and worthless securities (Claim these the year the debt becomes uncollectible or the security becomes valueless. The IRS gives you seven years to file these claims.)

Form 1040X
(Rev. November 1998)

Department of the Treasury—Internal Revenue Service

Amended U.S. Individual Income Tax Return
▶ See separate instructions.

OMB No. 1545-0091

This return is for calendar year ▶ 19____ , OR fiscal year ended ▶ _____ , 19____ .

Please print or type

Your first name and initial	Last name	Your social security number
If a joint return, spouse's first name and initial	Last name	Spouse's social security number
Home address (no. and street) or P.O. box if mail is not delivered to your home	Apt. no.	Telephone number (optional) ( )
City, town or post office, state, and ZIP code. If you have a foreign address, see page 2 of the instructions.		For Paperwork Reduction Act Notice, see page 6.

A If the name or address shown above is different from that shown on the original return, check here . . . . . . ▶ ☐

B Has the original return been changed or audited by the IRS or have you been notified that it will be? . . ☐ Yes ☐ No

C Filing status. Be sure to complete this line. **Note:** *You cannot change from joint to separate returns after the due date.*

On original return ▶ ☐ Single ☐ Married filing joint return ☐ Married filing separate return ☐ Head of household ☐ Qualifying widow(er)

On this return ▶ ☐ Single ☐ Married filing joint return ☐ Married filing separate return ☐ Head of household* ☐ Qualifying widow(er)

* If the qualifying person is a child but not your dependent, see page 2.

USE PART II ON THE BACK TO EXPLAIN ANY CHANGES

	A. Original amount or as previously adjusted (see page 2)	**B.** Net change—amount of increase or (decrease)—explain in Part II	**C.** Correct amount
Income and Deductions (see pages 2–5)			
1 Adjusted gross income (see page 3)			
2 Itemized deductions or standard deduction (see page 3) . .			
3 Subtract line 2 from line 1			
4 Exemptions. If changing, fill in Parts I and II on the back .			
5 Taxable income. Subtract line 4 from line 3			
6 Tax (see page 4). Method used in col. C_____			
7 Credits (see page 4)			
8 Subtract line 7 from line 6. Enter the result but not less than zero .			
9 Other taxes (see page 4)			
10 Total tax. Add lines 8 and 9			
11 Federal income tax withheld and excess social security and RRTA tax withheld. If changing, see page 4			
12 Estimated tax payments, including amount applied from prior year's return			
13 Earned income credit			
14 Additional child tax credit from Form 8812			
15 Credits from Form 4136 or Form 2439			
16 Amount paid with Form 4868, 2688, or 2350 (applications for extension of time to file)			
17 Amount of tax paid with original return plus additional tax paid after it was filed			
18 Total payments. Add lines 11 through 17 in column C			
Refund or Amount You Owe			
19 Overpayment, if any, as shown on original return or as previously adjusted by the IRS . . .			
20 Subtract line 19 from line 18 (see page 4).			
21 **AMOUNT YOU OWE.** If line 10, column C, is more than line 20, enter the difference and see page 4			
22 If line 10, column C, is less than line 20, enter the difference			
23 Amount of line 22 you want **REFUNDED TO YOU**			
24 Amount of line 22 you want **APPLIED TO YOUR 19___ ESTIMATED TAX │ 24**			

(Tax Liability; Payments — side labels)

Sign Here

Under penalties of perjury, I declare that I have filed an original return and that I have examined this amended return, including accompanying schedules and statements, and to the best of my knowledge and belief, this amended return is true, correct, and complete. Declaration of preparer (other than taxpayer) is based on all information of which the preparer has any knowledge.

Joint return? See page 2. Keep a copy for your records.

▶ Your signature _____ Date ____

▶ Spouse's signature. If a joint return, BOTH must sign. ____ Date ____

Paid Preparer's Use Only

| Preparer's signature ▶ | Date | Check if self-employed ☐ | Preparer's social security no. |
| Firm's name (or yours if self-employed) and address ▶ | | EIN | ZIP code |

Cat. No. 11360L

Form **1040X** (Rev. 11-98)

Form 1040X (Rev. 11-98)

Page **2**

Part I — Exemptions. See Form 1040, Form 1040A, or Form 1040-T instructions.

If you are **not changing your exemptions**, do not complete this part.
If claiming **more exemptions**, complete lines 25–31 and, if applicable, line 32.
If claiming **fewer exemptions**, complete lines 25–30.

		A. Original number of exemptions reported or as previously adjusted	**B. Net change**	**C. Correct number of exemptions**
25	Yourself and spouse	**25**		
	Caution: *If your parents (or someone else) can claim you as a dependent (even if they chose not to), you cannot claim an exemption for yourself.*			
26	Your dependent children who lived with you	**26**		
27	Your dependent children who did not live with you due to divorce or separation	**27**		
28	Other dependents	**28**		
29	Total number of exemptions. Add lines 25 through 28	**29**		
30	Multiply the number of exemptions claimed on line 29 by the amount listed below for the tax year you are amending. Enter the result here and on line 4.	**30**		

Tax year	Exemption amount	But see page 3 if the amount on line 1 is over:
1998	$2,700	$93,400
1997	2,650	90,900
1996	2,550	88,475
1995	2,500	86,025

31 Dependents (children and other) not claimed on original (or adjusted) return:

Note: *For tax year 1998, do not complete column (e) below. For tax years before 1998, do not complete column (d) below.*

(a) First name Last name	(b) Dependent's social security number. If born in the tax year you are amending, see page 5.	(c) Dependent's relationship to you	(d) ✓ if qualifying child for child tax credit (see page 5)	(e) No. of months lived in your home
			☐	
			☐	
			☐	
			☐	
			☐	

No. of your children on line 31 who:

- lived with you ▶ ☐
- did not live with you due to divorce or separation (see page 5) ▶ ☐

Dependents on line 31 not entered above ▶ ☐

32 For tax year 1995, if your child listed on line 31 did not live with you but is claimed as your dependent under a pre-1985 agreement, check here ▶ ☐

Part II — Explanation of Changes to Income, Deductions, and Credits

Enter the line number from the front of the form for each item you are changing and give the reason for each change. Attach only the supporting forms and schedules for the items changed. If you do not attach the required information, your Form 1040X may be returned. Be sure to include your name and social security number on any attachments.

If the change relates to a net operating loss carryback or a general business credit carryback, attach the schedule or form that shows the year in which the loss or credit occurred. See page 1 of the instructions. Also, check here ▶ ☐

Part III — Presidential Election Campaign Fund. Checking below will not increase your tax or reduce your refund.

If you did not previously want $3 to go to the fund but now want to, check here ▶ ☐
If a joint return and your spouse did not previously want $3 to go to the fund but now wants to, check here ▶ ☐

Printed on recycled paper

☆ U.S. Government Printing Office: 1998-435-249

FOURTEEN

DICTIONARY
OF TAX DEDUCTIONS

Can I deduct points I pay on a home equity loan?
Are my birth-control pills deductible?
Where should I deduct my accountant's tax-preparation fee?

If you've ever written a check and wondered if you can write it off, this chapter holds your answer. This should be a valuable reference for years to come. First, read how to shift income and expenses from one year to another, then how to deduct expenses before you actually pay the bill. Next, skim the dictionary to get a feel for the variety of tax deductions available. Finally, keep this book as a reference. You can run through the dictionary with your checkbook and credit-card statements at tax time, or use it as often as you have a question.

The Dictionary answers these questions:

What Can You Deduct?

What exactly can you write off against your income? What categories of deductions are available? What special breaks are out there? What are you missing? The Dictionary gives you a complete list of available deductions so that you don't lose a dime.

Where Can You Deduct It?

Generally, you'll report personal deductions on Form 1040 or one of its supporting schedules and forms. You'll report business deductions on Form 1040, Schedule C (sole proprietorships), Form 1065 (partnerships), or Form 1120 (corporations). The Dictionary will tell you which form you need to report a particular writeoff.

There are some deductions you can report in more than one place on your return. For example, if you pay tax-prep fees for your 1040 and your sole proprietorship, you can report the fees attributable to the proprietorship as a business deduction on Schedule C or as a miscellaneous itemized deduction on Schedule A. If you report it on Schedule C, you'll bypass the 2% floor on miscellaneous itemized deductions. The Dictionary will help you identify the best place to report your deductions.

What Are the Limits to the Deduction?

Many types of deductions are available only after you top a particular "floor" of adjusted gross income. For example, miscellaneous itemized deductions are available only after your total tops 2% of adjusted gross income. Similarly, medical deductions are available only after your total tops 7.5% of adjusted gross income. The Dictionary will alert you to these important limits.

How Do You Prove the Deduction?

Proving your writeoffs isn't important until you're audited. Then you'll be grateful you've got the required proof. Most deductions merely require a canceled check or credit-card receipt. Other deductions, such as some charitable contributions and volunteer expenses, require specific proof from the organization. The Dictionary will alert you to any unusual requirements so you won't be scrambling in case of an audit.

In some cases, you can substantiate a deduction without the regular proof. The *Cohan* rule, named for entertainer George M. Cohan, lets you approximate your deductions even without actual receipts. This works in cases where you obviously incurred a deductible expense but don't have the paperwork to prove it. But this is a shaky strategy for serious tax planning. To win with it, you'll have to convince the IRS that you incurred the expense, that it was reasonable, and that it was proper. You're much better off keeping decent records to start with.

YEAR-END TAX PLANNING

The end of the year brings chances for you to plan and cut your taxes, this year or next year. This is valuable if all you want to do is delay the tax. It's especially valuable if your tax rates this year and next will be different.

There are several classic strategies for shifting income. If you're self-employed, you can delay billing clients and customers, pushing back the income. And you can choose when to sell investments to realize gains and losses.

"Bunching" deductions is another valuable year-end strategy. Itemized deductions don't start cutting your taxes until your total itemized deductions top your standard deduction. For 1998, this is estimated at $4,250 for singles, $6,250 for heads of households, $7,100 for joint filers, and $3,550 for married couples filing separately. Many taxpayers find their itemized deductions just barely reach the standard deduction and don't give them real value. The solution here is to "bunch" as many deductible expenses as possible into a single year, taking maximum advantage that year and settling for the standard deduction the next. It's relatively easy to do this by prepaying property taxes, medical insurance, charitable gifts, and the like.

Let's say you're a retired couple, filing jointly, in the 28% tax bracket, and your itemized deductions total $7,200 per year. Since the standard deduction is $7,100, your itemized deductions save you just $28 per year (28% of the $100 difference). If you pay $9,200 of deductible expenses one year and $5,200 the next, you'll save an extra $560 the first year at no cost the second.

This strategy will help you maximize itemized deductions subject to the 2% floor on adjusted gross income, as well as medical expenses subject to the 7.5% floor. If your miscellaneous expenses don't top the 2% floor, prepay your safe-deposit box, your next year's subscriptions to investment publications, and similar expenses to get value for your deductions every *other* year. Similarly, if you have unusually high medical expenses in a single year, consider prepaying insurance and other predictable expenses to maximize your deductions that year.

Here are your available "bunching" candidates:

◆ Business expenses (you can buy equipment and pay employee bonuses before year-end, as well as prepay insurance and advertising costs)

- Casualty losses (unreimbursed casualty losses are deductible the year you settle with insurance, so time your insurance settlement for maximum tax advantage)
- Charitable contributions
- Medical expenses
- Moving expenses (even if your move will be next year, you can deduct house-hunting expenses this year)
- Taxes (you can prepay fourth-quarter estimated taxes that aren't due until January 15, plus state and local income taxes, and property taxes)
- Miscellaneous itemized deductions (you should always bunch these to exceed the 2% floor on adjusted gross income)

DEDUCT EXPENSES BEFORE YOU ACTUALLY PAY

◆ ◆ ◆

Ordinarily, you can't deduct expenses until you actually pay them. But, if you charge deductible expenses to a third-party credit card, such as Visa, Mastercard, American Express, or Discover (as opposed to a store card for purchases made at that store), you can deduct the expense the year you incur the charge. This is because you actually incur the obligation to pay when you make the charge. This strategy is useful for accelerating deductions to capture tax savings now, as well as bunching deductions for maximum effect.

AVOID AN AUDIT

◆ ◆ ◆

An examination, or "audit," is when the IRS examines your return to see if you've paid enough tax. An audit is a civil proceeding, not a criminal investigation. And an audit doesn't always mean extra tax. In fact, some 15% to 20% of audits result in a refund.

When the IRS receives your return, it checks to make sure you've included all income reported by third parties on Forms W-2, 1099, and the like. Then, the IRS scores your return based on a program developed to flag returns that seem likely to yield additional tax. This score is called the Discriminant Information Function (DIF). If your score falls in the audit range, the computer notifies your district office to pull your return and investigate. Local officials make the final decision to audit your return.

The formula used to calculate DIF scores is a closely guarded secret. However, Bentley College statistics professor Amir Aczel claims to have "cracked the code." His study states that you'll be flagged for audit if you report Schedule C deductions exceeding 63% of your Schedule C income or Schedule A deductions exceeding 44% of your adjusted gross income. Aczel's study found five other audit flags: (1) bad debt; (2) casualty losses; (3) medical expenses not exceeding 7.5% of adjusted gross income; (4)

"excessive" charitable contributions (including tuition payments disguised a charitable contributions and gifts over 10% of income); and finally, (5) the home-office deduction.

Does this mean you should forgo deductions if they push you into the "audit zone"? That depends on how much you're willing to pay to avoid an audit. Is fear of a possible audit reason enough to pay more tax? If your deductions are legitimate, and you can prove them, then by all means take what you deserve.

In the end, the IRS audits less than 1% of all returns. Taxpayers reporting Schedule C income are the likeliest targets. The IRS audits approximately 2½% of taxpayers with Schedule C incomes over $100,000. This confirms their focus on small business owners with the best chance to hide income and inflate deductions.

There are three kinds of audits. The simplest is a "correspondence audit." This just involves a letter asking for further explanation of some aspect or another of your return. For 1996, these audits averaged just over $1,700 in additional tax and penalties. The next step up is the "office audit." This is when you and your tax adviser bring your records and verification to the local IRS office. These audits averaged over $3,000 in additional tax and penalties. The final step is the "field audit," where the IRS visits you. The IRS reserves this course for businesses and cases involving more records than the taxpayer can practically deliver to the IRS. These audits averaged over $24,000 in additional tax and penalties.

Once the IRS finds you owe extra tax (plus penalties and interest), the collection process begins. It starts with a series of notices to "remind" you of your unpaid balance. From there, the IRS can summon you to examine your ability to pay, garnish your wages, and file liens and levies against your property. These are the cases that turn into horror stories that make the headlines. Some hapless victims have even committed suicide.

If the IRS suspects fraud, organized crime, official corruption, or other criminal offenses, the Criminal Investigation Division (CID) steps in. The IRS itself won't take you to court. Instead, CID refers cases to the Justice Department. CID also cooperates with investigations launched by the Justice Department. Remember, this is how the feds finally nailed Al Capone. Although many taxpayers fear CID as the IRS's ultimate weapon, in 1996 CID referred just over 3,600 cases for prosecution, and just 2,100 of these defendants wound up in jail. These numbers are a tiny fraction of taxpayers. Most of you will never see this side of the IRS so long as you don't hide income or accounts, take bogus deductions, or fail to file returns while receiving income. If you do find yourself in front of CID, most experts suggest you find a criminal lawyer schooled in tax, rather than a tax attorney or CPA. Here's a better solution. Show some respect for those of us that try to play by the rules.

AVOID THE ALTERNATIVE MINIMUM TAX
❖ ❖ ❖

The Alternative Minimum Tax, or AMT, is the tax system's answer to "the rich" who skate by with no significant taxes on large incomes. Unfortunately, it's creeping down to the middle class. Here are signs to watch for:

- Do you claim an unusually large amount of itemized deductions or credits? Many of these are "added back" to figure AMT income.

- Do you exercise incentive stock options? The difference between the fair market value and the strike price is included as AMT income.

- Do you earn income from private-activity municipal bonds? This income is included in AMT income.

- Have you donated appreciated assets to charity? The appreciation is included in AMT income.

Form 6251 lists the major adjustments and preferences for figuring AMT income. These include deductions for medical expenses between 7.5% and 10% of your adjusted gross income, state and local taxes, miscellaneous deductions (except for employee business expenses), accelerated depreciation exceeding straight-line depreciation, and passive losses you take against passive income.

If you're in danger of falling into the trap, here are steps to take to ease the bite:

- Review income and expenses to see how close you are. Plan your year-end elections regarding income and deductions according to your potential AMT liability as well as your regular tax liability.

- Defer exercise of incentive stock options if it makes investment sense.

- Avoid private-activity municipal bonds.

- If your regular tax rate is *higher* than the 26% or 28% AMT rates, *accelerate* income into a year when you pay the AMT. You'll save as much as 13.6% if you can shift income that would otherwise be taxed at 39.6% into an AMT year.

Form **6251**	**Alternative Minimum Tax—Individuals**	OMB No. 1545-0227

Form **6251**

Department of the Treasury
Internal Revenue Service (O)

Alternative Minimum Tax—Individuals

▶ See separate instructions.

▶ Attach to Form 1040 or Form 1040NR.

OMB No. 1545-0227

19**97**

Attachment
Sequence No. **32**

Name(s) shown on Form 1040

Your social security number

Part I   **Adjustments and Preferences**

1	If you itemized deductions on Schedule A (Form 1040), go to line 2. Otherwise, enter your standard deduction from Form 1040, line 35, here and go to line 6	1
2	Medical and dental. Enter the smaller of Schedule A (Form 1040), line 4 **or** 2½% of Form 1040, line 33	2
3	Taxes. Enter the amount from Schedule A (Form 1040), line 9	3
4	Certain interest on a home mortgage not used to buy, build, or improve your home . . .	4
5	Miscellaneous itemized deductions. Enter the amount from Schedule A (Form 1040), line 26 . . .	5
6	Refund of taxes. Enter any tax refund from Form 1040, line 10 or line 21	6 ( )
7	Investment interest. Enter difference between regular tax and AMT deduction . . .	7
8	Post-1986 depreciation. Enter difference between regular tax and AMT depreciation . . .	8
9	Adjusted gain or loss. Enter difference between AMT and regular tax gain or loss . . .	9
10	Incentive stock options. Enter excess of AMT income over regular tax income	10
11	Passive activities. Enter difference between AMT and regular tax income or loss	11
12	Beneficiaries of estates and trusts. Enter the amount from Schedule K-1 (Form 1041), line 9	12
13	Tax-exempt interest from private activity bonds issued after 8/7/86	13
14	Other. Enter the amount, if any, for each item below and enter the total on line 14.	

a Charitable contributions .	**h** Loss limitations	
b Circulation expenditures .	**i** Mining costs	
c Depletion	**j** Patron's adjustment . .	
d Depreciation (pre-1987) .	**k** Pollution control facilities .	
e Installment sales . . .	**l** Research and experimental	
f Intangible drilling costs .	**m** Tax shelter farm activities .	
g Long-term contracts . .	**n** Related adjustments . .	14

15	**Total Adjustments and Preferences.** Combine lines 1 through 14 . . . . ▶	15

Part II   **Alternative Minimum Taxable Income**

16	Enter the amount from **Form 1040, line 36.** If less than zero, enter as a (loss) . . . . . . ▶	16
17	Net operating loss deduction, if any, from Form 1040, line 21. Enter as a positive amount	17
18	If Form 1040, line 33, is over $121,200 (over $60,600 if married filing separately), **and** you itemized deductions, enter the amount, if any, from line 9 of the worksheet for Schedule A (Form 1040), line 28	18 ( )
19	Combine lines 15 through 18 . . . . ▶	19
20	Alternative tax net operating loss deduction. See page 5 of the instructions	20
21	**Alternative Minimum Taxable Income.** Subtract line 20 from line 19. (If married filing separately and line 21 is more than $165,000, see page 5 of the instructions.) . . . . ▶	21

Part III   **Exemption Amount and Alternative Minimum Tax**

22	**Exemption Amount.** (If this form is for a child under age 14, see page 6 of the instructions.)	

IF your filing status is . . .	AND line 21 is not over . . .	THEN enter on line 22 . . .	
Single or head of household	$112,500	$33,750	
Married filing jointly or qualifying widow(er) .	150,000	45,000	22
Married filing separately	75,000	22,500	

If line 21 is **over** the amount shown above for your filing status, see page 6 of the instructions.

23	Subtract line 22 from line 21. If zero or less, enter -0- here and on lines 26 and 28 . . . . . ▶	23
24	If you completed Schedule D (Form 1040), and had an amount on line 25 or line 27 (as refigured for the AMT, if necessary), go to Part IV of Form 6251 to figure line 24. **All others:** If line 23 is $175,000 or less ($87,500 or less if married filing separately), multiply line 23 by 26% (.26). Otherwise, multiply line 23 by 28% (.28) and subtract $3,500 ($1,750 if married filing separately) from the result . . . . . ▶	24
25	Alternative minimum tax foreign tax credit. See page 7 of the instructions	25
26	Tentative minimum tax. Subtract line 25 from line 24 . . . . ▶	26
27	Enter your tax from Form 1040, line 39 (minus any tax from Form 4972 and any foreign tax credit from Form 1040, line 43)	27
28	**Alternative Minimum Tax.** (If this form is for a child under age 14, see page 7 of the instructions.) Subtract line 27 from line 26. If zero or less, enter -0-. Enter here and on Form 1040, line 48 . . ▶	28

For Paperwork Reduction Act Notice, see separate instructions.   Cat. No. 13600G   Form **6251** (1997)

Part IV **Line 24 Computation Using Maximum Capital Gains Rates**

29	Enter the amount from line 23	**29**	
30	Enter the amount from Schedule D (Form 1040), line 27 (as refigured for the AMT, if necessary) **30**		
31	Enter the amount from Schedule D (Form 1040), line 25 (as refigured for the AMT, if necessary) **31**		
32	Add lines 30 and 31 . **32**		
33	Enter the amount from Schedule D (Form 1040), line 22 (as refigured for the AMT, if necessary) **33**		
34	Enter the **smaller** of line 32 or line 33	**34**	
35	Subtract line 34 from line 29. If zero or less, enter -0-	**35**	
36	If line 35 is $175,000 or less ($87,500 or less if married filing separately), multiply line 35 by 26% (.26). Otherwise, multiply line 35 by 28% (.28) and subtract $3,500 ($1,750 if married filing separately) from the result . . . . ▶	**36**	
37	Enter the amount from Schedule D (Form 1040), line 36 (as figured for the regular tax)	**37**	
38	Enter the **smallest** of line 29, line 30, or line 37	**38**	
39	Multiply line 38 by 10% (.10) . . . . ▶	**39**	
40	Enter the **smaller** of line 29 or line 30	**40**	
41	Enter the amount from line 38	**41**	
42	Subtract line 41 from line 40. If zero or less, enter -0-	**42**	
43	Multiply line 42 by 20% (.20) . . . . ▶	**43**	
44	Enter the amount from line 29	**44**	
45	Add lines 35, 38, and 42	**45**	
46	Subtract line 45 from line 44	**46**	
47	Multiply line 46 by 25% (.25) . . . . ▶	**47**	
48	Add lines 36, 39, 43, and 47	**48**	
49	If line 29 is $175,000 or less ($87,500 or less if married filing separately), multiply line 29 by 26% (.26). Otherwise, multiply line 29 by 28% (.28) and subtract $3,500 ($1,750 if married filing separately) from the result	**49**	
50	Enter the **smaller** of line 48 or line 49 here and on line 24 . . . . ▶	**50**	

✪ *Printed on recycled paper*   *U.S. Government Printing Office: 1997 - 419-414

TAX DEDUCTIONS A–Z

❖ ❖ ❖

Abdominal Supports are a medical expense subject to the 7.5% floor.

Abortion is a medical expense subject to the 7.5% floor.

Accounting Fees (other than for tax preparation) are generally deductible as a business expense on Schedule C, Form 1065, or Form 1120.

- ◆ Accounting fees related to capital transactions (buying or selling property) are not currently deductible. Instead, include them in the basis or adjusted sale price for figuring gain or loss on the sale.
- ◆ Accounting fees related to the organization of a new business are deductible over five years.
- ◆ Accounting fees relating to reorganization of a business are not deductible.

Acupuncture is a medical expense subject to the 7.5% floor.

Adjustments to Income are a specific group of expenses deductible on Form 1040:

- ◆ IRA contributions (subject to income limits)
- ◆ Moving expenses (subject to mileage requirements)
- ◆ One-half of self-employment tax paid
- ◆ Self-employed health insurance
- ◆ Self-employed Keogh and Simplified Employee Pension (SEP) retirement plan contributions
- ◆ Penalty on early withdrawal of savings
- ◆ Alimony paid
- ◆ Student-loan interest during the first 60 months that interest payment is required (subject to income limits)

Subtract adjustments to income from total income to figure "adjusted gross income." This figure is important for two reasons. First, your personal exemptions and itemized deductions phase out as your adjusted gross income tops certain thresholds. Second, many itemized deductions are available only after your total tops a certain "floor" percentage of adjusted gross income. For more information, see Chapter 1, What You Need to Know About the Tax System.

Air-Conditioner Costs are a medical expense, subject to the 7.5% floor, if prescribed by a physician to relieve a specific condition.

Alcohol-"Rehab" Inpatient Costs are a medical expense subject to the 7.5% floor.

Alimony Payments are an adjustment to income, deductible by the payor, and taxable to the payee so long as the payments meet certain rules. For more information on alimony, see Chapter 2, Your Family.

Allowance you pay to your kids may be deductible as a business expense on Schedule C, Form 1065 or Form 1120, if you pay your kids to work in your business.

Ambulance Expenses are a deductible medical expense subject to the 7.5% floor.

Appraisal Fees may be deductible as follows:

- ◆ Appraisal fees related to your trade or business are deductible as a business expense on Schedule C, Form 1065 or Form 1120.

- ◆ Appraisal fees related to charitable gifts over $5,000 are deductible as a miscellaneous itemized deduction subject to the 2% floor. Be careful not to report these as charitable contributions.

- ◆ Appraisal fees related to buying a capital asset (such as your house) are not deductible.

Arches for shoes are a deductible medical expense subject to the 7.5% floor.

Artificial Teeth/Eyes/Limbs are deductible medical expenses subject to the 7.5% floor.

Autoette Expenses (except for travel to and from work) are a deductible medical expense subject to the 7.5% floor.

Automobile Expenses may be deductible depending on the purpose of the travel.

- ◆ Travel for your trade or business is deductible as a business expense on Schedule C, Form 1065 or Form 1120. For more information, see "Business Use of Your Car," in Chapter 4.

- ◆ Travel on behalf of your employer is deductible as an employee business expense subject to the 2% floor on miscellaneous itemized deductions.

- ◆ Travel to and from medical facilities is deductible at 12 cents per mile, plus parking and tolls, as a medical expense subject to the 7.5% floor.

- ◆ Travel during a move is deductible as a moving expense. See Moving Expenses in the Dictionary.

- ◆ Travel to find a job is deductible at 31 cents per mile as a job-hunting expense subject to the 2% floor on miscellaneous itemized deductions.

- ◆ Travel to manage your investments is deductible at 31 cents per mile (up to investment income) as investment expense subject to the 2% floor on miscellaneous itemized deductions.

- ◆ Travel for volunteer or charitable causes is deductible at 14 cents per mile as a charitable gift.

Property taxes you pay on your car are deductible as an itemized deduction on Schedule A, regardless of how you use your car.

Back Supports are a deductible medical expense subject to the 7.5% floor.

Bad Debts are deductible from gross income in the year the debt becomes worthless.

- ◆ Business bad debts are deductible as business expenses on Schedule C, Form 1065 or Form 1120.

- ◆ Personal bad debts are deductible as short-term capital losses on Schedule D.

This appears to be an IRS audit "hot button," so be sure to document the debt and the loss. To prove a bad debt, you'll have to show that it was a valid debt arising out of a debtor-creditor relationship. The funds you use to make the loan had to come from your income or capital. Finally, you'll have to point to some identifiable event that convinces you the debt is worthless. Family bad debts are hard to prove; the IRS presumes they're actually gifts. You don't need to wait until the debt is actually due to deduct it. You can claim the deduction as soon as the debt becomes worthless. The amount of debt written off is taxable income to the borrower in the year written off by the lender.

Birth-Control Pills or devices prescribed by a doctor are a deductible medical expense subject to the 7.5% floor.

Blood Tests/Transfusions are a deductible medical expense subject to the 7.5% floor.

Braces for your teeth or your kids' teeth are a deductible medical expense subject to the 7.5% floor. This is one medical expense that may be large enough to break the 7.5% floor if you pay all at once rather than financing through the orthodontist. Here's one possible strategy. If you have a child that's old enough to need braces, you probably have home equity. Consider taking out a home-equity loan to pay for the braces up front. You'll get to write off braces, plus the interest you pay to finance them. This will cut your taxes even if the cost of the braces doesn't exceed the 7.5% floor by converting nondeductible personal interest into deductible home-equity interest.

Braille Books (excess cost over regular books) are a deductible medical expense subject to the 7.5% floor.

Briefcase costs are deductible as a business expense on Schedule C, Form 1065 or Form 1120, or an employee business expense subject to the 2% floor on miscellaneous itemized deductions.

Burglar-Alarm costs are a capital cost included in your property's basis for figuring gain or loss on a sale.

Business Cards for your trade or business are deductible as an advertising expense on Schedule C, Form 1065 or Form 1120, or an employee business expense subject to the 2% floor on miscellaneous itemized deductions.

Capital Gains are gains from the sale of property. Capital gains enjoy three significant advantages over ordinary income:

- Long-term capital gains are taxed at lower rates than ordinary income—no more than 20%, even for taxpayers in the top tax brackets.

- You don't pay tax until you "realize" your gain (actually sell your property), so you can choose when to pay the tax.

- If you hold onto appreciated property until your death, you avoid income tax entirely. Your heirs inherit the property with a basis equal to its value on your date of death. This "stepped-up basis" is an important tax- and estate-planning tool.

For more information, see Chapter 6, Tax-Advantaged Investments to Meet Your Needs.

Car-Phone costs are deductible under these rules:

- ◆ A car phone you use for your trade or business is deductible as a business expense on Schedule C, Form 1065 or Form 1120.
- ◆ A car phone you maintain for your employer's convenience is deductible as an unreimbursed employee business expense, subject to the 2% floor on miscellaneous itemized deductions.
- ◆ A car phone you install for medical emergencies is a deductible medical expense subject to the 7.5% floor.

Career Counseling for a new position in your same field is a deductible job-hunting expense, subject to the 2% floor on miscellaneous itemized deductions. See **Job-Hunting Expenses.**

Casualty Losses are deductible on Form 4684 to the extent that they exceed 10% of your AGI *plus* a $100 floor. Casualty losses are deductible in the year the casualty occurs or the year you discover the damage.

> ▶ **Example:**   In 1997 your adjusted gross income is $30,000. Your car is worth just $4,000, and you decide to save money by dropping your theft insurance. Naturally, someone steals your car. How much can you deduct? First reduce the loss by 10% of adjusted gross income, or $3,000. Next, subtract $100. Your deduction is $900.

Charitable Contributions are generally deductible up to 50% of your adjusted gross income on Schedule A. For more information, see Chapter 5, Make the Most of Charitable Gifts. Business contributions are deductible as a business expense on Schedule C, Form 1065 or Form 1120.

Chemotherapy is a deductible medical expense subject to the 7.5% floor.

Childbirth Expenses, including childbirth classes, are a medical expense subject to the 7.5% floor.

Child-Support Payments are a nondeductible personal expense. To write off these expenses, consider recharacterizing them as alimony. For more information, see Chapter 2, Your Family.

Chiropractor fees are a deductible medical expense subject to the 7.5% floor.

Christian-Science-Practitioner fees are a medical expense subject to the 7.5% floor.

Clothing Costs (see **Work Clothes and Uniforms**)

Clarinet Lessons prescribed for teeth defects are a medical expense subject to the 7.5% floor.

Commissions you pay on real estate or other investments aren't deductible when you pay them. Instead, include commissions in the cost of the property when you figure your taxable gain.

Commuting Expenses are nondeductible personal expenses. However, if you travel to more than one location in a day, your "commuting" expenses include travel from home to your first location of the day, and from your last location home. If you have a home-office or sideline business, your "commute" may be the trip from the kitchen to the office. Any further travel is a deductible business expense.

Computer expenses, including peripheral equipment such as printers and scanners, may be deductible depending on how you use the computer. Generally, use Form 4562 to claim depreciation and first-year expensing deductions, then carry the amount to the appropriate form or schedule.

- Computer equipment you buy for your trade or business is deductible as a business expense on Schedule C, Form 1065 or Form 1120.

- Computer equipment you buy on behalf of your job may be deductible as an unreimbursed employee business expense (subject to the 2% floor on miscellaneous itemized deductions) if your employer requires you to own it as a condition of your job. It's not enough that the computer merely makes you productive. The IRS requires you to show that your employer doesn't provide one powerful enough to do your job.

- Your computer is deductible as an investment expense subject to the 2% floor on miscellaneous itemized deductions, up to investment income, if you use it to manage your investments.

- There are several ways to write off the computer depending on how much time you use it for a deductible purpose. If you use it more than 50% for a deductible purpose, you can choose first-year expensing or Modified Accelerated Cost Recovery System (MACRS) "200% double declining rate." If you use it less than 50% for a deductible purpose, use straight-line depreciation. Finally, if you're subject to the AMT, your depreciation is limited to the MACRS's "150% double declining rate" even if your deductible use is more than 50%. First-year expensing should let you write off the full cost.

DEPRECIATION DEDUCTIONS (COMPUTER)

MACRS Depreciation

Year	1	2	3	4	5	6
Half-Year	20.00%	32.00%	19.20%	11.52%	11.52%	5.76%
Q1	35.00%	26.00%	15.60%	11.01%	11.01%	1.38%
Q2	25.00%	30.00%	18.00%	11.37%	11.37%	4.26%
Q3	15.00%	34.00%	20.40%	12.24%	11.30%	7.06%
Q4	5.00%	38.00%	22.80%	13.68%	10.94%	9.58%

Straight-Line Depreciation

Year	1	2	3	4	5	6
Half-Year	10.00%	20.00%	20.00%	20.00%	20.00%	10.00%
Q1	17.50%	20.00%	20.00%	20.00%	20.00%	2.50%
Q2	12.50%	20.00%	20.00%	20.00%	20.00%	7.50%
Q3	7.50%	20.00%	20.00%	20.00%	20.00%	12.50%
Q4	2.50%	20.00%	20.00%	20.00%	20.00%	17.50%

Let's say you spend $2,500 for the latest screaming-fast home computer tricked up with stereo speakers, 32X CD-ROM, and a 17-inch monitor. You use the computer 60% to manage a sideline business, 20% to manage your investments, and 20% to vaporize space aliens. Since business use tops 50%, you can claim first-year expensing of $2,000 (80% of the full $2,500 price). You could also claim depreciation of $400 (20% of the $2,500 purchase price, multiplied by the 80% deductible use). If you used it just 40% to manage investments and 60% to save the earth from the alien hordes, you could deduct just $100 (10% of the purchase price, multiplied by the 40% deductible use). If you continue to use it 40% for deductible purposes, next year you'll be able to write off $200 (20% of the purchase price, multiplied by the 40% deductible use).

◆ If business use falls below 50% in a subsequent year, you'll have to "recapture" and report as income any MACRS and first-year expensing that exceeds what you would otherwise have been able to deduct with first-year expensing.

◆ If you lease a computer, you can deduct whatever percentage of your lease payment equals your deductible use of the computer. However, if your business use is less than 50%, you'll have to report income based on the value of the machine according to tables published in IRS Publication 534.

Computer software is deductible according to similar rules depending on the purpose of the software. Programs with a usable life of just one year, such as tax-preparation software, are deductible the year you buy them. Other programs are depreciable over three years. Accounting software and similar programs for your business or job are deductible as business expenses or employee business expense. Investment-management programs, such as stock-charting programs, are deductible as an investment expense up to investment income and subject to the 2% limit on miscellaneous itemized deductions. Finally, tax-preparation software is deductible as a miscellaneous itemized deduction subject to the 2% floor on miscellaneous itemized deductions.

Contact Lenses are a medical expense subject to the 7.5% floor.

Continuing-Education Expenses for attorneys, accountants, physicians, real-estate and insurance agents, and similar professionals, are deductible as follows:

◆ Continuing-education expenses related to your trade or business are deductible as a business expense on Schedule C, Form 1065 or Form 1120.

◆ Continuing-education expenses incurred on behalf of your employer are deductible as an unreimbursed employee business expense subject to the 2% floor on miscellaneous itemized deductions.

Convention Costs are deductible as a business expense on Schedule C or an employee business expense on Schedule A if you can show that the convention is related to your trade or business. Convention costs include transportation, lodging, and 50% of meals and entertainment, as well as specific convention registration fees and costs. Conventions outside North America and the Caribbean are deductible only if you can show they're directly related to your trade or business and it's as reasonable to hold the convention abroad as it is to hold it here. Finally, you can deduct up to $2,000 per year for cruise-ship conventions on U.S.-registered ships if all ports of call are in the U.S. and U.S. possessions. Keep a log of convention sessions and business appointments you attend, as well as convention programs and materials.

Cosmetic Surgery is generally *not* deductible except for disfigurement related to a congenital abnormality, disfiguring disease, or accidental injury. However, a stripper once won a case in Tax Court arguing her breast implants were a deductible business expense.

CPA Fees (see **Accounting Fees** and **Tax-Preparation Fees**)

Crutches are a medical expense subject to the 7.5% floor.

Day-Care costs (including costs for a day-care center, day camp, nursery school, or in-home care, but not including school tuition for kindergarten and beyond or sleepaway camp) may qualify for the Dependent Care Credit. These expenses also qualify for pretax reimbursement through a dependent-care flexible spending account. For more information on the credit, see "Tax Breaks for Your Kids," in Chapter 2. For more information and dependent-care flexible-spending accounts, see "Flexible Spending Arrangements" in Chapter 4.

Dentist expenses are a deductible medical expense subject to the 7.5% floor.

Dentures are a deductible medical expense subject to the 7.5% floor.

Dependents are deductible from adjusted gross income in the form of personal exemptions. For more information, see "Claim All Your Personal Exemptions," in Chapter 2.

Dialysis is a deductible medical expense subject to the 7.5% floor.

Diets prescribed for specific medical conditions (to the extent the diet costs more than a regular diet) are a medical expense subject to the 7.5% floor.

Disability-Income-Insurance Premiums are deductible as a business expense on Form 1120 if your corporation pays the premium. However, if you write off the premiums now and wind up getting benefits, your benefits will be taxable. If you pay for the premium personally, any benefits you receive are tax-free. Consider this when you choose your business-perk package.

Doctor (see **Physician**)

Drug-"Rehab" Inpatient Costs are a medical expense subject to the 7.5% floor.

Dues you pay to business, professional, and social organizations may be deductible under these rules:

◆ Union dues are deductible as a miscellaneous itemized deduction subject to the 2% floor.

◆ Dues to professional organizations, chambers of commerce, and civic organizations (Kiwanis, and the like) are deductible as a business expense on Schedule C, Form 1065 and Form 1120. Business dues to charitable, religious, or educational organizations may be deductible as a business expense if you reasonably expect to gain some business benefit from your membership.

- Personal dues you pay to charitable, religious, or educational organizations are deductible as charitable contributions.
- Memberships you maintain on behalf of your employer are deductible as an employee business expense subject to the 2% floor.

Education Expenses include tuition, books, supplies, and fees, plus transportation (including parking and tolls). These expenses are deductible under the following rules:

- Education expenses may be deductible as a business expense on Schedule C, Form 1065 or Form 1120 if you take courses to enhance the skills you use to carry out your trade or business.
- Education expenses may be deductible as an employee business expense on Form 2106, subject to the 2% floor on miscellaneous itemized deductions, if you take courses to maintain or improve your current job skills.
- Qualified educational assistance from your employer is tax-free up to $5,000 per year.
- You can't write off education expenses intended to prepare you for a new trade or business. For example, you can't deduct the cost of attending law school to prepare you for a job as an attorney. However, you can write off education expenses to maintain or improve your current job skills. So, if you practice law for a period of years, then go back to school to get an advanced degree in, say, labor law, you can deduct the cost of getting the advanced degree. Similarly, if you go back to school for an MBA to improve your skills for your existing job, you can deduct the cost of the degree.

Education expenses may also qualify for the Lifetime Learning Credit. For more information, see "Claim the College Tax Credits," in Chapter 11.

Employment-Agency Fees for a new position in your same field are deductible as a job-hunting expense subject to the 2% floor on miscellaneous itemized deductions.

Employee Business Expenses are deductible as miscellaneous itemized deductions subject to the 2% floor.

If your employer reimburses your expenses under an "accountable plan" (one that requires you to report all expenses and return any excess reimbursement or allowance), your reimbursement will not count as income. So if your employer reimburses all your expenses, you don't need to bother reporting them. If you have unreimbursed expenses, report them on Form 2106, then subtract any partial reimbursement and carry the unreimbursed balance to Schedule A as a miscellaneous itemized deduction subject to the 2% floor. If your employer reimburses you under a nonaccountable plan, the reimbursement will be reported as income. Report your expenses on Form 2106, then carry the unreimbursed balance to Schedule A.

Specific deductible expenses include:

- Briefcase or attaché case
- Office decor (frames for diplomas, artwork for walls, and the like)
- Stationery/office supplies you purchase personally

- Business/greeting cards for business associates
- Subscriptions to professional publications
- Dues for unions or professional associations
- Bonding costs and professional liability-malpractice insurance
- Home-computer costs, if your employer requires you to buy it and use it for your job
- Business gifts (up to $25 per recipient)
- Business transportation (cabs, auto mileage, parking and tolls, and so on), plus air-fare, lodging, and 50% of meals and entertainment for trips out of town; if your employer reimburses you less than 32.5 cents per mile, you can deduct the difference directly
- Educational programs intended to enhance your skills in your current job
- Uniform and work-clothes costs (including laundry and maintenance) for clothing and protective gear not suitable for ordinary street wear)

Entertainment Expenses (See **Meals and Entertainment**)

Eyeglasses are a deductible medical expense subject to the 7.5% floor.

Financial-Planning Fees are deductible as an investment expense, up to the amount of investment income, subject to the 2% floor on miscellaneous itemized deductions.

Fluoridation Treatment is a deductible medical expense subject to the 7.5% floor.

Frequent-Flyer Miles you receive from business travel and redeem for personal use are supposed to be reported as income. However, the IRS has little way to verify this usage, and the attempt to tax frequent-flier miles has fallen short.

Gambling Losses are a miscellaneous itemized deduction subject to the 2% floor, deductible up to your amount of gambling winnings. No, you can't use gambling losses to offset ordinary income. But you can use gambling losses to shelter your wins. You can't carry forward losses to another year, and you can't deduct travel or associated costs to get to the gambling.

   The gambling-loss deduction is frequently abused by gamblers who win a big score, receive a W-2G (reporting the win to the IRS) and scramble for deductions to avoid paying tax on the win. So it's important to document your losses. If you play the lottery, keep your losing tickets. If you gamble at a casino, keep records of any markers or cash you receive at the casino. If you play the slots, join the casino's slot club so that the machines can record how much you play. (You'll even get some nice comps in the process.) And if you bet at the track, staple your losing tickets to the program.

Gifts are deductible as follows:

- Gifts you make on behalf of your trade or business are deductible, up to $25 each, as a business expense on Schedule C, Form 1065 or Form 1120.
- Gifts you make on behalf of your employer are deductible as unreimbursed employee business expenses subject to the 2% floor on miscellaneous itemized deductions.

- Gifts to charities are deductible up to 50% of your adjusted gross income as charitable contributions of Schedule A. For more information, see Chapter 5, Make the Most of Charitable Gifts.

Gum Treatments are a deductible medical expense subject to the 7.5% floor.

Health-Insurance Premiums are deductible as a medical expense subject to the 7.5% floor.

If you're self-employed, write off your health insurance premiums as an adjustment to income according to this schedule:

SELF-EMPLOYED HEALTH INSURANCE

Year	Deduction
1999–2001	60%
2002	70%
2003 on	100%

If you're self-employed, you can still deduct your health insurance as an itemized deduction subject to the 7.5% floor. The only way to know which saves you most is to try them both. Also, you can deduct the appropriate percentage as self-employed health insurance, and the remaining percentage as a regular medical deduction subject to the 7.5% floor.

Hearing Aids are a deductible medical expense subject to the 7.5% floor.

Heating Pads are a deductible medical expense subject to the 7.5% floor.

Hobby Losses are deductible up to hobby income.

Home Computer (see **Computer**)

Home Improvements generally aren't deductible. Instead, include the cost of the improvement in your "adjusted basis" when you figure your gain when you sell. See Chapter 3, Buying, Owning, and Selling Your Home. Home improvements for medical reasons may be deductible to the extent the cost exceeds the increased value for the home (see **Medical Expenses**).

Home-Office Expenses may be deductible as a business expense on Schedule C, Form 1065 or Form 1120, or as an employee business expense if you meet certain strict requirements. For more information, see Chapter 4, Your Job and Your Business.

Hospital Bills are a deductible medical expense subject to the 7.5% floor.

Hydrotherapy is a deductible medical expense subject to the 7.5% floor.

Insulin Treatments are a deductible medical expense subject to the 7.5% floor.

Interest Expenses may be deductible depending on the source or the purpose of the loan.

♦ "Acquisition indebtedness" of interest on up to $1 million of debt to buy your primary residence and one additional residence is deductible on Schedule A. For more information, see Chapter 3, Buying, Owning, and Selling Your Home.

♦ Home-equity indebtedness of interest on up to $100,000 of debt is also deductible on Schedule A. For more information, see "Cut Your Taxes with Home-Equity Debt," in Chapter 3.

♦ Interest you pay to buy or carry investment property, including stocks, bonds, mutual funds, and other securities (margin interest), is deductible on Form 4952 as an investment expense. You can deduct investment interest up to the amount of net-investment income (gross-investment income minus investment expenses in excess of 2% of your adjusted gross income). Investment interest is subject to the 2% floor, but not the 3% phaseout of itemized deductions. You have to be able to trace the borrowed money to the investment. Margin interest used for otherwise nondeductible personal uses is not deductible. So, if you use investment interest for both investment and personal purposes, segregate your loans so you can trace deductible proceeds back to the source.

If you need to borrow against your investments for otherwise nondeductible personal expenses, consider selling some or all of your investments to raise the necessary cash, then buying back your investment with borrowed dollars. That way, you can trace the borrowed money to the investment. Of course, you'll have to weigh the deduction against any capital-gains tax you pay when you sell the investment. And, if you sell an investment at a loss, then buy it back within 31 days before or after your original sale, your loss will be disallowed as a "wash sale."

♦ Interest you pay to buy or carry tax-exempt securities, single-premium life insurance, endowment, or annuity contracts, is not deductible.

♦ Prepaid interest isn't deductible until the year the interest is actually due.

♦ Student-loan interest within the first five years of loan repayment is deductible as an adjustment to income if your adjusted gross income is $60,000 or less. For more information, see Chapter 11, Investing for College.

Investment Expenses are a miscellaneous itemized deduction subject to the 2% floor. Your total investment-expense deduction may not exceed your investment income. Deductible expenses include:

♦ Legal and accounting fees relating to investments

♦ Fees for investment advice (fees paid to money managers or financial planners)

♦ Bookkeeping and secretarial fees relating to investments

♦ Books and periodicals relating to investments

♦ Custodial fees for IRAs, if paid separately from the account

♦ Account fees for dividend-reinvestment plans

♦ Safe-deposit boxes, if used to store investment information

- Investment-related travel (mileage to and from your broker, trips away from home to meet with investment advisers and manage investment property, and so forth)
- Fifty percent of meals and entertainment (lunch with your financial adviser)
- Interest on an unlimited amount of debt used to buy or carry investment property, including stocks, bonds, mutual funds, and other securities (see **Interest**)
- Home-computer costs for a computer you use to manage your investments (see **Computer**)

Commissions you pay to buy and sell investments are included in the cost of the investment for figuring gains and losses when you sell. You can't deduct the cost of investment seminars or the travel costs for shareholder meetings.

IRA Custodial Fees are a deductible investment expense subject to the 2% floor if you pay the fee separately by check, rather than letting the IRA sponsor deduct the fee from the account.

Job-Hunting Expenses for a new position in the same line of work are a miscellaneous itemized deduction subject to the 2% floor. Costs of finding your first job, or a job in a new line of work, are not deductible. Specific costs include:

- Expenses for resumés, cover letters, typing, printing, envelopes, and postage
- Fees for employment agencies, consultants, headhunters, and the like
- Magazines and newspapers you buy for job ads
- Costs of assembling portfolios of previous work
- Transportation to and from job interviews, headhunters, and so forth
- Phone calls
- Fifty percent of meals and entertainment associated with job hunting
- Out-of-town travel, including 50% of meals and entertainment
- Fees for legal, accounting, and tax advice regarding employment contracts

The Tax Court has allowed a deduction for costs of entertaining existing clients *between* positions when the job hunter intended to continue doing business with the client in his new position.

Labor-Union Dues are deductible as an unreimbursed employee business expense, subject to the 2% floor.

Laboratory Tests are a medical expense subject to the 7.5% floor.

Laundry Expenses (see **Uniforms and Work Clothes**)

Lead-based Paint Removal is a medical expense subject to the 7.5% floor. Sorry, there's no deduction for repainting costs.

Legal Fees are generally deductible if they are related to: (1) your trade or business, (2) production of income, or (3) determination of tax. Here are specific rules:

- Legal fees related to your trade or business are deductible as a business expense on Schedule C, Form 1065 or Form 1120.

- Legal fees directly related to your job (such as fees to defend your conduct on the job) are deductible as an employee business expense subject to the 2% floor on miscellaneous itemized deductions.

- Legal fees related to your investments are deductible (up to investment income) as an investment expense subject to the 2% floor on miscellaneous itemized deductions.

- Legal fees related to income-producing property are deductible against income from the property on Schedule E.

- Legal fees for guardianship or commitment proceedings are a deductible medical expense subject to the 7.5% floor.

- Legal fees for personal tax planning, including tax preparation, audits, and Tax Court cases, are a miscellaneous itemized deduction subject to the 2% floor.

- Legal fees for fixing taxable alimony are deductible as a miscellaneous itemized deduction subject to the 2% floor. (This fee is deductible by the party *receiving* the alimony, not by the party *paying* it.)

- Legal fees related to buying or selling property, including your home, are included in the basis or adjusted sale price of the property for figuring gain or loss on the sale.

If your legal service doesn't fall entirely within one of these categories, have your lawyer itemize the bill so that you can deduct whatever specific percentage is appropriate. For example, if your attorney prepares a sophisticated will with a marital-deduction bypass trust to eliminate estate taxes, have him or her itemize the portion of the fee relating to the tax planning so that you can deduct it. Similarly, if your lawyer negotiates a divorce that includes taxable alimony, have him or her itemize the portion of the fee related to the alimony. However, be aware that the IRS is on the lookout for taxpayers who deduct personal expenses and improperly shift nondeductible personal expenses onto business schedules.

Life-Insurance Premiums are generally not deductible for individuals. However, businesses can deduct life-insurance premiums as follows:

- Businesses can deduct the costs of group life provided for employees as a business expense on Schedule C, Form 1065 or Form 1120.

- Businesses can deduct the cost of VEBA contributions used to buy individual life insurance as a business expense on Schedule C, Form 1065 or Form 1120. For more information, see Chapter 4, Your Job and Your Business.

Local Taxes, including income, personal property, and real property taxes, are deductible as itemized deductions on Schedule A.

Long-Term-Care Insurance may be a deductible medical expense subject to the 7.5% floor. The policy has to cover long-term care for the chronically ill. It has to be guaranteed renewable and can't offer cash-surrender values. Your agent or carrier can tell you if premiums are deductible.

LONG-TERM-CARE INSURANCE

Age	Deduction
40 and below	$210
41–50	$380
51–60	$770
61–70	$2,050
71 and up	$2,570

Since the government determines when you are eligible for benefits under a deductible policy, you may wish to consider a nondeductible policy to take advantage of more liberal eligibility provisions. For more information, see your insurance agent.

Losses may be deductible as follows:

- Casualty losses are deductible on Form 4684 to the extent the loss exceeds $100 plus 10% of your adjusted gross income. See **Casualty Losses.**
- Gambling losses are deductible as a miscellaneous itemized deduction up to gambling winnings. See **Gambling Losses.**
- Investment losses are deductible against investment gains. See Chapter 6.

Mattress Expenses are a deductible medical expense subject to the 7.5% floor if a physician prescribes a new mattress for treatment of a specific condition.

Magazines (see **Subscriptions**)

Margin Interest (see **Interest**)

Meals and Entertainment may be 50% deductible depending on the purpose:

- Meals and entertainment related to your business are deductible as a business expense on Schedule C, Form 1065 or Form 1120. You have to discuss specific business at the meal; you can't simply sip martinis with prospective clients.
- Meals and entertainment on behalf of your employer are deductible as an unreimbursed employee business expense subject to the 2% floor on miscellaneous itemized deductions.
- Meals and entertainment related to your job search are deductible as a job-hunting expense subject to the 2% floor on miscellaneous itemized deductions.
- Meals and entertainment related to your investments are deductible as an investment expense (up to your investment income) and subject to the 2% floor on miscellaneous itemized deductions. (This includes lunch with your broker, meals you eat while traveling to manage investment property, and so forth).

Meals and entertainment are 50% deductible if they're directly related to the active conduct of your business or directly before or after substantial, bona fide discussion directly related to the active conduct of your business. This includes "goodwill" meals and entertainment, entertainment at home, and spousal costs. Specific deductible expenses include meals and drinks, taxes and tips, and the face value of tickets to sporting and theatrical events.

Meals and entertainment away from home are 50% deductible for overnight trips. The IRS allows a $30 per diem for travel to most locations within the continental United States. Some more expensive locations, including big cities and resort towns, qualify for $34, $38, and $42 per diems. The per diem is divided into quarters for days you leave and arrive back home. If you leave between midnight and 6:00 A.M., you qualify for the entire allowance; if you leave between 6:00 A.M. and noon, you qualify for three quarters of the allowance, and so on. Record the time, place, and business purpose of the trip to claim the full allowance, even if your actual costs are less.

You'll need to keep two sets of records to prove your deductions. First, you'll need a diary, day planner, or similar log to record your business appointments. Include the names of guests, the business purpose, the business relationship between you and your guests, and the place of your meeting. Second, you'll need receipts or bills for expenses over $75. Credit-card statements are fine if you record the business purpose of the expense.

Medical Expenses are deductible to the extent they exceed 7.5% of AGI. Deductible medical expenses generally include any cost of diagnosis, cure, mitigation, treatment, or prevention of disease. These expenses are reduced by any reimbursement you receive from insurance, Medicare, or Medicaid. Expenses must relate to a *specific* disease or condition; you can't deduct the cost of weight-loss treatments taken simply to improve general health. Cosmetic surgery isn't deductible except for disfigurements related to a congenital abnormality, disfiguring diseases, or accidental injuries.

Here are several ways to make the most of medical deductions:

♦ Health-insurance premiums, including Medicare Part "B" premiums, are deductible as a medical expense. If you are self-employed, you can write off 100% of your health-insurance premium as an itemized deduction if it gives you a greater benefit than writing off a percentage as an adjustment to income.

♦ If you undergo a medical examination for your employer or for your business (such as to qualify for life insurance you buy to secure financing), you can deduct the cost as a business expense. This will avoid the 7.5% floor on adjusted gross income.

♦ Long-term-care-insurance premiums may be deductible up to certain limits based on your age and the amount of coverage. Many people are reluctant to buy this coverage, fearing it will go to waste if they don't wind up in a home. One way to avoid that risk is to buy a combo life/long-term care policy, a life-insurance policy with a long-term-care rider. You substantially increase funds available for long-term care; your policy cash values grow tax-deferred; and death benefits pass tax-free to your heirs if you don't use the long-term-care coverage. However, premiums for this kind of policy aren't tax-deductible.

♦ Nursing-home costs are deductible if the patient is confined for medical treatment.

♦ Medical expenses provided by a nursing home are deductible even if the patient is not confined for medical treatment.

♦ Private-nursing expenses are deductible, including a nurse's salary, any employment taxes paid on behalf of the nurse, extra rent to make room for a nurse or attendant, and a nurse's travel costs if the nurse is required on the trip.

♦ Home improvements made for medical reasons, such as swimming pools and elevators, are deductible to the extent the cost exceeds the increased value for the home.

> ♦ **Example:**   Your doctor recommends you install a lap pool for exercise. The pool costs $10,000 and adds $4,000 to the value of the house; $6,000 is deductible.

♦ Travel costs for medical care are deductible medical expenses. These include your transportation (actual costs or 10 cents per mile, plus parking and tolls), plus lodging on trips to receive medical treatment.

♦ If one spouse has particularly heavy medical expenses in a single year, it may pay to file separately to cut that spouse's 7.5% floor on AGI. However, this will subject more of your combined income to higher rates. It might also wipe out other tax breaks, such as the low-income-housing tax credit. The best way to see if this works is to figure your tax both ways.

Medical Savings-Account contributions are deductible directly on Form 1040. For more information, see "Special Breaks for Business Owners" in Chapter 4.

Medicare Part "B" premiums are deductible as a medical expense subject to the 7.5% floor.

Miscellaneous Itemized Deductions are a "catchall" set of writeoffs. They include investment expenses, job-hunting expenses, tax-preparation fees, and unreimbursed employee business expenses.

Miscellaneous itemized deductions are deductible only to the extent that the total exceeds 2% of your adjusted gross income. Add up all your deductions before you subtract the floor. Don't apply the floor to each deduction, or even to each category of deduction.

> Your 2000 income is $50,000. You contribute $2,000 to an IRA, so your adjusted gross income is $48,000. Your miscellaneous itemized deductions include $400 for tax preparation, $500 for a job-hunting seminar, and $175 to print and mail resumés. Total miscellaneous itemized deductions are $1,075. But 2% of your adjusted gross income is $960, so you deduct just $115.

Moving Expenses are deductible on Form 3903, then carried forward as an adjustment to income on Form 1040 according to these rules:

♦ The distance between your new job location and old home has to be at least 50 miles.

- You have worked as a full-time employee in the area of your new job for at least 39 weeks during the 12-month period immediately following your move (78 weeks if you're self-employed or a partner).

Moving expenses include:
- The actual cost of packing and moving your belongings
- Lodging costs for one night at the beginning of the move, all nights of the trip, and one night at arrival
- Transportation costs, including gas, oil, and repairs (or 10 cents per mile) plus parking and tolls
- The cost of finding a new house at the new location

Nanny Wages may qualify for the dependent-care credit. For more information, see Chapter 2, Your Family.

Native-American Healing Rituals are a medical expense subject to the 7.5% floor. Presumably, voodoo rituals and Santeria animal sacrifices (for medical purposes) are deductible under the same reasoning, although no formal support exists for this position.

Newspapers (see **Subscriptions**)

Nursing Costs are a deductible medical expense subject to the 7.5% floor. Registered-nurse fees are generally deductible; practical-nurse fees are deductible for medical services only.

Nursing-Home Costs are a deductible medical expense subject to the 7.5% floor if the patient is confined for medical treatment. If you pay an up-front entrance fee to a continuing-care facility, you can deduct whatever portion of the fee you can show relates to medical costs. If the fee is refundable, however, part of it is considered a "loan" to the facility. You might owe tax on imputed interest if the "loan" tops $131,300 (1997 tax years; this figure is indexed for inflation). The facility will tell you how much of this "interest" is taxable.

Nursing-Home Insurance (see **Long-Term-Care Insurance**)

Nylon Stockings or Pantyhose prescribed for varicose veins are a deductible medical expense subject to the 7.5% floor.

Office Supplies are deductible as a business expense on Schedule C or a miscellaneous itemized deduction subject to the 2% floor if you buy them for investment recordkeeping or similar purposes.

On-Line Services (AOL, Internet providers, and so on) may be deductible under these rules:
- On-line services you use for your trade or business are deductible as a business expense on Schedule C, Form 1065 or Form 1120.
- On-line services you use on behalf of your employer are deductible as an employee business expense subject to the 2% floor on miscellaneous itemized deductions.
- On-line services you use to find a new job in your same line of work are deductible as a job-hunting expense subject to the 2% floor on miscellaneous itemized deductions.

♦ On-line services you use to manage investments are deductible as an investment expense, up to investment income and subject to the 2% floor on miscellaneous itemized deductions.

Optician fees are a deductible medical expense subject to the 7.5% floor.

Optometrist fees are a deductible medical expense subject to the 7.5% floor.

Organ-Donor Costs are a deductible medical expense subject to the 7.5% floor.

Organ Transplants are a deductible medical expense subject to the 7.5% floor.

Orthopedic Furniture (the difference in cost over regular furniture) is a deductible medical expense subject to the 7.5% floor.

Orthopedic Shoes (the difference in cost over regular shoes) are a deductible medical expense subject to the 7.5% floor.

Osteopathic fees are a deductible medical expense subject to the 7.5% floor.

Over-the-Counter Drugs are a nondeductible personal expense, even if your doctor writes a prescription for the drug.

Oxygen Equipment is a deductible medical expense subject to the 7.5% floor.

Passport Fees may be deductible if you get your passport for business travel:

♦ Passport fees for your trade or business are deductible as a business expense on Schedule C, Form 1065 or Form 1120.

♦ Passport fees on behalf of your employer are deductible as an unreimbursed employee business expense subject to the 2% floor on miscellaneous itemized deductions.

Penalty on Early Withdrawal from Savings is deductible as an adjustment to income on Form 1040.

Phone Calls may be deductible under the following rules:

♦ Calls you make for your trade or business are deductible as a business expense on Schedule C, Form 1065 or Form 1120.

♦ Calls you make on behalf of your employer are deductible as an unreimbursed employee business expense subject to the 2% floor on miscellaneous itemized deductions.

♦ Calls you make to find a job are deductible as job-hunting expenses subject to the 2% floor on miscellaneous itemized deductions.

♦ Calls you make for medical care are a deductible medical expense subject to the 7.5% floor.

♦ Calls you make to manage your investment are deductible as investment expenses, up to investment income, subject to the 2% floor on miscellaneous itemized deductions.

♦ Calls you make to manage rental property, and the like, are deductible as rental expenses on Schedule E.

Physical Therapy is a deductible medical expense subject to the 7.5% floor.

Physician fees are a deductible medical expense subject to the 7.5% floor. Deductible physician fees include any licensed medical doctor.

Points you pay to buy or improve your primary residence are deductible if paying points is an established practice in your geographical area and the points charged don't exceed the points generally charged in the area. The amount must be figured as a percentage of the loan amount and specifically itemized as points, loan-origination fee, or loan-discount fee. Finally, points must be paid directly to the lender. If your points don't meet these tests, you can still amortize them over the life of the loan. Your lender will report the amount of deductible points on Form 1098.

Points you pay on a second home, home-equity loan, or line of credit are deductible over the term of the loan. If you prepay the loan, deduct any remaining amount the year the mortgage ends.

Political Contributions, alas, are a nondeductible personal expense. President Clinton's aide Harold Ickes apparently learned this the hard way after faxing a Texas donor instructions for disguising political contributions as charitable gifts.

Prenatal and Postnatal Care are deductible medical expenses subject to the 7.5% floor.

Prescription Drugs are a deductible medical expense subject to the 7.5% floor.

Professional-Association Dues are deductible as follows:

- ◆ If you maintain membership for your trade or business, dues are deductible as a business expense on Schedule C, Form 1065 or Form 1120.
- ◆ If you maintain membership for benefit of your employer, dues are deductible as an employee business expense subject to the 2% floor on miscellaneous itemized deductions.

Professional-Education Expenses are deductible as follows:

- ◆ If you run your own business or practice, professional-education costs are a deductible business expense on Schedule C, Form 1065 or Form 1120.
- ◆ If you take courses for your employer, costs are an unreimbursed employee business expense (subject to the 2% floor on miscellaneous itemized deductions).

Property Taxes on your primary residence and any additional residences are deductible on Schedule A. You can also deduct any property tax you pay on automobiles. Property taxes on business property are deductible as a business expense on Schedule C, Form 1065 or Form 1120.

Psychologist fees are a deductible medical expense subject to the 7.5% floor.

Radial Keratotomy surgery to correct vision is a deductible medical expense subject to the 7.5% floor.

Radium Treatments are a deductible medical expense subject to the 7.5% floor.

Reading Classes for a child suffering from dyslexia are a deductible medical expense subject to the 7.5% floor.

Safe-Deposit-Box Fees are deductible as an investment expense subject to the 2% floor if you use the box to store investment-related papers.

Sales Tax is not deductible. However, you can add any sales tax you pay to the cost basis of the item.

Seeing-Eye-Dog Expenses are a deductible medical expense subject to the 7.5% floor.

Self-Employment Tax is 50% deductible as an adjustment to income on Form 1040. For more information, see Chapter 4, Your Job and Your Business.

Seminar Fees may be deductible depending on the purpose of the seminar.

- ◆ Seminars you attend for your trade or business are deductible as a business expense on Schedule C, Form 1065 or Form 1120.

- ◆ Seminars you attend on behalf of your employer are deductible as an employee business expense subject to the 2% floor on miscellaneous itemized deductions.

- ◆ Job-hunting seminars are deductible as a job-hunting expense subject to the 2% floor on miscellaneous itemized deductions.

- ◆ Investment seminars are no longer deductible as an investment expense.

Sex Counseling prescribed by a psychiatrist is a medical expense subject to the 7.5% floor. This includes hotel-room and even travel costs.

Sixty-Minute Tax Planner is a miscellaneous itemized deduction subject to the 2% floor.

Software (see **Computer**)

Smoking-Cessation Program is a deductible medical expense subject to the 7.5% floor. This includes physician fees and prescription drugs, but not over-the-counter medication.

State Taxes are an itemized deduction on Schedule A.

State-tax refunds are tax-free if you took the standard deduction the previous year. If you itemized, refunds are taxable up to the difference between your actual deductions and the standard deduction you could have claimed. In that case, report the refund as income on Line 10, Form 1040.

Sterilization Costs are a deductible medical expense, subject to the 7.5% floor.

Student-Loan Interest is deductible as an adjustment to income during the first five years of loan repayment if your adjusted gross income is $60,000 or less. For more information, see Chapter 11, Investing for College.

Subscriptions to newspapers and magazines may be deductible depending on why you subscribe.

- ◆ Subscriptions you take for your trade or business are deductible as a business expense on Schedule C, Form 1065 or Form 1120.

- ◆ Subscriptions you take on your employer's behalf are deductible as an unreimbursed employee business expense subject to the 2% floor on miscellaneous itemized deductions. For example, stockbrokers who read *The Wall Street Journal*, lawyers who read *The National Law Journal*, and real estate agents who read the classifieds can deduct those subscriptions.

- ◆ Subscriptions you take for help-wanted ads are a deductible job-hunting expense subject to the 2% floor on miscellaneous itemized deductions.

♦ Subscriptions you take for investment advice are a deductible investment expense, up to your investment income and subject to the 2% floor on miscellaneous itemized deductions.

You don't actually have to subscribe to deduct the cost of papers and magazines. You can deduct single-copy purchases as well.

Tax-Preparation Fees are deductible according to these rules:

♦ Personal tax-preparation fees are deductible as a miscellaneous itemized deduction subject to the 2% floor on Schedule A.

♦ Tax-preparation fees for your trade or business are deductible as a business expense on Schedule C, Form 1065 or Form 1120.

♦ Tax-preparation fees for rental property or farm income are deductible in full as a rental property or farm expenses on Schedule E or Schedule F.

Tax-preparation fees include the costs of IRS rulings, plus fees for audits and Tax Court cases. Since personal tax-preparation fees are subject to the 2% floor on miscellaneous itemized deductions, have your tax preparer allocate fees to specific schedules to take maximum advantage of the deduction. However, be aware that the IRS is on the lookout for taxpayers who improperly shift personal expenses onto business schedules.

Teeth cleaning, extracting, filling, or straightening are deductible medical expenses subject to the 7.5% floor.

Telephone (see **Phone Calls**)

Theft Losses are deductible on Form 4684 to the extent the value of the stolen property exceeds 10% of your adjusted gross income plus $100. For more information, see **Casualty Losses.**

Transfusions (see **Blood Tests/Transfusions**)

Travel Expenses may be deductible depending on the nature of the trip. Travel costs generally include transportation, lodging, and 50% of meals and entertainment.

♦ Travel for your trade or business is deductible as a business expense on Schedule C, Form 1065 or Form 1120.

♦ Travel on behalf of your employer is deductible as an employee business expense subject to the 2% floor on miscellaneous itemized deductions. This includes living costs for temporary assignments lasting less than a year.

♦ Travel to and from medical facilities is deductible as a medical expense subject to the 7.5% floor. This includes meals and lodging for out-of-town travel to medical providers such as the Mayo Clinic or Betty Ford. You can deduct 12 cents per mile for auto expenses, plus parking and tolls.

♦ Travel for investments is a deductible investment expense, up to your investment income and subject to the 2% floor on miscellaneous itemized deductions (for example, if you travel out of state to acquire investment property). You can deduct 31 cents per mile for auto expenses, plus parking and tolls.

- Travel on behalf of a volunteer or charitable organization is deductible as a charitable gift on Schedule A. You can deduct 14 cents per mile for auto expenses, plus parking and tolls.

- If you bring a spouse or dependent, his or her costs are deductible only if there's a business purpose for bringing the person. If there's no business purpose, you can still deduct the full cost that you could deduct if you had traveled alone. Let's say your hotel costs $50 a night for you, but $70 for you and your spouse. You can deduct the full $50 that you would pay if you had traveled alone. Don't simply divide the $70 by two and claim $35.

- If you add a personal trip to the business trip, the cost of personal travel isn't deductible. Let's say you spend a week in Boston for business, then a weekend visiting family on the Cape. There's no deduction for the cost of your stay on the Cape.

Travel outside the United States is deductible if the primary purpose of the trip is for business and you don't have control of the trip. However, if you're in charge of the business—you're a managing executive, self-employed, related to your employer, or own more than 10% of the business—travel abroad is deductible only if the trip lasts a week or less, or you spend less than 25% of the trip vacationing. If you spend more than 25% of the trip vacationing, allocate your travel expenses to deductible business travel and nondeductible vacation travel.

TTD and Television Close Captioning for a deaf person are deductible medical expenses subject to the 7.5% floor.

Uniforms and Work Clothes may be deductible as follows:

- Uniforms and work clothes you buy for your trade or business are deductible as a business expense on Schedule C, Form 1065 or Form 1120, if they are not suitable for street wear.

- Uniforms and work clothes you buy on behalf of your employer are deductible as an unreimbursed employee business expense, subject to the 2% floor on miscellaneous itemized deductions, if they are not suitable for street wear.

- Clothing you buy and wear for volunteer activities (Boy Scout and Girl Scout uniforms, and the like), are deductible as a charitable gift on Schedule A.

- Laundry and dry-cleaning expenses for any deductible clothing are also deductible.

- Laundry and dry-cleaning costs you incur for business travel are deductible as a business expense or unreimbursed employee business expense depending on whether you travel for your own trade or business or for an employer.

The IRS or Tax Court have specifically approved deductions for airline pilots, baseball players, bus drivers, firefighters, letter carriers, and nurses. However, the IRS disallowed deductions for a tennis pro and house painter because both uniforms were suitable for ordinary street wear.

Unreimbursed Employee Business Expenses (See **Employee Business Expenses**)

Vacation Expenses may be partially tax-deductible if you combine a business trip with a vacation. If the primary purpose of a trip is for business, your transportation costs to your destination are deductible even if you spend additional vacation time at your destination (lodging and meals are deductible for the duration of your business stay, but not for vacation time). If you tack vacation days onto a business trip to qualify for an airline "Saturday-stay" discount, your lodging and meals for the extra days are deductible even if you use them for vacation. Keep a log or diary to prove the primary purpose of your trip. For more information, including rules for foreign travel, see **Travel Expenses** and **Convention Costs.**

Vasectomy Costs are a deductible medical expense subject to the 7.5% floor.

Volunteer Expenses are deductible as charitable gifts on Schedule A. These include:

- Meals and lodging on trips away from home
- Travel expenses to and from volunteer and charitable activities (actual expenses or 12 cents per mile, plus parking and tolls)
- Telephone calls and office supplies
- Convention expenses
- A portion of organizational dues (the organization can tell you how much)
- Clothing expenses, including laundry and dry-cleaning expenses, for clothing not usable as ordinary street clothing (Girl Scout uniforms, for example)

For more information, see Chapter 5, Make the Most of Charitable Gifts.

Weight-loss Programs are a deductible medical expense subject to the 7.5% floor if the program is prescribed by a doctor for a specific medical purpose, not just to improve general health.

Wheelchairs are a deductible medical expense subject to the 7.5% floor.

Wigs are a deductible medical expenses if prescribed by a doctor for mental health after losing hair to disease.

Worthless Securities are deductible as a capital loss on Schedule D the year that they become completely worthless. To claim the loss, you have to show that the security had some value the previous year (such as trading on an established exchange) and became completely worthless the year you claim the loss (such as ceasing to do business or insolvency). If a security is nearly worthless—trading for pennies a share, for example—consider selling for what you can get and taking a regular loss, rather than waiting for complete worthlessness. You have seven years from the date of worthlessness to file an amended return to claim the loss. If you're in doubt whether a security is completely worthless, go ahead and claim the loss. You can always amend your return later. (For more information, see "Find Gold in Old Returns," in Chapter 13.) Securities are deemed to become worthless on the last day of the year for purposes of figuring whether losses are short-, mid-, and long-term.

X-Rays (including CT scans and MRIs) are deductible medical expenses subject to the 7.5% floor.

INDEX